Imperial Constantinople

NEW DIMENSIONS IN HISTORY

Historical Cities

Series Editor: Norman F. Cantor

John Wiley & Sons, Inc., New York · London · Sydney · Toronto

IMPERIAL CONSTANTINOPLE

DEAN A. MILLER

10 9 8 7 6 5 4 3 2 1

Library of Congress Catalog Card Number: 69-19233
Cloth: SBN 471 60370 8 Paper: SBN 471 60371 6
Printed in the United States of America

PREFACE

Every historian knows that in reconstructing even the smallest fragment of the past he is undertaking an act of unforgivable *hubris*. He goes on anyway, excusing himself as best he can; he has, after all, plenty of company. He begins, at any rate, with what he hopes is an insight, and ends with a prayer that he has not betrayed the dead.

This study has as its center the capital of the Byzantine Empire, a state we no longer have any reason to make excuses for or misunderstand. I have tried to describe Constantinople at the height of its powers: not the tragic, embattled remnant of tattered glories, but the living New Rome of its best years, when it was the exemplification of an important unitary theory of politics, spirit, and secular life—an imperial city reflecting an imperial theory. According to this theory the city—the capital—must be more than an aggregation of human bodies and the services that they require; the city is above all the solid, archetectonic metaphor of eternal order and harmony, peace, justice, and life. Its ruler, following this plan, exercised powers and controls that we no longer feel are suitable; but we have to recognize that the Imperial City fitted its day, and that the perceptions that created it are not so much invalid in modern times as occluded or hidden. In my reconstruction I hope I have had an insight; as I hope that I have not betrayed the dead.

I would like to acknowledge the aid I received at various times in the progress of the manuscript: from colleagues, especially Sidney Monas, R. J. Kaufmann, and Loren Baritz of this department; and Norman O. Brown. I was extended the privilege of using the library of the Dumbarton Oaks Research Center and Library by Dr. Ihor Sevcenko, Director of Studies of the Center. During a sabbatical leave spent in Athens I was materially and spiritually assisted by Mr. Francis Walton and his staff, of the Gennadeion Library, by Henry S. Robinson of the American School of Classical Studies and his staff, and by John and Mary Zelia Phillipides, *philoi kai meletetai.* There are others who are aware of the help they extended and may think that I have forgotten: I have not. Finally, I want to publicly recognize the patience and understanding of my wife, an occasional critic of style and an unfailing and invaluable critic of the historical task and profession.

D. A. MILLER

Rochester, New York, 1968

CONTENTS

LIST OF ILLUSTRATIONS

LIST OF MAPS

Maps by John V. Morris

Imperial Constantinople

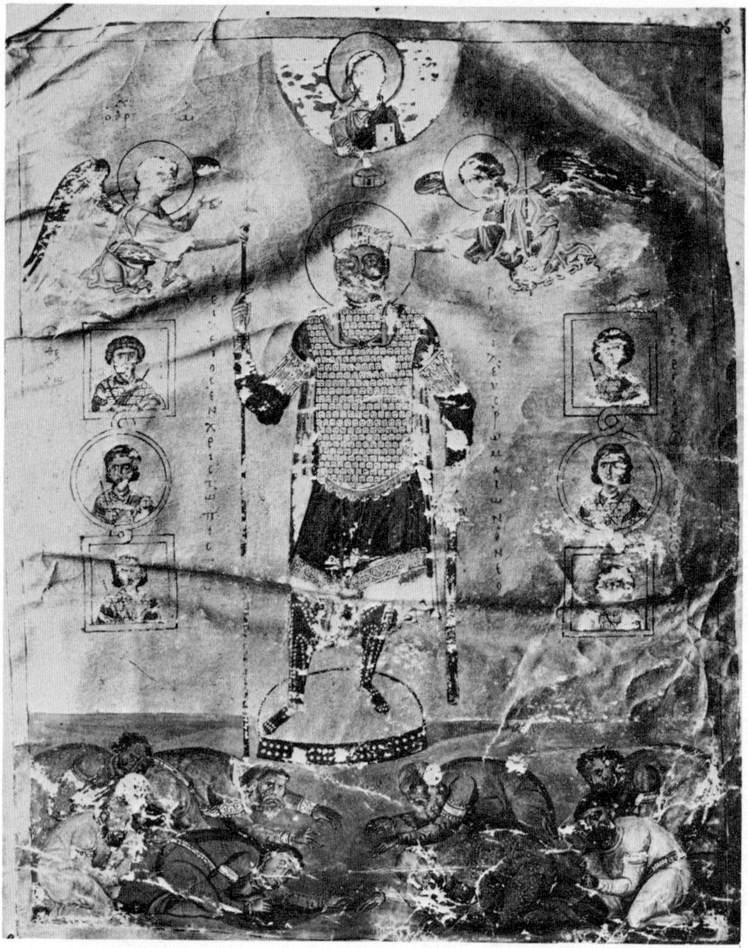

Portrait of Basil II triumphing over the nations, from the Psalter of Basil II. (Biblioteca Marciana, Venice; Bohm—Art Reference Bureau.)

ONE

The City

The city of Constantinople is situated in the sixth climate, at 49° longitude and 45° latitude. It is a great and important city which none can surpass. It has three gates and three sides of which two are turned toward the sea, and the third toward the continent in the direction of the land of Rome and (the city) of Rome the Great. It is fortified with very powerful walls. Rome is subject to it although Rome is more ancient. It was built by Constantine, son of the king of the Romans, for the following reason: the first time that he, believing in Jesus and being converted, made profession openly of the Christian faith, the people of his kingdom of Rome condemned this action. He then left Rome and founded Constantinople which he called by his own name. The Romans were brought there and it became the capital of his empire and his residence.

Ishaq ben Al-Husain, *Kitāḇ ākām al-marğān fi dikr al-madā'in al-mašhūra fī kull makān*

THE CITY

Cities appeared, and the world changed: this is the "Urban Revolution," and we are only just beginning to realize the extent of the revolution and its traumata. The originator of the term, V. Gordon Childe, was constrained to show the necessary control of —and desire to control—the material environment that had to lie behind the transformation. But the very act, the hubristic intent, of placing man in charge of nature caused reverberations that have not yet ceased.[1]

[1] V. Gordon Childe, "The Urban Revolution," *Town Planning Review* **21** (1950), 3–17.

The transformation of village into city is not ony unclear as to cause, but is precisely the point where a purely economic determinism fails, for too many phenomena evade its net. At some point, traceable and untraceable elements precipitate the city. This city—whatever it *is*—from the first is *not* merely a more complex, oversized village. Man raised, and moved into, a multiplex structure that immediately began to pose psychic problems and take a psychic toll, at the same time that it optimized his production of goods and freed his mind from certain old controls. There *is* original sin here: the sin of isolation, of differentiation, of the appearance of the mental attitude that separates Subject and Object—Man from his psychically nutritive environment once extensive with him. The pathos of this discovery has touched even archaeologists, who ask whether the archetypal Paradise is not the preurban archaic village, with its putative balance, order, and calm submergence in nature.[2]

The city begins with separation, with the creation of "the other": the shell or carapace, however intangible, is the first and most significant urban fact and artifact. Robert Redfield, in *The Primitive World and Its Transformations*, calls this the appearance of the "technical" as differentiated from the "moral" human order, but the first point here is that this separation sets up psychic pressures that are perdurable and intense.[3] The *security* of the city was paid for, the ambition of man in creating it was paid for, the very act of ordering and composing Nature was paid for with unendurable anxieties. The neutralizing and dissipation of these anxieties, their sublimation, took and presently takes many forms, but I am concerned here with one early and powerful sublimatory mode: the metaphoric-symbolic.

However, sublimatory mechanisms are not always successful, if in fact "success" is ever possible in the ancient human conflict between inner and outer. The unnatural or wicked essence of the city continues to be underscored and excoriated by those who support the moral order outside the city's more or less real walls.

[2] L. Mumford, *The City in History* (New York, 1961), 30, 71; R. Girshman, *Iran* (Penguin Books, 1961), 32.

[3] R. Redfield, *The Primitive World and Its Transformations* (Cornell Univ. Press, 1957), 20.

Thus the pedigree of St. Augustine's *City of God,* in the Judaeo-Christian tradition, goes back as far as the Israelitic prophets, who spoke against the city not only on behalf of the excluded peasant, but for the old anti-imperial Israel.[4] There exists as well the actuality and the tradition of the Greek *polis,* where the order of the city was made supremely ethical—a tradition that continues to inhere in some aspects of Byzantine civic life—and of Rome, which is too often remembered for the misleading tradition expressed by Cicero: *Urbs ipsa moenia sunt, civitas autem non saxa sed habitores vocantur,* "A city is only walls, but the real city is its dwellers not its stones."[5] Graeco-Roman civic traditions make up a bulk that is difficult to set aside lightly. However, I judge this development more on the basis of its failures than its successes. It was, furthermore, the "successful" Hellenistic city rather than the "failed" Hellenic city which was St. Augustine's target, and it was the Augustinian antinomy—the City of God set over against the City of Man—that the Byzantines seemed compelled to ignore.

This readhesion of man in nature is achieved in the following manner: the city is described, and essentially becomes, the simulacrum of a total order, a cosmic system. Its appearance or epiphany must then be "natural," for Nature itself is now become Organization. The creation of Order in the face of a felt reality is excused by a reaction-reversal, so that Order becomes Reality, and that outside of Order is chaos—the disjunct, the wild, and therefore the evil. A battery of images is made available to support this conceit, and out of them are gradually chosen the macrometaphors of the city, the prepotent word-signs that attempt to render old doubts harmless by the reverberatory power of the masks they create. The very materiality of the city is made to show and ratify its place in the universe. The names of concrete masses and shapes, transmuted, attach it to the divine plan. These words are the necessary preritual: the reinducement of sacrality, the setting of the great stage. They are dramaturgic *nomena* which consistently recur as the city shapes itself: as the Cosmic

[4] G. Pedersen, *Israel: Its Life and Culture* (Oxford, 1926), 23, 82 ff.
[5] According to Isadore of Seveille, *Etymologies,* **XV**, 2.

Shape or outline, as the Wall, the Gate, the Tower, the Dome, and the Hill.[6]

Imperial—Byzantine—Constantinople is a special case. As a city it catches and magnifies all the paradoxical attributes of the Empire it commanded. The Byzantine Empire was "Roman," the heir to the power of the Augusti, and Constantinople was New Rome. Byzantium was Greek in language and Hellenic in its cultural inheritance, and Constantinople was conceived to be the continuator of the pride of Athens—the *polis* nonpareil. Byzantium was "Oriental" in its spiritual affiliation with the revelations of Christianity, and Constantinople was the New Jerusalem.[7]

Of course, the act of analyzing Byzantium into its cultural components raises more problems than it solves. Don't the categories of order, duty, and control, which are centrally "Roman," cancel or at least conflict with the characteristics of the Greek free citizen? And how can either secular tradition be successfully combined with the Gospels or with "Oriental" revelation and mystery? It is not that we force Byzantium into categories not its own, for terms like New Rome and New Jerusalem *are* its own. Almost certainly we are missing a vital power: the synthetic and prismatic ability of a civilization, a civilization capable of richly combining metaphors—for "Roman," "Greek," and "Oriental" must be understood thus—in a manner we see imperfectly. And, in Constantinople, we have a focus for this synthetic and combinatory power; a *topos* where the substance and accidents of the civilization are concentrated.

In the typology of cities, Constantinople is truly Imperial. By this I mean that although inevitable organic change is visible, the ruling and shaping patterns and metaphors came from a view of a cosmos having a unity and singular teleology. This cosmos was reflected in a unitary political schema in which the Empire was totally and uniquely possible and necessary, and this Empire

[6] Compare M. Eliade, "Centre du monde, Temple, Maison," in *Le Symbolisme cosmique des monuments réligieux* (Serie Orientale Roma **XIV**, Roma, 1957), 63–64.

[7] For the usual statement of the three cultural ingredients see e.g., N. Iorga, "L'Homme byzantin," in his *Études byzantines* (Bucharest, 1939), 313–325.

was headed by, concentrated in, and iconically and symbolically represented by its center and city, *and* in and by the creator of that city. This Imperial conceit presumes, first, that there is a perceptible cosmic pattern and, second, that the city as *artifice* reflects that pattern in complex ways. As artifice the city is the creation of the king-emperor, the demiurge, representative, and vicegerent of God. Orderer and ordered, protector and protection —God, Emperor, Empire, City—are made to merge.[8]

Constantinople is Imperial not only because it commands a certain extensive space, then, but because it is the creation of the Emperor, the imitator of the cosmos. "Imperial" rings as well of physical size and mass, of architectural devices chosen for their grandiloquence, of sheer bulk and even what has been called the "bureaucratic" style of official monument.[9] In fact, the relationships between citizen-subject or city dweller and the architecture of an Imperial city are dominated by twinned concepts: distinctive *size,* which shows more than the mere mastery or monopoly of material resources, and effective *control,* the placing of specifically designed masses and spaces. The Imperial city is—must be—a planned city, and as such Constantinople is in the line of descent from both the rationalized city-type of the Hellenistic age and the older cosmogenic and symbolic cities of the empires of the Near East.[10]

The interplay between city and citizen is only now beginning to be studied, more or less imaginatively, and extrapolation of an historical dimension—the reconstruction of attitudes and influences, flavors, ambiances—for any particular city is extraordinarily difficult to achieve. A combination of the sensitivities and paraphernalia of the psychologist and the perceptiveness of the sculptor would be helpful, as well as more data than we are ever likely to find available.

[8] For the merging of King and city see the "wall" images collected in I. Engnell, *Studies in Divine Kingship in the Ancient Near East* (Oxford, 1967), 194; the regalian representation of this idea is the "mural crown."
[9] K. Wittvogel, *Oriental Despotism* (New Haven, 1957), 43.
[10] On the Hellenistic city see Mumford, *City,* 197; M. Poëte, *Introduction à l'Urbanisme: L'Évolution des Villes: La Leçon de l'Antiquité* (Paris, 1929).

One modern town planner has suggested the following series of categories under which to examine and classify urban life: size, density, grain, shape, and internal pattern.[11] Useful as these are, we are kept from using all of them in examining Constantinople of the 10th century A.D., because, among other lacks, we have no sure idea of the population of the city at that time. The *shape* of the capital we know (excluding the suburban extensions), and we have fairly clear notions of its internal patterns of use and specialization, but even approximate densities of habitation, quarter by quarter, are difficult to arrive at.[12] And, as we know, congestion, once it passes a point differing from society to society, begins to act on the social fabric itself: the ambiguousness of life in the city becomes more marked and less bearable; the neuroses of the true mob appear. Did 10th century Constantinople endure these pressures? Where, on a scale of stress, did the push of numbers meet the countervailing force of containment and control? We don't know.

A great many of my conclusions on attitudes and reactions within this Imperial City will spring from my interpretation of certain characteristics of the civilization of Byzantium itself. The most important of these was the predilection of the Byzantines for one symbolic relationship, that is, what Lewis Mumford (in his view of the city) calls "materialization," the solidification of an idea in material.[13] In Constantinople, the collocation of material masses seems to provide or underlie a tension or ambiguity in the Byzantine concept of "city" itself, for on the one hand solidity, physicality, presentness is and shows *power,* and yet all physical outlines tend to shift, blur, vibrate, disappear in the radiant Reality behind them. True iconizing, that "picturing" which always maintains the idea as a Real Presence behind or beyond the material, is a complex construction, one probably beyond the minds of

[11] K. Lynch, "The Form of Cities," *Scientific American* **190–191** (1954), 55–63.

[12] On the population of Constantinople, see A. Andreadès, "De la population de Constantinople sous les empereurs byzantines," *Metron* **I,** 2 (1920), 7, n. 1, 32; J. L. Teall, "The Grain Supply of the Byzantine Empire: 330–1025," *Dumbarton Oaks Papers* **13** (1959), 105, 134–135.

[13] Mumford, *City,* 113.

most Constantinopolitans, but some sense of the world as hierarchy, a feeling of the interpenetration of visible and invisible, a consciousness of the ancient powers now demonic, a dependence on the efficacy of magic—all these, it seems to me, will be seen in the ordinary citizen's reaction to his Byzantine urban environment.

Beyond this, I intend to take (not for granted, but as valuable guides) and use those data and conclusions that point to certain architectural forms and massed arrangements, considering them to be evocative in the deepest sense, as tentacular contacts, or at the very least stage settings, for the most basic and oldest of human concerns. So every city must be a step from paradise—that warless, stable, womblike archaic village which is one of the few dreams that archaeologists permit themselves—and every city must attempt to create another paradise: a paradise of artifacts, not given but made. And every city must be prepared to accept the risks inherent in this attempt.

Finally, the city must be placed in time as well as in space. However much a true Imperial City resists this temporal-historical pressure, its life must yield to the life and drama of men. In the case of Constantinople, the paradox and tension are acutely visible, for this city and the Empire it stood for, towering so high in the 10th century, the sixth century of its existence, did not survive the next hundred years intact. The perfect florescence of power, conceived of as ultimate and static, faded so suddenly that we must recognize how many resistant human problems had *not* been solved.

Within the *saeculum* there are beginnings and endings. The created city, in its own view, sacralizes itself and so removes itself from time, for it *is* creation, the place of replicated creation, and within its sacred boundaries time has no leverage or hold.[14] This idea finds firm support in Byzantine visions of their capital, and especially in their ceremonial reification of its timeless potency, but we know that time eventually revenged itself. If the 10th century was the century when this city was indeed the image of all, it was also the century when the surrounding fabric

[14] M. Eliade, *Patterns in Comparative Religion* (New York, 1958), 377.

was torn, when the social cement that had kept all the classes and élites pressed into service broke, when the shapes of decadence and destructive neurosis were first clearly seen.[15]

The view of the Imperial City from the inside—from within the core of radiant power—cannot be enough. Every source of power excites opposition, and each city meets ambivalent and ambiguous reactions to its actuality or to its fictions. It may be enriched by these reactions or, sclerotic in pride and self-confidence, reject and despise them, to its own loss and downfall. Not every citizen accepts the city at all times as Utopia—the "Good Place"—and, outside its walls, outside the literally charmed circle or circuit, there were others. These were the masses of peasants in their harassed but symbiotic relationship to the center; the landed aristocracy with its own hierarchy and jealous mythology; the self-excluded monks representing yet another view, another world set over against the power of the New Jerusalem. All oppositions, of course, can work themselves out in the broadest spectrum of political action, or in social forms detached from the city, but in this study I want to explore at least one of them as it refracts directly from the Byzantine capital. And, in exploring the reactions of those who withdrew or were rejected, I must show a brilliant and fruitful human construction fading.

The brilliance of the construction is there, whether or not it fell at last. Other sacred cities had gone before or served, in ritual memory, as patterns, and the Byzantine combinatory and conservative mode was such that names and shapes were often retained with a totally new substance flowing inside them. But, from the first, an extrordinary unity was conceived of and accomplished. Constantinople was created in the 4th century A.D. as a Christian-Imperial city, as one locus where the two powers could be made to join and not conflict. Constantinople was the apotheosis of Rome—*the* Center—not a Second Rome in any serial sense.[16] It shook free almost immediately from the skein of history, even Christian history, and laid claim to the most absolute dominance simply because it *was* (not had become) the eternal

[15] See *Epilog* at the end of the book.

[16] On Philofei of Kiev and the idea of the "Third Rome" see V. Malinin, *Starets Eleazarova Monastyrya Filofei i ego Poslaniya* (Kiev, 1901), 50, 55.

Center, where the prime symbols of time and space were conjoined and reinforced by multivalent ritual, and the world bowed down.

Even if this idea could not endure, even if time and history had their revenge, the nobility—even the arrogance—of the series of concepts that formed Constantinople have to be demonstrated. The variety of impacts the city had, the obtrusion it made into men's minds and actions, the cooperation it managed to elicit by whatever means, and the failures it had, are my themes here. I am going *eis ten polin*—to the city—again.

THE CREATION AND THE CREATOR

Setting and Description

By the 10th century A.D. the City of Constantine, viewed from our vantage point, had passed through four stages, taking some of its affects and character from each of them, to reach its peak of strength and influence. The stages are as follows:

(a) *Founding and fortification.* Under Constantine, the replication of a "Roman" Imperial capital and the first drawing of the bounds; the definitive fortification by Theodosius II; the shaping by Justinian of the major masses and outlines in monumental architecture and the last flash of self-consciously Roman images in the capital (to the end of the 6th century).

(b) *Isolation.* With the advance of Islam and tribal enemies from the north, a strong flow of energies *outward* into the threatened provinces (the formation of the theme system); an absolute and relative loss of population in city and Empire; the city defers to its defensive needs and returns to the status of *castrum*; the city lives its history rather than recording it (to the mid-8th century).

(c) *Secularization and sacralization.* Overlapping the last period, a strong reaction *inward* and toward centralized power; attempt by Iconoclastic emperors to subvert other sources of authority and to sacralize their own position within city and Empire (to mid-9th century).

(d) *Centralization.* Basing their efforts on Iconoclastic patterns, succeeding houses (especially the Macedonian) take the

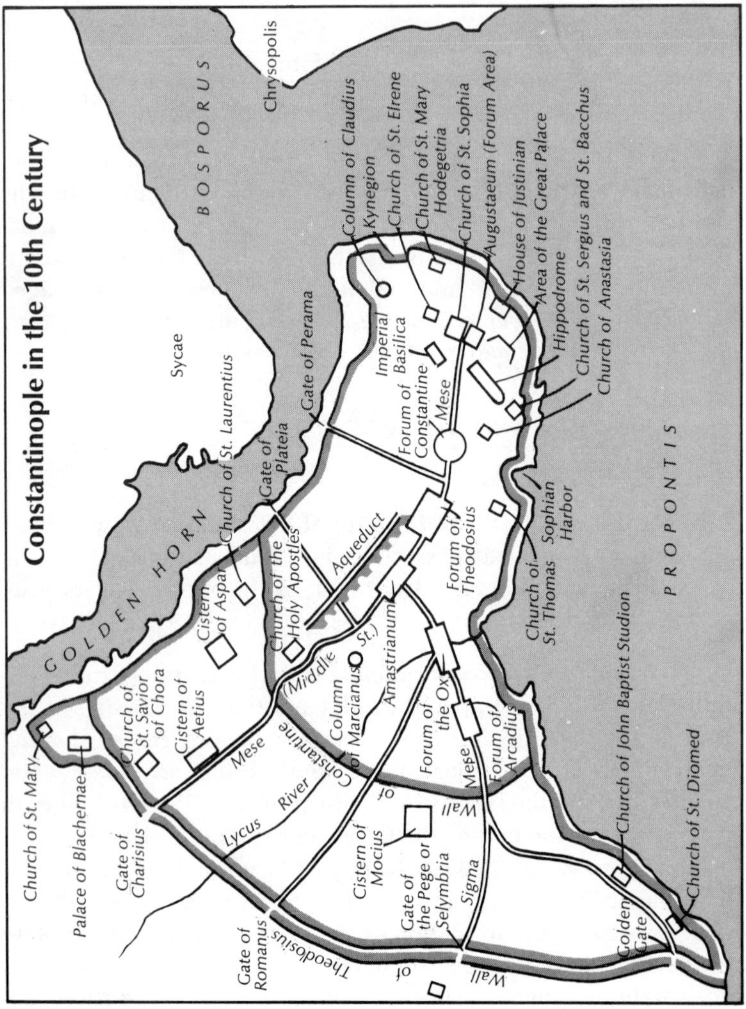

Constantinople in the 10th Century
GOLDEN HORN
BOSPORUS
Sycae
Chrysopolis
PROPONTIS
Church of St. Mary
Palace of Blachernae
Gate of Charisius
Church of St. Savior of Chora
Cistern of Aetius
Cistern of Aspar
Church of St. Laurentius
Gate of Plateia
Gate of Perama
Church of the Holy Apostles
Aqueduct
Mese
(Middle St.)
Column of Marcianus
Amastrianum
Lycus River
Constantine
Wall of
Gate of Romanus
Theodosius
of
Wall
Cistern of Mocius
Gate of the Pege or Selymbria
Sigma
Forum of the Ox
Forum of Arcadius
Forum of Theodosius
Forum of Constantine
Imperial Basilica
Column of Claudius
Kynegion
Church of St. Elrene
Church of St. Mary Hodegetria
Church of St. Sophia
Augustaeum (Forum Area)
House of Justinian
Area of the Great Palace
Hippodrome
Church of St. Sergius and St. Bacchus
Church of Anastasia
Sophian Harbor
Church of St. Thomas
Church of John Baptist Studion
Church of St. Diomed
Golden Gate

city to its supreme position; external enemies are reduced; the symbols and rituals of power are worked out to their fullest (to the 11th century).

To this, in fairness, we must add the coda:

(e) *Fragmentation, miniaturization.* A dissipation of power at the Center; centrifugal movement of authority into the hinterlands and beyond the borders; injection and triumph of the Medieval West with the loss of the city to the Fourth Crusade; reduction of territory; concentration of creativity into the city and a reduction of the scale of that creativity. Transmission of the culture, and end of the city/Empire (to 1453).

By the 10th century, then, Constantinople's unique form was clearly marked. The natural setting, with all its defensive strength, has been perhaps stressed too often; a glance at the map, at any rate, shows the city on a peninsula shaped like a tenderloin steak, about 8 km along its southern and eastern shore, 4½ km along the northern seawall, and protected and delineated on the landward side by the great Wall of Theodosius (5½ km long). So outlined and so protected by the Propontos of the Sea of Marmora, the Bosporus, and the deep estuary called the Golden Horn, and by its Land Walls, Constantinople was neither invulnerable nor impregnable, but its defenses had to be, and generally were, effective.[17]

However, Constantinople, as a world capital and great urban complex, could not be merely a fortress. The interchange, the "concentration and withdrawal" which helped to define it as a city not only filled it with every sort of people and their business of the day, but also made it more of a target. The water barriers which guarded it and carried its merchandise also brought hostile fleets from the Black Sea and the Mediterranean. This city could not be perpetually on guard, yet its enemies came at it again and again, by sea and land. In the 10th century alone it was laid under siege by Bulgars, by Russians, and by great rebels from among its own supposed defenders. In its power and wealth it

[17] R. Janin, *Constantinople Byzantine: Dévelopement urbaine et répertoire topographique,* 2e ed. (Institut Français d'Études Byzantines, Paris, 1964), 1–20, 260 ff.

was more than a magnet for the careerist and the peaceful opportunist; it was an object of envy on a worldwide scale, and was forced to defend itself frequently against this simple envy or more grand ambitions. Unlike Old Rome, Constantinople had to be walled and guarded from its birth, and the shell erected against the symbolic menace of Chaos had its uses in fending off a long list of enemies.[18]

In erecting the material outline of the city, its builders defined it in several senses. The life in and the continued existence of this urban center would depend on and be limited by these and other physical features, on the maintenance of a whole *protective* regime and on a system of *provisioning*. There were also—seeing the city as the restrictive and manipulatory system that it must be—special features for *concentration* of the population and for *control.* Taken all together, these vital physical patternings produce a large part of the macrotexture of the city, providing direction, restriction, spacing, and mass, and also—of equal importance—producing certain psychological threats and assurances.

Protection. Certain basic defenses, a protective shell, allowed the city to continue to function. Most of the Land Walls that sealed off the peninsula were complete by the middle of the 5th century and are impressive to this day: the complete system consisted of a stone-lined ditch (seven meters deep by 20 broad), a glacis, an outer wall, a second glacis, and the main or inner wall. Ninety-six small towers on the exterior wall covered the spaces between 92 larger towers on the main defensive work. There were subsidiary fortifications covering the main gates, and the northern hinge of the wall (nearest the Golden Horn) was protected by special works that eventually included a palace complex, the Blachernae, as well. The city possessed seawalls, portions built before Constantine but mainly put up in the 9th century. On the northern shore, facing the Golden Horn, this wall was built back some distance from the actual littoral, and the space between wall and shore contained most of the city's wharves and shipping facilities (and probably most of the "Frankish" (i.e. Italian) merchants' factories).[19]

[18] Mumford, *City,* 42.
[19] Janin, *Constantinople,* 245–249, 260 ff.

The restrictive presence of the city as Fortress is the natural reverse of the protective presence. Walls bulk and close off as well as guard, and manned towers overlook and overawe the interior of the city as well as standing against the enemy outside. The necessary police function which the regular garrison of Constantinople could perform, quite apart from its guard duties, must have been always clear to the people. Access and egress, movement to and from the city, was channeled and supervised; certain gates, for instance, were restricted to the use of the military only. But irritation and ambiguity must have disappeared when the city was threatened, when the city "Guarded of God" expressed one aspect of divine custody in its massed defensive manpower and technical expertise. At this time the regular regiments, the artillerymen and engineers with their wicked and effective devices, and the Imperial Fleet were joined by militia battalions drawn from the *deme* organizations—the "people" in arms fulfilling an ancient civic obligation and right, to defend their own walls.[20]

Provisioning. Under this heading comes the facilities provided or available for offloading goods and supplies, for storage (especially grain), for concentrating and displaying goods or services for readier or more accessible use or sale, for transport strictly speaking, and for the supplying and storage of water—the literal "water of life."

The dependence of part of the Imperial city population has often been noted, mostly with a moral judgment implied; *panem et circenses* has been a cliché among historians describing a pandering to the irresponsible desires of the urban mob, a craven or vicious response of the despot. There is good reason to suspect, however, that the essentials of life *had* to be supplied in some measure by the King-Emperor. In this he acted not merely from charitable instincts, nor to calm the mob's anarchic spirit—he acted to recreate, to continue life. The economic area and impulse in Byzantine life was, as surviving evidence shows, very closely circumscribed. Profit was suspect, and was scrutinized

[20] M. Manojlovic, "Le peuple de Constantinople de 400 à 800 après J.C. Étude spéciale de ses forces armées, des elements qui le composaient et son rôle constitutionelle pendent cette périod," *Byzantion* 11 (1936), 621.

and limited from above. It was the Emperor's task, and that of his bureaucracy, to intrude themselves between his subjects and economic need. They were to equalize, to provide, to perform a series of miracles of loaves and fishes. The munificence and beneficence of the Emperor had to be continuously proven as part of his viceregal *philanthropia*: in his city the categories and necessities of economic man were partly dissolved. This is shown in the great ritualized largesses that followed the recreatory rite of coronation, on the one hand, and in the everyday provision of bread and water, on the other. In either case it was necessary that the "body of citizens" be fed.[21]

This city, after all, *is* of the Type of Paradise; it can be regarded as a sacralized place, where man's existence is continued as ritual, not by work. The sense of this must pervade the city, and be especially localized in the monumental "provisionary" structures even when these (like the granaries and covered cisterns) were not obtrusively visible.

The most visible evidence would have been the great aqueduct of Valens, which cut the city on its longitudinal axis from the Adrinople Gate to the Palace complex, bringing water from sources 50 km away in Thrace. The principle *nymphaion* or fountain-reservoir which the aqueduct filled was near the Forum of Theodosius; there were many others, and water was drawn off from this system to fill the numerous underground cisterns and the several open "tanks." The baths, served by the waterworks, provided another public necessity.[22] Open or invisible, the structures described act in the city as proof of fullness or plenitude, as springs or sources of life itself. They combine with the private sector of provisioning—located in its set quarters and policed by Imperial overseers—to give a kind of visceral richness to the city, an impression of the most basic vital substance, accessible to all. The possibility of a land flowing with milk and honey finds concrete images here.

Concentration. Another aspect of the macrotexture of the city is caught up in the spaces, shapes, and masses that direct or catch

[21] On the Mob, see E. L. Hobsbawm, *Primitive Rebels* (Manchester Univ. Press, 1959), 118–125; on *Philanthropia*, see E. Barker, *Social and Political Thought in Byzantium* (Oxford, 1957), 84, 148.

[22] On baths and the provision of water, see Janin, *Constantinople*, 198–224.

and hold the people, which place or vector—that is, concentrate —their "going and staying." Concentration is many times identical with control, but concentration may be internal and organic, as in the voluntary microtexture—street and house pattern and use, siting of shops and small services—of the ward or neighborhood. There may also be points of voluntary concentration provided by the creating authority; this is true of Constantinople's Hippodrome, the great popular locus where the Emperor openly encountered his subject-citizens.

The most prominent concentrating spaces or masses appear to impinge on the populace from outside and are *designed,* not organic; they are the ganglial system of streets and squares. Main streets, in a city of the Imperial type, are qualitatively different from simple streets, the ways of the neighborhood. These latter, in a city built in a Mediterranean or Near Eastern setting, will be narrow and probably tortuous, conforming to the scarcity of land-space and the power of the climate, but the *broad* street is, invariably, a Sacred Way. Its size and its orientation take it into another category: it is primarily a stage for an instrumentality of power, not a convenience.[23]

The design or internal pattern of the city is strongly shaped by these obtrusive features, and in Constantinople the main ways are radial from (or confluent on) the complex of power-laden structures at the apex of the city's roughly triangular outline. This happens to be a plan that makes practical sense, and certainly some of the main thoroughfares, such as the portico-lined street "of Maurianos" which led from the *Mése* to the port area on the Golden Horn, were economically and logistically useful. The point is that these boulevards were patterned to create a significant effect, one that shifted their economic utility, or even their usefulness to the military or police, to a secondary place at best. Constantinople does not exist because it is at the juncture of great land and sea routes—at a "crossroads"—but because a Center *must* be, and roads (whatever their true or "historical" date of construction) come later.[24] The *Mése* or Middle Way, leading from the Golden Gate eastward to the *omphalos* of the

23 Mumford, *City,* 94.

24 R. Lopez, "The Crossroads within the Wall," *The Historian and the City,* Handlin and Burchard, eds. (Cambridge, Mass., 1963).

world, the Milion, in the great square of the Augusteon, was not a continuation of the Via Ignatia, the Imperial route which ran from the Adriatic to the Golden Gate. The *Mése* was a ritual way or, more precisely, *more* of a ritual way than the Via Ignatia was; the *Mése* was a boulevard where ritual was concentrated and flowed. The ritual was one of movement or progression, and as passersby moved on or crossed the stage upon which this kinetic ritual took place, they were made conscious of a radiating power, one of whose rays they had intercepted. The size, the force of direction, and the quality of being unlike simple streets which the *Mése* and its primary tributaries had, should have, and, I believe, did elicit these reactions.

The fora, spaced along the Sacred Way, had other concentrative purposes. There were points of interchange and intercourse, business, leisure—and, in their size, spacing, and decoration they vibrated to the power of stronger currents. These currents became more perceptible, seemingly, when the Forum Amastrianum was reached; here two branches of the *Mése* joined, and we know that the Amastrianum was a place of execution, filled with pagan statues (and thus with demons).[25]

The Forum of Theodosius lay upward, half a kilometer along the *Mése*. One of its prime features was a triumphal arch, signifying the place of the King's *adventus*, his entrance-and-transformation, and the forum also boasted the first of the great Imperial equestrian statues. It was the largest of the fora.[26] Still farther (inward and upward) was the Forum of the Founder—Constantine's forum—distinguished by its shape, which was that of the sun-shield, the ovoid representation of solar elevation and power. This forum was dominated by monumental statues of the First Emperor, his mother St. Helena, and the Cross.[27] From this forum the *Mése* took the name of Regia, the "royal way," in recognition of its increasing potency. It ended, finally, in the Augusteon, a reverberating space dominated by the Sacred Palace

[25] Janin, *Constantinople,* 68–69.

[26] *Ibid.,* 64–68; on the Adventus, see A. Grabar, *L'Empereur dans l'art byzantine. Récherches sur l'art officiel de l'empire d'Orient.* (Paris, 1936), 234–235; E. Kantorowicz, *Selected Studies* (Locust Valley, New York, 1965), 48, n. 47.

[27] Janin, *Constantinople,* 62–64.

and the Haghia Sophia. Here also were the materializations of the power of measurement: the Horloge, the Great Clock, and the Milion, or navel-stone, marking the point from which all secular distance must be calculated.[28]

The special use and nature of each of these spaces must have been clear to the citizens of Constantinople. The ritual-architectural additions—particularly triumphal arches and columns—were signs of the external agency under whose aegis the people gathered or moved. On the occasions of the great processions, when the Emperor and his retinue toured and reconsecrated the city, the great squares became neural points in a sacralized ganglion—or rather, this meaning was reinforced.[29]

Smaller nuclei of concentration were seen in all the "basilicate" or governmental, administrative, and public buildings, in the baths, the hippodromes or games areas (other than the Great Hippodrome, which was a unique phenomenon), and, of course, in the churches of whatever size. Baths (and theaters, though how long these continued to exist in Constantinople is not known) are redolent of the ancient *polis,* or of that supreme distillation of the *polis,* Rome. Evidently Byzantium reacted against the pagan tone of the secular theater, or saw other possibilities and other necessities for dramaturgic creation. Baths, on the other hand, with all their accumulation of devices and symbols relating to the care of the body and of service to the body of city-dwellers, not only survived into the 10th century, but were built or rebuilt. There is good reason for expecting a Christian reaction against these gathering-places—not only on moral grounds, or even theological ones (those stressing the unimportance of the physical body's care), but on grounds recognizing the possible confusion or opposition of symbols. Christianity, after all, with its baptismal rite and its battery of hydraulic images (especially in connection with the cult of martyrs) had other uses for water. Yet the bath, with its recreative space and comfortable, enclosing forms, seems to have been too valuable a proof of the Imperial will and beneficence—and too great a convenience—to forego.

28 *Ibid.,* 59–62, 102, 103–104.

29 O. Trietinger, *Die ostromische Kaiser- und Reichsidee nach ihrer Gestaltung im hofischen Zeremoniell* (Jena, 1938), 152 ff.

An immediate link between munificence, power and provision, and popular use seems to have persisted here.[30]

Control. Control, or the exercise of power to protect itself and its further exercise, may be made materially visible in the city by various forms. These may be (a) dominating structures specialized for the control function or overtly demonstrating this purpose; (b) ambiguous or "doubled" structures, where a consciousness of some aspect of control which reverses a second use or aspect is apparent; (c) larger spatial elements marked by regulatory attitudes and measures, especially the highly visible and specialized producing or selling quarters, and the equally visible segregatory sections, where exotic (in the Byzantine usage, heterodox) peoples were quarantined.

(a) The prime material sign of the police power of the state was evident in the form of the Praetorion, located on the *Mése* between Constantine's Forum and the Augusteon. It was headquarters for the Eparch or Prefect of the City, court, and prison. Its position was clear; through it flowed the effective punitive strength of the Emperor, whose own precincts rose beyond it. (There were other prisons closer to the Palace, the larger and more important under the jurisdiction of the regiments of the Guard.) Probably a certain amount of careful awe surrounded other administrative buildings, especially the Basiliké, with its courts, which faced on the Augusteon.[31]

(b) The ambiguous or mixed impressions elicited by the walls of a city so protected have already been sketched; the walls compress, rigidify, restrict movement (especially after nightfall, when the entire city was sealed off so far as the ordinary citizen was concerned). These vertical, overlooking masses had their repressive connotation and ambiance; so did the broad ways, especially the *Mése,* for along its straight, open courses passed the Imperial eye, an efflux of force, reinforced by the massive images of dominion—arches, columns, monumental statues—in the successive fora. The sense of radiation was felt equally with the practical thought that broad, straight streets brought the regular soldiery of the Guard quickly within reach of any civil disturbance.[32]

[30] Janin, *Constantinople,* 216–224.
[31] *Ibid.,* 165–173.
[32] On the city walls, see Mumford, *City,* 39 ff.

(c) The rationality and regularized rhythm or texture of economic development in an Imperial city made for visibility, handiness, and ease of access so far as the city dweller, as customer or consumer, was concerned. The hint of control, however, could never be far removed. The physical or topographic dimension of this control—the prescription of the quarter where a trade or specialty was concentrated—reflected a number of desiderata. A purely economic rationale would see here the pattern of the *oikos-oeconomie* clear in the concentration of certain goods and services around their principal market, the Palace complex.[33] Simple security or police precautions made sensible the placement of workers in precious metals or other restricted and valuable goods next to the Praetorion or even in the Palace itself. Symbolic perceptions, however, have their own logic, and this logic, too, stands behind the arrangement of specific materials or services close to the radiant source. Thus certain finely-worked silks (the "forbidden" silks and brocades) which had no true market value, since they were not sold, were produced for the Treasury in a factory located within the Great Palace. Other merchants dealing in Syrian silks, considered a precious but not a forbidden commodity, were placed under the porticoes of the *Mése,* probably near the Praetorion.[34] Goldsmith-jewelers had their place on the *Mése* east of the Forum of Constantine, and bronze workers were quartered just below Haghia Sophia to the west.[35] Sellers of perfume were ordered to set up their booths in the stoa of the Augusteon itself, to "make pleasant the porches of the palace."[36] The logic that concentrated richness and preciousness around the Palace precinct worked itself out both in multisensual and polysymbolic forms.

Occasionally economic segregation and other varieties of separation and control merge or are confused; for example, Syrian (by place of origin) silk merchants and native dealers in Syrian

[33] M. Weber, *The City* (Trans. Martindale and Truewirth, Free Press of Glencoe, 1958), 72–74.
[34] R. Lopez, "Silk Industry in the Byzantine Empire," *Speculum* **XX.1** (January, 1945), 7.
[35] Janin, *Constantinople,* 95–96.
[36] "*The Book of the Prefect*" (Translated by A. E. R. Boak), *Journal of Economic and Business History* **1** (1929), 611, sect. X.

silks shared a quarter by law. Italian and other "Frankish" merchants make a special case; their numbers at this time were not large. True ghetto regulations, however, ordinarily had as their basis the Byzantine fear of religious contagion. Separation, exclusion, the enforcing of marks of visibility were the remedies prescribed for whatever harmful contact might occur between the orthodox and the heterodox—the latter including Jews and Moslems.

In the 10th century the Moslems of the city seem to have been gathered into a residential and commercial quarter very near the Praetorion, where there was a mosque, and where the protection of the Emperor was presumably unquestionabily clear. All Jews were excluded from the city proper, though they could conduct business there during the day; their residential quarter was probably in Pera, across the Golden Horn. The Armenians, or those who kept to their own version of the faith, had a church of their own, a "corporation of merchants," and presumably a quarter; its location we do not know.[37]

It is certain that Bulgar traders, though presumably orthodox, were not allowed to settle permanently in the city, and that the pagan Russians of the early 10th century, and the more or less Christianized and fumigated Russians later, were all restricted to summer quarters on the Bosporus, well out of the city.[38] All those, in fact, who came from outside the circle of the oecumene were allowed into the city, the metaphor of the oecumene, only on sufferance. This would be true whatever the rank of the outsider, for diplomatic representatives were closely guarded and separately housed. It would be true even of the inner security force of the Palace formed of barbarian Turkic tribesmen—Ferghanese, Khazars, and others—who, like tamed wild animals, were kept on a short leash.

The most apparent macrotextural effect achieved by the archi-

[37] On the Moslems, see Janin, *Constantinople*, 257–259; on the Jews, *Ibid.*, 259–260, also J. Starr, *The Jews in the Byzantine Empire* (Athens, 1939); on the Armenians, Michael the Syrian, *Chronique universelle* (Ed. et trad. J.-B. Chabot, Paris, 1901), **III**, 185.

[38] Janin, *Constantinople*, 255–257; on the Russian quarter, J. Pargoire, "St. Mamas, le quartier russe de Constantinople," *Echoes d'Orient* **XI** (1908), 203–210.

tectonic and spatial plan devised by the Emperor as protector, provider, concentrator, and controller was: regularity and predictability. A strong secondary effect was *richness*, as a fabric is rich; the city formed a brocade of symbols, all gathered into the knot of power, of radiant gold, on the Imperial acropolis. Potentiality and effective strength suffused the whole, all surrounded by the mass of walls and the "proud towers."

The Emperor's Rôle

The Byzantine Imperial office has been frequently examined and analyzed in its constitutional or structural-legal dimension.[38a] In the following pages I want to emphasize another aspect of this office, and take other data and other analyses that bear on this aspect: that of the King-Emperor in his *creating* rôle or rôles. Obviously, to recreate these rôles our perceptions, though they need not necessarily be ahistorical, are focused on areas of the human experience that are resistant to proof and even to logic, and yet these perceptions can clarify and vivify the nature of the most important single expression of Byzantium.

The city as Creation cannot be legitimately separated from the King-Emperor as Creator. In the tradition that peaks in Byzantium, the city as sacralized point or place, place-of-the-god or of God, must be in the possession of the god's viceroy. Possession becomes identification, for as the city is divinized—becomes a place of power—by extension it becomes the King as well who, always conquering or annihilating time, creates and recreates the city.[39]

The psychological ambiguities that cluster in the city are intensified in the person of the King-Emperor, the more so since his "creative" rôle attracts to him all the enigmatic and perilous properties of the act of creation itself. It would seem, first, that only with difficulty can the act of creating the city-as-shelter be regarded as a *male* act; that is, proper to or possible for the male

[38a] See the bibliography collected by Charanis in C. Diehl's *Byzantium: Greatness and Decline* (New Brunswick, New Jersey, 1957), 333–336; also Ensslin's bibliography appended to his section of the new *Cambridge Medieval History*, **IV**, part II, 403–408.

[39] H. Frankfort, *Kingship and the Gods* (Chicago, 1962), 237 ff; M. Eliade, *Images and Symbols*, 39.

King. The creation, especially of the artificial womb which the City is, becomes a possibility for a King only after significant adjustments have been made in the nature of kingship itself.[40] The King is understood to be "Father of His People," and with the integrity of his maleness clear; but actually the maleness of the King is thoroughly denatured in the very ritual act that makes him King—in his coronation.[41] Coronation arms the ruler-figure with signs of an undeniably phallic and masculine (and thanatic and coercive) meaning, such as the Sword and the Scepter. But the ceremony also *robes* the King, covers him with fabric, and transmutes him, within the resistant vestments of state, into a container of power as well as its wielder; i.e., into a half-female figure. Uncovered, unrestrained maleness too blatantly contradicts what must be: the magical process of creation can never be completely shifted from the realm of the mother.[42]

The purely male ruler, in Byzantium as in Imperial China, is *tyrannos*; he has, in our phrase, "naked power"—Latin *vis*—undiluted aggressive male potency.[43] A tyrant is not so much an illegal ruler (in the classical view) as he is an unnatural one. He actually has law (as coercive force) on his side, but not magic, for it is only the crowned, robed, hermaphrodized King who can command the twinned instrumentalities of coercion *and* magic. The true King becomes the "nursing father," and his creativity is an act of *couvade*, an imitation-ritual.[44]

This conception stands behind, or is disguised in, the doubled sovereignty which the French scholar Georges Dumezil sees in certain regal and imperial institutions. The "Varunal" sovereignty

[40] S. Freud, *Civilization and Its Discontents* (Trans. J. Strachey, Norton, New York, 1962), 45 ff.

[41] A. M. Hocart, *Kingship* (Oxford, 1927), 77–79, 89.

[42] L. Mumford, in *City Invincible, A Symposium on Urban Civilization and Cultural Development in the Ancient Near East* (Chicago, 1960), 229.

[43] For the connection of *vis* to the supermale boar, see Onians, *Origins of European Thought* (Cambridge, 1951), 177, n. 9. A strong case can be made for the interpretation of the ancient Chinese *BAK* (*pa*) or "tyrant" as penis-king, a ruler by brute male force: I am indebted for this information to G. W. Kent, of the University of California at Irvine (communication of 8 November 1967).

[44] T. Reik, *Ritual: Psycho-analytic Studies* (New York, 1958), 27–89, for expressions and interpretations of *couvade*.

which Dumezil isolates is an *etherialized* aspect of mother-magic, a *mysterium tremendum* that spiritualizes the old, limitless expansive strength and creativity of the female. The supplementary power of the magistrate, of law-as-order (Dumezil's "Mitral" sovereignty) persists as, possibly, the fossilized remnant of an intrusive male force: that of the Hunter-King.[45]

The King, from his coronation-elevation, takes control of all processes of life, space, and time, and among these the building (or rebuilding: the act of repetition or replication does not, in this theory, involve a "space of time," since the divinized King's work comes into being as a sacred, timeless act) of cities or of the city, is paramount in importance. The Myth of the City and the Myth of the King are perfectly complementary; that is, the city must be the dwelling place of the god, who turns his authority over to his icon-viceroy, the King. Beyond this, we find in the symbolic arrangements of a culture like Byzantium's that God-and-King, on the one hand (the ordering power) and City-and-Oecumene, on the other (the ordered space) are made equal:

$$\text{GOD} \longleftrightarrow \text{KING} \longleftrightarrow \text{CITY} \longleftrightarrow \text{OECUMENE}$$

In this scheme, the metaphoric equalization of God and city is immediately possible.[46] This transposition is made even easier in Byzantium, where the city "guarded of God" is most intimately tied up with the cult of the Virgin, the *chora*; that is, the "Place." She, the womb in which man's salvation took human shape, returns, as protectress of the capital, to revive or continue the most archaic depiction of what the city is: the saving womb. Her pure soteriological force and significance stands next to and supports that of the Christ-imitating King.

In the city, the King must perpetually reinforce through his own prismatic image and activity the image of the city as source and refuge of Economy—of Order. His very existence is a substantiation of some part of a divine plan: the sheep are given a

[45] G. Dumezil, *Mitra-Varuna, essai sur deux réprésentations indo-europées de la soveraineté* (Paris, 1948), 94.

[46] See Eusebius of Caesarea, *Ecclesiastical History* (Loeb Classical Library, 1953), **X. iv.** 21.

shepherd.[47] But the King is more truly an actor, and must act, in an eternal drama of salvation, where salvation is considered in all its permutations, from the defensive and physical through the theological. His important rôles are builder, hunter-warrior, focus of ceremony, and prescriber of law; in each he plays against the daemonic unknown, the force of the Outer, or Other.

The King as builder imitates, and so continues, the plastic order that was begun in Creation itself. In ancient Mesopotamia the erection of a reed hut by the King established the "peace of God."[48] Yearly festivals marking the continuation and renewal of life must be marked (as in the Egyptian Sed festival) by special constructions—stage-settings—for the renewing god-king and his divine relations.[49] What was caught up in the act of building (temple=city, for "a house and a city" must be provided to a god) is clear in an Assyrian text:

> For life, for length of days, for the stability of my reign, for the welfare of my prosperity, for the safety of my priestly throne, for the overthrow of my enemies, for the success of the harvest(s) of Assyria, for the welfare of Assyria, I built it.[50]

This is not a formulary expressing the relationship *do ut des,* a serial or causal relationship where the divine powers accept the temple as offering and grant favors in return. The logic is both simpler and more complex: the act of building corresponds with, rather than induces or leads to, "long life," "safety," and "welfare." In this construction all the beneficent currents of life run *through* the rebuilt temple, where they are made to fit with its own solidity and mimetic order.

In another tradition seen as more directly affecting Byzantine conceptions of Creation and Creator, the ancient Judaic imperial city is at one time "the city of our God . . . this holy mountain" and "the city of the great King" which "God will establish . . . for

[47] On the paradigmatic Mesopotamian type, see Frankfort, *Kingship and the Gods,* 217 ff, 237, 238 ff.

[48] I. Engnell, *Studies in Divine Kingship in the Ancient Near East,* 32.

[49] Frankfort, *op. cit.,* 79–80.

[50] D. D. Luckenbill, *Ancient Records of Assyria* (Chicago, 1927), II, para. 702.

ever," and whose walls, towers, palaces give witness to the power of Judah's God.[51] These Psalms were used by Eusebius of Caesarea in his panegyric on Constantine's decoration of Jerusalem, especially the erection of the Church of the Holy Sepulchre. Thus, according to Eusebius, was confounded "the demon that loveth the evil" with his "ferocious (*thēriōdē*) madness" and his allies of "beasts in men's shape" (*anthrōpomorphon thēra*) and "every kind of savage thing (*agrion*)."[52] The greatest victory in Constantine's Christ-directed war against these malign—unordered—forces (in the case of the root-meaning of *agrios,* forces "from the countryside") is won when the Name of Christ is recorded on monuments, and His victories "inscribed in imperial characters in the midst of the city that is Empress among the cities of the world."[53] As Jerusalem is Empress, so must Rome (or New Rome) be Emperor, but Constantinople will eventually combine both, the paternal and the maternal modes of effective authority.

So far as the physical history of the city itself is concerned, Justinian's *renovatio* of the Roman Empire is described by the secular historian Procopius in terms that clarify the act of divine mimesis. The great Emperor was, according to Procopius, given a commission to remake (*metapoieisthai*) the Empire.[54] This physical reconstruction at all times proceeded according to divine or superhuman plan, and the Emperor was made to intervene and solve particular problems of an architectural or technical nature with divine guidance.[55] Haghia Sophia receives this grace, and impossible things (*amēchanois*) are done elsewhere.[56] Cities are founded as specifics against the Old Adam, the beast in man which is more than "pagan" (as "pagan" refers to the non-Christianity of the conservative countryside); it is utterly outside the order of things. For example, the Tzani, a tribe of eastern Anatolia, were "independent . . . without rulers (*anarchoi*) . . . living a savage-like manner of life" and went so far as to worship the

[51] Psalms, 48.1.2; Psalms, 48.8.
[52] Eusebius, *op. cit.,* X.iv.14.
[53] *Ibid.,* X.iv.16.
[54] Procopius of Caesarea, *Buildings* (Loeb Classical Library, 1954), II.vi.6.
[55] *Ibid.,* II.v.11.
[56] *Ibid.,* I.i.71 ff, V.iii.10–11, V.vi.15–21.

very wildness—birds and trees—that surrounded them.[57] They were tamed not only by defeat, and by guardian fortresses and vigilant garrisons, but by the founding of a city as example, which immediately brought and thereafter preserved order (*eukosmia*) in their country.[58]

At one terminus of his empire Justinian fortified the Mesopotamian frontier; Procopius' comment, with accurate reflection caught in the hyperbole, is that one would say "it was solely for this purpose that he succeeded to the imperial power."[59] At the other end of the world the "threshhold of the Empire," the Straits of Gibraltar, were made impregnable by his founding of a church dedicated to the Theotokos, the threshhold to salvation. In either case, or in any of his constructions, all sacred edifices, Justinian solidified the idea of creative jurisdiction and power, imitating God, and following the pattern set by the first imitator and founder, Constantine the Great, the arch-emperor in every sense.

The most valuable record of Imperial constructions to survive in a readable form is the circuit-wall of Constantinople itself. Separating the city from the Outside, the Great Walls were a primary focus of the cosmos-imitating imperative, and one revealing, in the strata and succession of inscriptions, a solidified chronology running through the life of the Empire. The identifiable inscriptions on wall, gate, or tower—the "imperial letters" mentioned by Eusebius—which show the euergetic and creative (or cosmetic) urge of the Christ-imitating emperor, run in time from Theodosius II, the original builder, through John VIII Paleologos (who died in 1448, five years before the end).[60] The great rebuilders, according to this record, were the Iconoclasts, Leo III and Constantine V, the Macedonian Basil II (with his supernumerary brother, Constantine VIII), and John VIII; other foundations are credited to Leo IV, Constantine VI and Irene, Justin II, Comneni, Angeli, a Romanus, and lesser officials. The surviving bits of the seawall fortifications are most frequently credited to Theophilus.[61]

57 *Ibid.*, III.vi.3 ff.
58 *Ibid.*, III.vi.19.
59 *Ibid.*, II.xx.11.
60 Janin, *Constantinople*, 269.
61 *Ibid.*, 265–286.

The briefest but most potent signification is the Byzantine monogram

IC	XC
NI	KA

"Jesus Christ, Conquer" is not a pious wish, nor completely a prophylactic slogan: Christ *does* conquer in the raising of the masonry against malign forces.[62] The theme of victory is explicit in inscriptions that proclaim "victory to the fortune (*Nikā hē tychē*)" of Leo and Constantine (or, in another place, of an unidentified Constantine).[63] The victory is an eternalized and transcendent victory actualized in stone; the "fortune," at the same time, must be both that of the two emperors and that of the city, combined in one image.

This victory, the wall proclaims, is won over time as well as over hostile (or amoral, anarchic) space. The destructive force of the cycling years—the *kyklikē kinēsis* of one inscription—is counteracted. But the act of building is a verification of timeless rule as well. The cry "many years" in Byzantine ceremonial responses is repeated on and in the Imperial buildings, and is even more concretely charged with a significance of eternal life and authority, created anew with every creation, every materialization.[64] The most sacred of the ten gates piercing the Great Walls, the Golden Gate which concentrated in itself the most potent threshold-magic and divinizing power, bore Theodosius's words: "Who builds the gate of gold re-founds the Age of Gold (AVREA SAECLA GERIT QVI PORTAM CONSTRVIT AVRO)."[65] The Golden Age was in fact refounded wherever and whenever an Imperial figure caused stones to take shape, for whatever use.

The wall complex which made concrete Constantinople's boast that it was *Theophilaktos*—"Guarded by God"—was an *opus mixta* in a meaning beyond the technical. In its effective mass and length it undoubtedly "saved" the city, but it was as well a

[62] *Ibid.*, 268, 295.
[63] *Ibid.*, 277, 279.
[64] *De ceremoniis aulis byzantinis* (Ed. Reisk, Bonn, CSHB, 1829); Janin, *Constantinople*, 270, 273.
[65] Janin, *Constantinople*, 269.

vessel of life in a true soteriological sense. Built by King-Emperors acting as Christ, it was actually (that is, metaphorically) built by Christ himself (one graffito says "God raised thee well"), whose protective beneficence inhered in the stones, and who was at the same time iconically represented by it.

Hunter-king; warrior-king. The Byzantine ruler-generalissmo followed a pattern and tradition shaped approximately as follows: the King as Hunter or as Warrior acts in the place of the god, or as God, to defeat the dark powers—powers regarded as identical in either hostile confrontation. The role is the most masculine the King is called upon to play; though magic may have its part in the scenario of the combat or hunt, the King relies upon *weapons*—tools, instruments of phallic extension and force—to overthrow the enemy. The King acts in his form and capacity as the "armed Mithra," the tool-and-weapon wielding sovereign, rather than as the magician, and acts *against* magic, against the encompassing fluid, the shapeless, the dark—actually attributes of his own Varunal aspect: his own feminine side.[66]

Separation of the city from its natural matrix and the inevitable and eternal conflict between them pits the King-Emperor against that called the Outside, whose original form was the Dragon. So the war may still be represented, in a pictorial tradition whose mythic roots go deep into Near Eastern king-and-godship. The god, armed with a ritualized "tool" (often a tool—a hammer or bludgeon—metaphorically crossed with the thunder) casts down Leviathan (Asag, Tryphon, Illuyankas, Azi Dahak).[67] The hero, as a distinct type and with a distinct aetiology, will be engrafted onto this myth.[68] The King, however, must perpetuate and reenact the victory, not only to ensure the life and progression of the year (on which Gaster, with his theories of the "topocosmic ritual," concentrates) but to continually "draw the bounds" and demonstrate his effective control.[69]

[66] Dumezil, *Mitra-Varuna,* 137.

[67] T. Gaster, *Thespis: Ritual, Myth, and Drama in the Ancient Near East* (2nd ed., Doubleday Anchor, New York, 1961), 137–138.

[68] On the hero: M. Eliade, *Cosmos and History, the Myth of the Eternal Return* (New York, 1959), 37, 40, n. 70.

[69] Gaster, *op. cit.,* 17–19, 24; for Orphic-Dionysian connections see R. Eisler, *Orphisch-Dionysisch Mystereingedanken in der christlichen Antike* (Hildesheim, 1966), 12 ff, 52–53.

The King-Emperor, in Byzantium's case, is associated with the hunting-ritual (a) in its symbolic, iconized form—the pictorial representation that connects the ruler with *victory* in all its forms, (b) as an observer (and possibly as an actor) in the *ludi* or hunting-scenes presented in the Hippodrome, and (c) as a participant, "in times of profound peace (*en eirēnē batheia*)" to prove the Imperial energy in hunting as in war (*en . . . polemois kai thēroktoniais*).[70]

The symbolic-artistic representation of ferocity, in Byzantium as in Mesopotamia-Iran, ordinarily was not the dragon or serpent but the lion. The hunter is mounted on horseback, not on the sun-chariot as in the Mesopotamian tradition, and carries a lance, not the Babylonian-Persian bow and sun-arrows (though there are exceptions). The combat, where the horsed hunter is clearly an Emperor, is a solemn, sacred balance of hieratic gestures: the Emperor wears his full ceremonial equipage, and strikes majestically at an heraldic lion. This equestrian Hunter-Warrior seems to have survived as an Imperial iconic type when the equestrian statue itself, with its burden of classical associations, fell out of the iconic vocabulary.[71] The lion, though one of its associations is daemonic (the lion-Satan of I Peter, "seeking whom he may devour") is less effective as an image of dark energy than the snake-monster is; the lion is more a representation of fierce but predictable, virile (and eventually royal) power. In its adoption as adversary is caught up an idea of knightly combat, of a duel between equals. By association it will become a royal beast and, finally, a proof of royalty, a beast that sinks into obedience only before the true King.[72]

The Hunt, of whatever beast or game, will remain royal and thus a pursuit tabooed to some extent. Wild beasts retain their quality of utter alienation from the human, and to follow them lays one open to risks as much spiritual as physical. Folklore is

[70] Grabar, *L'Empereur dans l'art byzantine,* 57–62, plates IX.1, X.2; Eustathius of Thessalonika, *Oratio ad manuelem imperator* (Ed. Regel, *Fontes rerum byzantinarum* I.1, Petropoli, 1892), 40; John Cinnamus, *Historiae* (Ed. Meineke, Bonn, CSHB, 1836), **IV**,266–267.

[71] Grabar, *op. cit.,* 47.

[72] M. Bloch, *Le roi thaumaturge: étude sur le caractère surnaturel attribué à la puissance royale particulièrement en France et en Angleterre* (Paris, 1961), 256 ff.

full of examples: the King or Prince crosses daemonic boundaries while hunting; the Forest masks the Realm of Faerie, out of mortal space and time; the hunted beast itself is an instrument of enchantment, and so on. The eternal or Wild Huntsman is a well-known folkloric type, and occasionally is specifically identified as a King who challenged deep and magical powers too often.[73] For the commoner, hunting was sufficiently risky without supernatural interference, especially if the game were "royal." To hunt the King's deer was not to encroach on royal property, but to interrupt and blaspheme against a protective ritual, to commit *lésè majesté* and even treason.

The Emperor, in taking his place in the *kathisma,* the Royal Box, in the Great Hippodrome, moved the "games" presented there into a special category. These games might be mock-hunts, or *ludi* of a nearly gladiatorial type, or they might be the more familiar chariot-courses, but in any case the Emperor could not be merely a highly-placed spectator. The mimetic war between men and beasts, or men and "other" men—men of the noncosmos, barbarians—reflected his own deadly prerogative, delegated for the occasion: his subjects were shown an eternal conflict and an eternal, protective victory. In the races another aspect of the same theme was demonstrated, for these contests were qualitatively similar recapitulations of the drama of man contending for victory, for the agonic proof of excellence. The victorious charioteer was regarded as the receiver of divine favor in a contest whose form was the "round of life," the circular track of the universe's accidents. This favor and this victory were so highly appraised, the *ludus* so charged, that it is hinted that the Emperor himself took part in the course.[74] Probably he did not—not, at least, in the great races of the Hippodrome. The charioteer, however, by *his* success had to be identified with the overreaching, essential victory that the true Emperor embodied, and the two identities were metaphorized and crossed: in every crowned athlete the Imperial crown was authenticated. The Emperor may thus be defined as victorious actor and benign *choregos,* presenter of the drama, in one.

[73] G. Roheim, *Gates of the Dream* (New York, 1952), 334, 511.
[74] Grabar, *op. cit.,* 63–64.

The third part of the hunting-ritual pattern, in which the Emperor actually followed the sport itself, is easy enough to chronicle. We may take it that every ruler hunted, and some were notorious blood-sportsmen: among the Emperors in the 9th century, Michael III was a great hunter, Basil I died as the result of a hunting accident; in the 10th century Romanus II hunted more than he ruled.[75] We cannot distinguish in the sport of these monarchs their subjective enjoyment as contrasted to the sense of ritual they felt; these must have been conjoined. What is true, though, is that the lust for hunting which seemed to possess Michael (however Michael's bad reputation might be the work of his assassin-successor, Basil the Macedonian) and Romanus passed a certain set limit of propriety in popular opinion. The aggressive-phallic, supermasculine pursuit, the too-often repeated challenge to the Wild, rebounded against them. They overbalanced and disrupted the patterns of kingly behavior and suffered for it, as in an Arthurian legend (and elsewhere) the King who rode after game once too often was sentenced by the divine powers to follow his passion forever.[76]

The Warrior-King seeks a victory quantitatively, not qualitatively, different from the victory of the Hunter-King. The enemy, called (ordinarily) the barbarian, may be represented in a daemonic or bestial guise, and is defined as of the same exotic and excluded genus. Pressing in his feral strength against the borders, he was met by the Emperor, his armies, and the Victory-bearing Cross. In this battle—defined as ritual combat in a special sense—the soldier-emperor gambled on the continuing potency of his viceregal status, for he as seeker of victory was the lens through which the piety of the oecumene shown and the light as well in which it was concentrated. Failure and defeat, perhaps even the smallest setback, could be of the gravest moment, for they meant that the divine hand had been taken away. Victory, on the other

[75] Theophanes Continuatus (Ed. Bekker, Bonn, CSHB, 1838), 248; Cedrenus (Ed. Bekker, Bonn, CSHB, 1839), I, 1157; *Vita St. Euthemii* [Trans. R. Karlin-Hayter, in *Byzantion* 25–27 (1955–57)]. See E. Brehier, *Civilisation byzantine* (Paris, 1950), 67–68.

[76] G. Roheim, "Die Wilde Jagd," *Imago* XII (1926), 465; R. Sebillot, *Le Folklore de France* (Paris, 1904), I, 168.

hand, proved the imperial office valid and its occupant effective, and was so celebrated.

The nature of this *agon* and the Emperor's place in it was iconographically represented in a fashion very similar to the iconic styles of the "hunting King." The spear of the ruler was presented against a fallen foe (as in the actual Triumph Ceremony recorded by Constantine Porphyrogenitus).[77] Or, the protective vigilance of the mounted, lance-bearing Emperor, in another surviving representation, was paired by the artist with a scene of the hunt, thus firmly attaching the two actions to one another. Perhaps these scenes show too much a "historical," overtly dramatic scenario. The most Byzantine depiction of victory must be that of the Psalter of Basil II, where the fully armed and armored *Basileus,* supported by two Archangels and crowned by Christ, stands on a cushion over eight miniature Bulgars, all abject in the *proskynesis.*[78] Here the Triumphator, in the gear of the Byzantine heavy cavalryman, contains in himself the total potential of the victorious; without a movement on the part of the Emperor his enemies are stilled into submission, borne down by the power which must be contained on the Christ-crowned.

The triumphant Emperor is raised up over his city as over the prostrate enemy; he is *victor omnium gentium,* but his triumph is significantly different from that of the older Empire and the older Roman tradition. For one thing, the Emperor is *victor,* like the Cross, not *invictus,* the "unconquered" ruler of the pagan oecumene, tied by this label to the cyclical, everreturning pattern of the sun and tied as well to the burden of negation or, at least, doubt.[79] In *victor* or *nikator* there is no doubt. Even more notable is the form of the triumph: pictorialized, as the 5th century Column of Arcadius, it was already a triumph concentrated into procession and ritual, swinging far from the series of dramatic encounters or fragments of history carved, for example, on Trajan's monument.[80]

By the 10th century the hieratic, nonhistoric aspect of the

[77] Grabar, *op. cit.,* 55 n. 2; *De ceremoniis,* 609, 613.
[78] See e.g. D. Talbot Rice, *The Art of Byzantium* (London, 1959), 26, plate XI.
[79] Compare L. Brehier, *Les institutions,* 57.
[80] Grabar, *op. cit.,* 42.

Byzantine triumph-show was even more emphatic, though the processional "entrance" triumph, which is predicated on victory as punctual and historical—that is, over an identified enemy—rather than atemporal, was still seen. The two complete Triumph-rituals contained in the Book of Ceremonies can be dated (in the 10th century), but their dominant tone is static, timeless.[81] One is set in the Forum of Constantine, a *locus potentissimus* inferior only to the Acropolis itself; stage-center is the stepped-base Cross of Constantine.[82] The second takes place in the Hippodrome, with the Emperor seated in the *kathisma,* replicating the sculptured scene of triumph on the base of the Obelisque of Theodosius which stood on the *spina* of the Hippodrome below him. In the first ceremony the Emperor is led by the Cross to the Forum and his triumph (as Constantine had been).[83] The hymnody for the occasion includes the Mosaic *figura* of the Crossing of the Red Sea and the miraculous vanquishing of both the enemy and nature. The "Chief Emir" of the hostiles is trampled under the Imperial foot with exquisite ceremony. At the conclusion of the set-piece the Emperor, as a trophy, leaves the *stolē* which he wore in the Church of the Theotokos nearby.[84] In the second or Hippodrome triumph the Patriarch is absent; the tone is more military and even secular, and a votive element is added. In both, the acclamations of the Demes are heavily weighted with the cry *polla te etē*—"many years"—the *vivat* that victory makes authentic, as the undying Empire finds its support in Christ eternal: "Son of God, life to them [the Emperors], Son of God, rule with them; Son of God, make us rejoice through them; Son of God, multiply their years . . ."[85]

With all of the symbols of war and victory, and despite the undisputed importance of a successful defense of the Empire, there are set limits to the activity of the Warrior-King. The military leadership of the ruler is taken for granted. The cooperation

[81] *De ceremoniis,* 607 ff.

[82] For the significance of the "stepped cross" as cosmic hill, see W. Müller, *Die Heilige Stadt: Roma quadrata, himmlischen Jerusalem und die Mythe vom Weltnabel* (Stutgart, 1961), 196 ff.

[83] Kantorowicz, *Selected Studies,* 44, n. 30, on the Adventus.

[84] *De ceremoniis,* 610; Grabar, *op. cit.,* 236–237.

[85] *De ceremoniis,* 612–615.

of God is accepted as the proof of "pious" rule, and the form of the triumph follows. Yet the armed might of the Empire serves, in theory, only to protect order from chaos; it is a force for rebalancing, and its leader is *eirēnopoios,* the Peace-Maker, whose type is the Prince of Peace. Imperial war, in this view, cauterizes and heals the wounds of the world.[86]

The King-Emperor in ritual. A definition of ritual, chosen arbitarily from a variety of definitions, is: an action or (in another remove) the imitation of an action that attaches the players or actors to a "significant" act in another time—that other time being either previous or atemporal. The other act, in its other time, was, in Byzantium and its state ritual, connected to the creative or controlling act of the founding deity or his first representative, the founding king—that is, Constantine the Great. This is one ritual level; there is another, in which the crises in the personal-extensional life of the monarch—birth, marriage, coronation, death—are attached to the vital symbols of both the faith, the Christian passion, and to the ongoing year with its generational but vulnerable strength.[87]

The Emperor both created and followed ritual in order to imitate and so to recreate the secular but iconic harmonies at whose core he stood. These secular harmonies reflected, as icons, Types which were eternal and divine as he, the King-Emperor, followed the Type of Christ. In ritual the Emperor had to both be and do —as Christ was both being and will. The Emperor-centered rituals moved from harmonic resolution to harmonic resolution, each bringing state and society into balance and consonance with the forces that fed them, but that also had the power to destroy them. The Emperor's rôle could be delegated but never divided, for one of his metaphors is that of the mirror, reflecting the truth, and another, more actively, is the shuttle: "While the ritual unfolds, the king moves like a shuttle in a great loom to recreate the fabric in which people, country, and nature are irrevocably comprised."[88] The act of ritual, which both connects and dissolves, is shown in this image working its most essential magic: making the

[86] Treitinger, *Kaiser und Reichsidee,* 230.
[87] *Ibid.,* passim.
[88] Frankfort, *op. cit.,* 84–85.

substitution of an order for the randomness and threats of life, weaving a societal fabric that enfolds and protects—again, separating the Inner from the Outer. So the essence of power, if tamed, must be predictability, and even the inevitable and necessary changes in rulers, dynasties, régimes can be immediately converted to *safe* energy, to productive-protective force: the ritual intervenes and mediates and change becomes no change; history and time, ritualized, are made impotent; dissonance and disharmony are simply not accepted as possible.

To say that the Byzantine King-Emperor acted in ritual seems to separate a function that could not be separate: if the Emperor *was* he was a ritual, walking and acting. His individual acts were all of the same fabric. There were no "prime" ceremonies, and no ceremony was ever truly lost: the compendium of ceremonial left us by the encyclopedist-Emperor Constantine VII recalls a "history" of ceremony in the form of datable rituals celebrating the reception of Persian ambassadors in the 6th century, or Russians, Arabs, and Bulgars in the 10th, but the ritual's power was not connected with time or circumstance: harmony rules all.[89] Its tones might be stronger or fainter; more or less complex. There were "simple" rituals of delegation, and there were the rituals where all the symbols of Imperial existence coalesced, as in the Coronation, but none were extraneous as none were "merely" ritual, in the sense of purposeless play or habit without content. Let me give two examples.

The Emperor celebrated the Nativity (*Christougennos*) with a processional ceremony, with six foci or "receptions" (*dokhai*) at points in the process.[90] The ritual begins with the predictive, scene-setting chant of the cantors: "a star foretells the sun, Christ, born in Bethlehem of a Virgin"; the Emperor then stands forth and is greeted with the acclamation of duration—"many years!" —and its variations. At the second reception the chants ask God to grant the Emperor long life. In the fourth the liturgical chorus connects the Incarnation, which eliminated the sin of Adam, to the guardianship of the Romans, granted for a "length of time"

[89] See the Proem to the *De ceremoniis,* 3–5, trans. in Barker, *Social and Political Thought,* 100.

[90] *De ceremoniis,* 35–38.

(*mekos khronōn*). In the sixth *dokhé,* which is held by the Horloge or Great Clock in the Augusteon, the Bethlehem image returns; in the chants the Virgin is in both Eden and Bethlehem, Christ appears from her to save mankind: at this point the Emperor stands forth again and the chants reidentify him: "O Lord and Despot of all," "Many years to thee, O born of a holy virgin."

This ceremony, with its striking conclusion, is a time-ritual, one in which all the concepts (Ideas) of time are collapsed into one. The chants that merely seem to wish the ruler "long life" become effective; the Emperor is first associated with Bethlehem and the Birth, when "old" time (the time of the Fall) was negated, then with both Eden and Bethlehem, the loci of no-time or paradise. As a supporting image the Virgin is given to both Eden and Bethlehem, since she too is a *paradeisos,* an "enclosure." At last the Emperor stands forth, and the chants make clear that linear time is dissolved: primordial time—Eden and the Fall—and figural-historical time—Bethlehem—are translated into the complete timelessness of ritual. All points come together, Savior (*Soter*) and Guardian (*Phylax*) are conflated; the Emperor then must become Christ: "Many years to thee, O born of a holy virgin." The God-King, standing by the Great Clock, assumes control over the *khronos.*

A second paradigmatic ritual celebrates the Feast of the Ascension with a procession and thirteen *dokhai.*[91] The procession itself, though always important, is less so than are the reception points, which taken in total describe the spiritual skeleton of the city. The Ascension of the Theotokos is not only the proximate cause of the ceremony, but all its metaphors radiate from her, especially the metaphor of salvation that she—and the city—project together. The acclamations call on her to guard the walls; yet she *is* the wall, the container or *chora,* as well as the fountain or source of life. She, in the city, becomes all providence or the space that both provides and is provided. The Emperor passes into both metaphorical containers: he, the Virgin, and the Walls guard the city as one. The protective symbols are visible, the place or space of each reception exists only by and through the

[91] *Ibid.,* 54–58.

ceremony when the Emperor brings the light that defines it; then the procession moves—without direction—onward or, actually, the procession *becomes* elsewhere. There is neither movement nor direction except as we reconstruct it.

This ceremony is twinned with that of the Nativity: space with time. Both show the rich combination of metaphors that shift, merge, and reinforce one another. As Christ and the Christ-imitating Emperor subdue and negate time in the first liturgy, so the Theotokos and the Emperor subdue and define space, a sacral expansion, in the second. There are no allegories, and the figural element is not strong, but the direct and dynamic metaphorical crossing or exchange is continually repeated. The Emperor, bearing light (which itself in the Byzantine view has materiality) lets this light flow into the city, so that he too is the generator of good and of salvation, a male *theotokos*; or, in another prismatic image, the paradise-city, Eden and Bethlehem, is recreated as a cycle of time brings the New Year and the Emperor stands forth to claim it.

The "fabric" described comes partly from the creator-King, partly from the material-emotional setting, partly from the resonating people, symbolized by the Demes. The whole is vibratory and reverberent, not stable, as the word, the effective acclamation, rings new changes and permutations, interacting with the liturgical occasions, the divine actors, the human representatives, the treasure of stored and evocative images. When each ceremony draws on the same source, none can be separate in quality or most effective and none is "simply" ritual. The least meaningful definition and use of ritual, in a civilization where ritual is a dominant, is its definition as a stabilized, solidified substitution for active, essential, or organic reality. In Byzantium, ritual set the boundaries of reality.[92]

The King-Emperor in law. The weight of law was heavy in Byzantium, and still affects our analyses of this state. *Romanitas* or "Romanness" was carried, it seems, not only in the name and exterior form of the empire (*Basileiōn Rhomaiōn*) but in the law codes that were quintessentially Roman, carrying with them the

[92] Treitinger, *Kaiser- und Reichsidee,* 1 ff.

explicit notion of the necessity of man's control of man; of a solid, definitive *jus* marking off the limits of man as a legal, and therefore a civilized, being.[93] The Roman law *is* Byzantine, inasmuch as Justinian, from Constantinople, ordered a final recension of the codified law already put in order by the Emperor Theodosius, his predecessor, and Justinian's Latin *Corpus Juris Civilis* is the monolith upon which the leaves of legal commentary and exegesis still gather, since it is the legal core around which most Western European law develops.

The fact of Justinian's great work, the massive subsidiary blocks of codified law added by his Byzantine successors, and the presence of certain legal definitions of the Imperial office itself often stand behind an argument for a "Roman" component in Byzantine civilization, set over against other constitutive elements. The fact of autocracy, in this argument, is somewhat blunted, and a *Rechtstaat,* a state-in-law appears.[94] True, if the eye is focused on law and on the legal definitions alone, Byzantium can be called a *Rechtstaat.* The Emperor, according to the *Epanagogē* which was ordered drawn up by the Emperors Basil I and Leo VI themselves, had to "enforce and maintain, first and foremost all that is set forth in the divine scriptures, then the doctrines laid down by the seven holy (General) Councils, and further, and in addition, the received Rhomaic law."[95] In interpreting the laws the Emperor must pay attention to "the custom of the State," to tradition, to precedent.[96] However, the Imperial office is not *formed* from these legal parts or segments; it stands with them, not because of them. All the legalistic descriptions of kingly power that can be extracted from the law codes leave intact the titlature of the King-Emperor: the law is enacted in the name of the *Autokrator kai Basileus Rhomaiōn,* and insofar as *autokrator* describes the "operative force" of the Emperor, it must mean that

93 Compare Brehier, *Les institutions,* 173 ff.

94 M. Dendias, "Études sur le gouvernement et l'administration à Byzance," *Atti del V Congresso Internazionale di Studi Bizantini* (Studi Bizantini e Neoellenici V) (Roma, 1939), 128.

95 E. von Lingenthal-Zepos, *Jus graecoromanum,* IV, 182; trans. in Barker, *Social and Political Thought,* 90.

96 *Ibid.*

no earthly power—including the power of law—stands above *his* power.[97]

The term *Rechtstaat,* then, must be considerably bent and reshaped before it can be properly fitted over the Byzantine political matrix. The Emperor was (a) a source of law; his acts had power in law from the moment of their pronunciation, though they might be codified later. No legislative power devolved on any separately consituted organ or agency of government, which was clear long before Leo VI abolished the antique *Senatus consultum.*[98] Therefore, since a creator is superior to that which he creates, the Emperor stands above his creation, law. "Some say," writes the commentator Nikulitzas in the 11th century, "that the emperor is not subject to law, but *is* law. I agree."[99] Yet (b) the Emperor was constrained to conform to a certain behavioral pattern, and this pattern was, in Byzantine eyes, more important than the substance called law. Barker remarks perceptively that "there was no single *thing* he could not do, in theory; but there were *ways* in which he could not act."[100] The King-Emperor was to act "like an Umpire making awards in a game";[101] he was not to act against the "laws of piety," which Nikulitzas sets as the limit to the Emperor's power in law.[102] The Emperor might take the Hellenistic kingly appellation of *nomos empsychos*—the Living Law—but his charge over law did not extend to Justice, of which laws—and the Emperor's laws included—were only a part.

The Byzantines conceived that written or enacted law was but one aspect of natural (*dikaios*) law—the ruling principle of both secular and sacred cosmos.[103] The Emperor was limited in his actions not by "constitutional" or codified restrictions, but by his

[97] J. B. Bury, *The Constitution of the Later Roman Empire* (Cambridge, 1910), 20–21.
[98] Leo VI, *Novella* 78, in P. Noailles et A. Dain, *Les Novelles de Léon VI le Sage: Texte et traduction publié* (Paris, 1944), 270–271.
[99] In Barker, *Social and Political Thought,* 125–126.
[100] *Ibid.,* 29.
[101] *Epanagogè,* tit. II, in *Jus graecoromanum* **IV,** 181; Barker, *Social and Political Thought,* 89.
[102] Barker, *op. cit.,* 126.
[103] Dendias, "Études sur le gouvernement," 127.

participation in the wider harmony of natural law which, when he acted in justice, he perfectly reflected. Justice, then, is thought of as the reflection in law of what *is*: natural in this case can mean not contrary to nature—as Nikulitzas says, no one need obey an Emperor who demands that his subjects drink poison, or commands them to "go to the sea and cross it like a diver."[104] Obedience in these instances would violate the "natural" desire for life. But *dikaios* has an added shade of meaning, that of "righteous," and righteousness as a moral quality is certainly demanded of the Emperor even though he is Living Law. Moral rectitude stands behind that section of the *Epanagōgē* which notes that "wrong decisions" shall not be confirmed "even by long custom."[105] *Dikaiosyne* or righteousness went far beyond the correcting of "wrong" decisions. As Christ, whose imitator the Emperor was, displayed love of man (*philanthropia*) and in displaying this love set aside the normative way of the world—in other words, performed miracles, including the raising of the dead—the Emperor, acting to the limit of his human powers, also occasionally set aside the processes of secular justice, in the name of mercy or *philanthropia.*[106] The commutation of a sentence can be considered a secular miracle, a relaxation of the inexorable power of the sword of justice, and this secular miracle confirmed the Christ-imitating Emperor in his "righteous" office or rôle.

The Byzantine Emperor acted in law as he acted elsewhere, to secure harmony, and law was regarded as an extension of the power of harmony, not of force. The *machinery* of law was in the Emperor's hands entirely; though the system of courts was divided according to status—that is, lay or clerical—the last appeal was to Caesar.[107] The primacy of the Emperor as judge is not

[104] Barker, *op. cit.,* 126.

[105] *Epanagogè,* tit. II.13, in *Jus graecoromanum* IV, 182; Barker, *op. cit.,* 91.

[106] For the transmission and Christianization of the concept of *philanthropia* by Eusebius of Caesarea, whose sources were Hellenistic political theorists, see N. Baynes, "Eusebius and the Christian Empire," in his *Byzantine Essays and Other Studies* (London, 1960), 170–172. Baynes takes his conclusions from Eusebius' *Triakontaeterikos* (Ed. Heikel, Leipzig, 1902).

[107] *Epanagogè,* tit. XI, in *Jus graecoromanum* IV, 184; Barker, *op. cit.,* 95–96.

clear in documents such as the *Epanagōgē*, but the Byzantine tendency to subject the ecclesiastical area to Imperial control at the highest level would make the Emperor's final intervention or adjudication likely. The great theoreticians of icon-worship, John of Damascus and Theodore of Studios, had demanded the separation of Church and State in their attacks on iconoclastic Emperors, but although iconoclasm had failed the Emperor remained powerful in the church, and retained his semipriestly function and oversight.[108]

The Emperor, even in his rôle in "Roman" law, could not escape completely into an instrumental or causative area free from the metaphoric and the symbolic, for though the law contained the procedural aspect of justice, the higher Law was reached in the Emperor's reflection of the miraculous and the magical. No one could flee into the law and escape Imperial justice—the law was not a sanctuary—but at the same time the Emperor could not himself escape the dictates of *dikaiosyne* and act arbitrarily or tyrannically. As *autokrator*, in law, he adjusted procedure to the pattern of societal reality as he saw fit, and reviewed his own decisions, but he could not evade his twinned title: as *basileus*, the King, he was connected to eternal forms and to the magic-working, creating, and maintaining Type of the King-Christ as All-Ruler, whose will sustained the order of the world.

[108] For the views of Theodore and John, see Barker, *op. cit.*, 86–87.

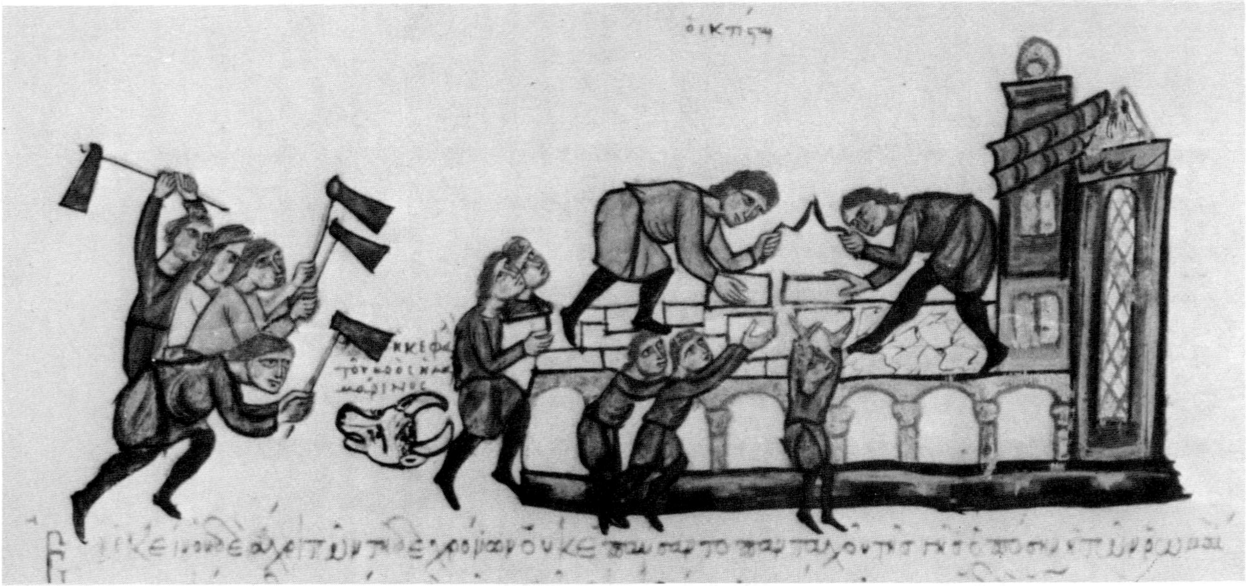

Builders at work in the city, from the Skyllitzes Matritensis. (Courtesy of Dr. S. Cirac Estopanan.)

TWO

The Economy of the City

> As for applied arts (al-sana'i al-mihaniya) they are indisputable masters in them and no one surpasses them excepting the Chinese.
>
> Marvazi, *Tabāii al-ḥayawān*

THE ECONOMIC FUNCTION IN THE CITY

The Specific Economic Gravity of the Empire

At the present time no city is, or can be, described only as a product of economic forces. This development, which is a reaction from various kinds of model-building simplicism—not necessarily Marxist—has taken strong support from recent theories of urban formation that try to show that the magnetic power of the market is complexly related to other magnetic forces, as strong or sometimes stronger. It is suggested, in fact, that the history of the city as a human artifact, the act of permanent congregation and coalescing *preceded,* in the protocity or eopolis, the agricultural-economic revolution which had been thought to be the absolute precondition for urban settlement. In other words, in the ancient Near East men were in cities before they were on farms.[1]

In this anomalous reversal, the city seems to construct itself as a power-referent and a ritual center *before* its population can be fed on the basis of crop-agriculture—that is, by reasonably predictable resources. Eventually the concentration of population

[1] See, e.g., J. Mellaart, *Earliest Civilizations of the Near East* (Library of the Early Civilizations) (London, 1965), 36, on Jericho. But see R. Adams, *The Evolution of Urban Society,* (Chicago, 1966), 38–39.

would produce a market, not the reverse.[2] In any case, the non-economic aspect continued not only to be seen but to dominate in the supercities of all the Imperial polities; in cities older than Constantinople the economic imperative was downgraded and the infallible logic of the market put by in favor of other imperatives and other considerations. This is willful blindness to human nature or human fact—and yet in the Imperial cities the perversion was accepted. These cities were highly complex economically, but they tended to insist that economic complexity could not be allowed to command a civilization, and should be vigorously restricted and controlled. Economic complexity was not to be a self-determining element in human affairs, in fact, and the "laws" of competition, pricing, and profit simply were not permitted to have what we would say would be their usual force. The economy was "mobilized," in one phrase—bent by the Imperial sovereigns to their own uses and desires.[3] Or we could say that the economy was ritualized; the various transactions and acts that made up the economic aspect of life were moved from their singular, independent plane to another, to that sacralized plane where all transactions and acts reflected a higher scheme and sempiternal order. If, in the end, this produced a distortion in the life of the city that had certain consequences, we must examine that distortion and its consequences in their turn.

Constantinople has in the past served as a better-than-average proof of the old arguments for urban-economic man and the city as Market. If the city is indeed always the "crossroads," then Imperial Constantinople qualified unreservedly. It was founded (as a captial city) where Europe touched Asia, where the great lines of communication and trade had to cross, where two seas met—the Mediterranean providing manufacturing and a complex market of its own, the Black or Euxine funneling raw material from its hinterlands. It had a superb harbor.

Yet Byzantium was neither a thalassocracy nor a trading empire, ruling the seas from its impregnable harbor-fortress. Its sea frontiers were properly guarded and patrolled only at intervals,

[2] Mumford, *City*, 71.

[3] Eisenstadt, *The Political Systems of Empires*, 46, 121 ff.

for the Byzantine fleet had an off-and-on existence. In this ephemerality it resembled its Imperial Roman predecessor, but Rome had faced no formidable naval threat after Carthage had been eliminated, except pirates and its own dissident fleets in the civil wars. Byzantium needed a strong naval arm at all times. From the 7th century on she was repeatedly challenged by Arab seapower either under the Caliphate or taking the orders of illegitimate pirate-emirs (in Sicily or Crete); there were also unexpected threats from strange quarters in the 9th and 10th centuries, as from the half-vikings of Kievan Russia. Byzantium needed a fleet but rarely made the effort to build and sustain it, though there were sea-themes supposedly founded to provide naval strength.[4]

In the 10th century the naval arm was revived enough to support the successful rollback of Islam and the great Bulgarian wars, but when the Eastern Mediterranean was cleared the fleet died again. Nor, at this propitious moment, was a renaissance of Byzantine sea- or carrying-trade seen; on the contrary, merchant-venturers from Italy were granted wider trading rights and privileges. The carrying-trade of East Rome shifted steadily into the hands of foreigners and the Imperial government did not object to this dependence, but encouraged it by discouraging mercantile ventures among its own citizens.[5] There were exceptions (such as the emperor Nicephoros I, who had an acutely developed and widely misunderstood "economic" sense) but ordinarily the Emperor thought it right that the largest proportion of the goods brought into the city or shipped out of it be handled by the *ethnoi*—the Gentiles.[6] The assumptions behind this rejection, among other things, of venture-capital and long-range mercantile activity were not aristocratic—there was no reaction of blood-and-breeding against mere money or money-making, nor any

[4] L. Brehier, "La marine de Byzance du VIIIe au XI siècle," *Byzantion* **19** (1949), 1–16.

[5] See F. Dölger, *Corpus der griechischen Urkunden des Mittelalters und des Neuern Zeit.* Reihe A: *Regesten.* Abt I: *Regesten der Kaiserurkunden des oströmischen Reiches.* 1 teil: *Regesten von 565–1025.* (Munich and Berlin, 1924), 781/100.

[6] E. Frances, "L'Empéreur Nicéphore Ier et le commerce maritine byzantine," *Byzantinoslavica* **XXVII/1** (1966), 41–47.

assumptions of racial superiority or caste. Trade, like all economic activity, was an obvious concern of the state, and the head of state kept the prerogative of telling his subjects which activities were necessary and which were not—or which derogated from the nature of a true subject and citizen, and which reinforced that role. This produced a controlled economy, but not in order to further the broader economic plans of the government nor, really, to fulfill overreaching social goals or desiderata. Again, the economic aspect of life was subordinated to the idea of balance and harmony, and therefore had to be encased in the ritual by which balance and harmony were forever achieved and eternally maintained.

The city could not be merely a crossroads; the sign of the cross had other meanings, and one of them was the Center of the World. More, the possibilities of exchange, sale, profit, and economic gain which made up the magnetic quality of the city-as-market were limited in every area, not only in import-export trade.

Sources and Resources: *Agriculture*

Byzantium, like almost every land-based polity of the ancient or medieval world, was "underdeveloped." Of its resources, figured in an approximation of modern statistical-economic surveys, fully 90 percent had to come directly or indirectly from the land. The state rested on an agricultural base: most of its population was fully occupied in feeding itself and providing enough of a significant surplus to feed the remainder. From the land, too, came the largest part of the tax revenues, which were calculated on the basis of land use.[7]

It was not uncommon in Imperial polities for the land itself to be considered a resource of the state, a resource that could not ever be considered alienated from the state into another category of private ownership. In Pharaonic Egypt the land under the fructifying sun was obviously the sun-god-king's, and the Ptolemies who succeeded to the Double Crown rationalized and extrapolated this principle to its extreme, so that the earth was indeed the Lord's and the fullness thereof, down to the last pig

[7] G. Rouillard, *La vie rurale dans l'empire byzantin* (Paris, 1953), 90 ff.

and chicken: the land was *gē basilikē*—the personal estate of the divinized ruler.[8] Evidence from Egypt and elsewhere has led some observers to claim that in Imperial or "despotic" systems there was no possibility of private property at all.[9]

In Byzantium neither the theory nor the practice of monarchic-personal totalitarianism is visible, and yet true private property, based on an unmistakable legal definition, is not visible either until late in the history of the Empire. In the ordinary course of events the economic fabric of the land, and of property in general, was allowed to develop its own personal-legal structure and continuity. The Emperor and the Imperial family directly "owned" large estates and vast properties, which were controlled and exploited by a separate branch of the fisc. The resources of that land held otherwise could be tapped by various kinds of taxation or, occasionally, by direct requisition. At any time, however, the ordinary continuity, this illusory privateness, could be interrupted by the Imperial vicegerent of God in the name not only of military necessity or security, but in the name of divine harmony. A too large accumulation of property, or especially blatant conspicuous consumption, could be drastically readjusted by the sequestration of all properties and resources.[10]

The Emperor was at all times concerned with the land. Again a necessity backed by stringency is seen, for the usable land surface of the Empire was not so great that any sizable amount of it could be allowed to go to waste. At least through the 11th century all land was considered to be within the administrative control of the Emperor. He granted title and could revoke the grant. He could insist on a joint communal responsibility for vacated land.[11] In the case of widespread desertion by the rural popula-

[8] D. Zakythinos, "Étatisme byzantin et expérience hellénistique," *Annuaire de l'institut de philologie et d'histoire orientales et slaves* X (1950), 674; W. W. Tarn, *Hellenistic Civilization* (Third ed., London, 1959), 187–204.

[9] Wittvogel, *Oriental Despotism,* 71 ff.

[10] On "social justice" see G. Ostrogorsky, "Agrarian Conditions in the Byzantine Empire in the Middle Ages," *Cambridge Economic History,* I, 194–203, 209.

[11] E. Bach, "Les rois agraires byzantines du XIème siècle," *Classica et Medievalia* V (1942): 70–91; J. de Malafosse, *Les lois agraires à l'époque byzantine: Traduction et exégèse* (Toulouse, 1949).

tion, or devastation, he could and did transfer people from elsewhere in the Empire to the deserted areas, by simple fiat (although the transfer of population was used for other reasons of state as well). He could demand that land be distributed and farmed so as to support certain valuable members of the society —the *stratiotai* or thematic soldiery—who formed the primary defense of the state.[12]

In summary, the Emperor's policies affected the agricultural sector (a) through the allocation of land, and the control of land as a resource; (b) through a taxation that drew resources indirectly from the land. There was also (c) the pressure that other policies might put on the individual farmer such as, specifically, the regulations affecting the price he might ask for his exportable surplus, if any. For example, the Imperial policy of controlling bread prices, so that cheap bread might always be available to the urban population, is well known. The major part of the wheat imported into Constantinople came (after the 7th century) from Bulgaria, Macedonia, and Asia Minor, but there were wheat-growing areas in the immediate vicinity, and farmers who expected to sell their grain in the city had to obey the pricing regulations and submit themselves to the government monopoly.[13] Pricing regulations also affected other products of the land, such as livestock sold for meat.[14]

Briefly, the agricultural sector of the Byzantine economy fed great resources into the State. It was not, however, a rich sector—rich, that is, in massive surpluses to be exported or easily available to expand the living standards of the populace. Agricultural products, tax revenues, and the other services that the farmer was supposed to supply were forthcoming on a slender margin. War, drought, and other man-made or natural disasters might powerfully affect the total. In the two hundred years when these disasters, especially war, were all too frequent the Byzantine state still managed to mobilize and control its agricultural resource, for the lines of control and response that led from the city outward

[12] On the transfer of population, see also Chapt. 4, footnote 107.

[13] J. L. Teall, "The Grain Supply of the Byzantine Empire: 330–1025," *Dumbarton Oaks Papers* 13 (1959), 117–125.

[14] A. E. R. Boak, "The Book of the Prefect," *Journal of Economic and Business History* 1 (1929), 615, sect. XV, XVI; 617–18, sect. XXI.

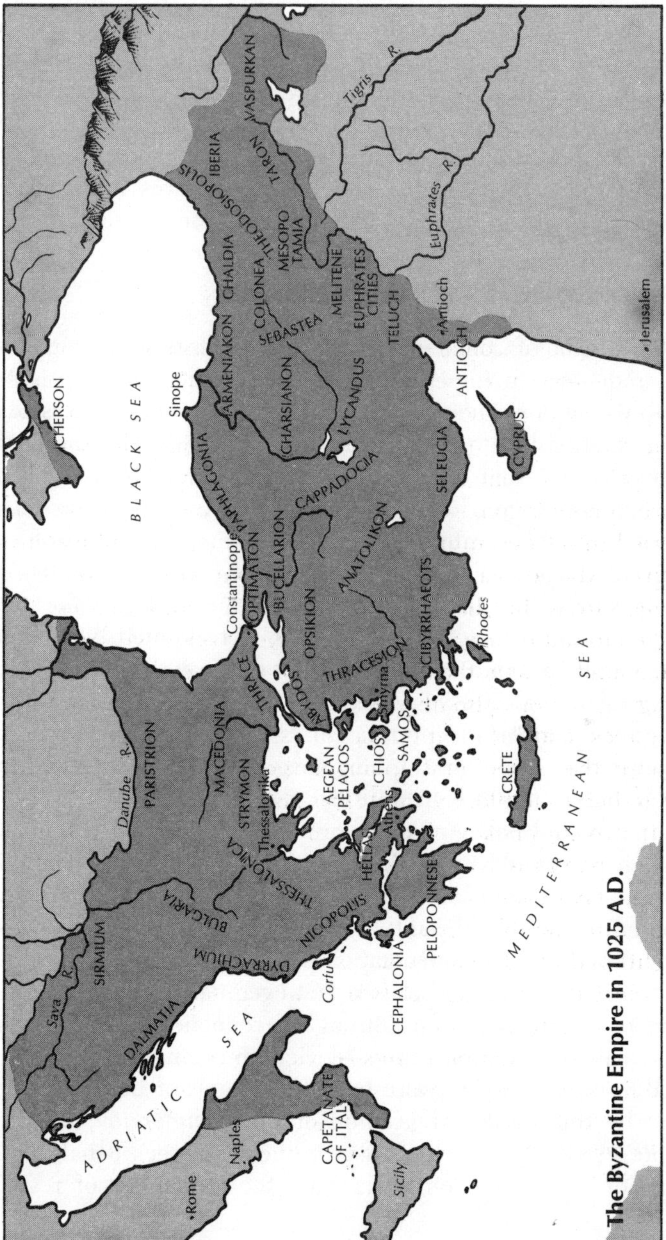

The Byzantine Empire in 1025 A.D.

and inward were continually adjusted. Part of the crisis that struck down the Empire in the 11th century, and that was prepared in the 10th, involved a rupture in these lines, so that city and countryside were split. The economic effects of this split would not be visible for a time because of a general revival in trade, but the effect on the national *morale* was more serious, since it showed the Imperial City isolated from its roots.

THE ECONOMY: TRADE AND TAXATION

The impact of commerce—especially a large-scale import-export trade—on an Imperial city of Constantinople's type is predictably complex. The size and activity of a merchant class has a direct relationship to the total wealth of a city: the capital investments and profits of this class raise the Gross National Product, and the range of their transactions points to a more rather than a less sophisticated economy, with a wider range of economic activity, opportunity, and mobility. In Constantinople's case it is clear that the economy of the state, and thus the range of choices and transactions in the city, were limited by Imperial interposition and interference, and that the growth of a mercantile class *within* the city was discouraged, while the prosperity of foreign mercantile adventurers was subsidized. Commerce—the import-export trade, or shipping in general—had to move into foreign hands and foreign ships.[15]

The Imperial policy of reducing the social and economic definitions and complexity of the city by action from the Throne—through measures calculated to disadvantage the competitive position of native merchants—was based on a point of view already described. The effectuation of this point of view not only involved individuals and classes, but eventually reduced the revenues of the Imperial fisc, through a reduction in the indirect taxes—sales and customs taxes—levied on commerce at the Center. Byzantine shippers were to be driven out of business, inevitably, by the absolute relaxation of the *kommerkion,* the most important sales-and-customs tax, on the foreigner's behalf, or by a considerable reduction in this tax: the initial loss of revenue

[15] H. Antoniadis-Bibicou, *Recherches sur les Douanes à Byzance* (Paris, 1963), 40.

then grew more severe as the number of taxable transactions declined. The elimination of Constantinople as a market for the native mercantile class did not come in the 10th century, but it had to follow, especially as the Venetians, moving upward to a new and ambitious economic stage, took a favored position.

The *kommerkion* was levied all over the Empire, though Constantinople, in terms of population and power, was obviously the prime market. As a customs-and-sales tax the *kommerkion* was also sometimes considered a tax on the *right* to sell. It ordinarily was a levy of 10 percent *ad valorem* on all goods imported or exported except those specifically privileged—the personal effects of merchants, materials belonging to the fisc, the court, or the army, goods destined for certain religious foundations, or the goods of other favored persons such as diplomats.[16] The *kommerkion* replaced older taxes and an older terminology, though in the 10th century the *dekata* or "tenth" was still mentioned; other taxes of the general type were the *praktikon*, which may have been a simple sales tax, and a number of lesser charges—on livestock, a toll for "passage," docking charges, and so on.[17]

The tax was collected by *kommerkiarioi*, who fell under the control of the General Logothete; in Constantinople their jurisdiction—as marked by the official sealing of goods taxed and passed—was not clearly differentiated from that of the Eparch of the City, who held responsibility for overall economic supervision there.[18] Most seaborne goods were evidently checked, taxed, and sealed elsewhere, at the approaches to the city: at Hieron for goods arriving from the Black Sea; at Abydos for goods coming from the Mediterranean.[19] The capital was hedged, in fact, with provincial customs posts, which not only taxed and controlled trade between provinces (or between the designated customs jurisdictions, which did not correspond precisely to provincial boundaries) but also served to limit passage into the city and control the amount of goods flowing into it.[20]

[16] *Ibid.*, 42, 48, 116.

[17] *Ibid.*, 99 ff.

[18] "Book of the Prefect," 617, sect. XX.

[19] Antoniadis-Bibicou, *Recherches sur les Douanes*, 203.

[20] *Ibid.*, 204. Bibicou believes that the aim of the provincial customs stations was to create provincial autarky and encourage private commerce, but the *effect* was to decisively limit mercantile activity in the Center.

There is no source to give us the proportion of tax revenues drawn from the *kommerkion* and other indirect taxes. They were fed into the General Treasury along with the larger sums that were collected directly, in the form of land and head taxes. The structure and operation of the Byzantine direct taxation is still a matter of controversy, the more so as it is related to the complexities of the system of land-tenure, the range of status, and the economic changes and new economic currents of the late 9th and early 10th centuries. We know that the compulsory "joint" land-and-head taxes of the Old Empire were long forgotten by the 10th century, and had been replaced by a separate land tax (*synone*) and a head or hearth tax (*kapnikon*).[21] The head tax was the chief extractive device used by the Empire, and was paid by all classes on the land—that is, by both individual free peasants in their rural communities, and by the military property holders: the thematic soldiery (*stratiotai*).[22] The free peasantry paid both an individual land tax and a "common" tax levied on their entire community; the soldier-farmers paid neither. The government collected an additional type of tax on abandoned land, making the adjacent village commune responsible. This tax, the *allelengyon*, eventually created pressures severe enough to help fracture the class of small holders and force them more and more into a disadvantageous position, compared with that of the larger landholders.

The taxes collected in the provinces were expected, first, to meet the expenses of the province in which they were collected; the surplus went to Constantinople. The land and head taxes, like the *kommerkion*, were received by the General Treasurer—the Logothete *tou genikou*—and by his associate, the Treasurer of the Soldiers (*tou stratiotikou*). These two officials were, by the 10th century, supervised by a Comptroller General, the *sakel-*

[21] K. M. Setton, "On the Importance of Land Tenure and Agrarian Taxation in the Byzantine Empire, from the Fourth Century to the Fourth Crusade," *American Journal of Philology* **76** (1953), 232; G. Ostrogorsky, "Das Steursystem im byzantinischen Altertum und Mittelalter," *Byzantion* **XI** (1931), 232.

[22] F. Dölger, *Beitrage zur Geschichte der byzantinischen Finanzwerwaltung besonders des 10. und 11. Jahrhunderts* (Byzantinisches Archiv, Heft 9) (Leipzig, 1927), 48–51; Ostrogorsky, "Steuersystem," 234.

larios; or rather their function as receiving agents was separated, and the *sakellarios*, after recording the sums received, had responsibility for overseeing the storage and disbursement of state funds.[23] A considerable degree of structural rationalization was extended into the rest of the *sekreton* or bureau of the *sakellarios*: two *chartularii* supervised the sections of the Purse proper—the store of coined money—and the Wardrobe, which contained a variety of items regarded as state treasure, including military hardware, prisoner's chains, sails, hemp, and the *kekolymena*—"forbidden" silk fabrics—in addition to the equipment of the Mint.[24]

Quite separate from the *sakellarios* and his control of the financial bureau of the state was the Palace (*oikeianon*) Wardrobe, which was the repository and recording agency of the "private" resources of the Emperor and the Imperial family. Income derived from all the Imperial estates came into this storehouse, which was administered by the Private Treasurer (the Logothete *tou eidikou*), and which also contained all the items used in the daily life of the Palace, including the collections of plate, a library, and a cabinet of *objets d'art*.[25]

The complexity and the putative rationalization of the Byzantine financial bureaucracy is impressive but misleading. All resources that flowed into the Center, whatever their nature or origin, however they might be separately recorded, counted, and administered, were part of the *treasure* of the state, to be used as the Emperor might see fit. Treasure is any accumulation, any amount of those substances that not only support the activities of the state, but stand as golden proof of its potency. The precise quantity of received funds is not really significant, and in the name of *sophrosyne* and *philanthropia* these funds can be reduced either through all the established or informal types of charity or direct largess, or by remitting taxation (as the "Emperor" Irene did in the last part of the 9th century).[26] The Emperor was not required to be an economic illiterate, but he was

[23] Dolger, *Finanzverwaltung*, 16–17.
[24] *Ibid.*, 24–30.
[25] *De ceremoniis*, 519; Dolger, *Finanzverwaltung*, 33–34.
[26] On the "Emperor" Irene, see Zepos-Von Lingenthal, *Jus Graecoromanum*, I, 45, 49.

not required to balance a budget, either. Overconcern with a precise rendering of income and expenditure did not win an Emperor popularity—the Emperor Nicephoros I, once a financial officer, who tried to rebalance the state's economy after Irene had crippled it, was violently criticized for his pains.[27] Again, during the reign of Theophilos a sizable amount of gold bullion seems to have come into the treasury, presumably mined gold from some new lode, and the Emperor responded by sharply increasing the number of gold coins minted.[28] Theophilos, in ordering the new mintings, seems to have had no other objective than to increase the number of visible signs of his own good fortune and providence, ignoring the inevitable economic reverberations of the move. The figures we are occasionally given estimating the accumulated treasure of the realm—1090 *centenaria* of gold and 3000 of silver in the early 9th century, or 200,000 talents during the reign of Basil II—are approximate indicators of the wealth the Emperor disposed of, and cannot even be used as an index to general prosperity or economic health.[29]

ECONOMIC ACTIVITY IN CONSTANTINOPLE

Manufacturing: Special Products

The needs of the citizenry of Constantinople and its suburbs were met by the number and variety of crafts and workshops one would expect in a major city, always conditioned and limited by the general level of prosperity and the technical achievements and possibilities of a particular time and place. A complete list of these necessary crafts cannot be drawn up for Constantinople, or not without some economic imagination, for the sources are fragmentary. The most valuable, the *Book of the Prefect,* is incomplete, and is not in any case a census of business or manufacturing but a compilation of government regulations bearing on the most sensitive or socially important guilds.

[27] For the vexations of Nicephoros see Theophanes, *Chronographia,* Ed. de Boor (Leipzig, 1883), 486–487; E. Bratianu, "La politique fiscale de Nicéphore Ier (802–811) ou Ubu roi à Byzance," in *Études byzantines d'histoire économiques et sociale* (Paris, 1938), 183–216.

[28] R. Jenkins, *Byzantium: The Imperial Centuries* (New York, 1966), 147.

[29] Theophanes Continuatus, 17; Michael Psellos, *Chronographia* (Translated by E. R. A. Sewter, London, 1953), I, 31.

We know of the existence of copperworkers (though the exact location of their quarter after the 6th century is unknown), candlemakers, soapmakers, nailmakers (but not ironworkers in general), crafters of sieves, and fur-workers, and artisans in lead.[30] There was a guild of harness-and-strap makers.[31] There was a quarter where fabrics, presumably common not precious, were dyed, a street of combmakers (*ktenaria*), and a factory for oars located, predictably, near the Golden Horn.[32] All these enterprises existed in the city but obviously they make up only a fraction of the total of local manufacturing—we have to assume the existence of shoemakers (only a quarter where military boots were made is mentioned, and that in a late source),[33] makers of ordinary clothing, ironmongery, common lamps, household utensils, and so on. All these objects were necessary to the daily life of the mass of city dwellers and few would have been imported. Some crafts, however, have been identified in the suburbs, which is a special subject.

In addition to mass market or localized specialized manufacturing, about which we know little, Constantinople was the center of a considerable textile industry; most of it destined for internal use, some exported. Linens were made up, but silk was the cloth produced in quantity. As a manufactured item silk had a peculiar character that has attracted much attention, for the silk industry was bifurcated: ordinary commercial production was carried on by the five ordinary guilds (*somata*); special production for special purposes was the province of the Imperial guilds (*demosia somata*), whose cloths were "forbidden" (*kekolymena*) and passed from commerce into another category entirely.[34]

The five private silk guilds, each rigorously differentiated in its processing of the silk, took cloth from its raw material—the silk-

[30] For copper workers, Janin, *Constantinople,* 96; for candlemakers, Janin, *op. cit.,* 96, "Book of the Prefect," 612; sect. XI; for soapmakers, "Book of the Prefect," 613, sect. XII; for nailmakers, Janin, *Constantinople,* 97; for sieves, *ibid.*; for workers in lead, Janin, *Constantinople,* 98.

[31] "Book of the Prefect," 614, sect. XIV.

[32] Janin, *Constantinople,* 371 (fabrics); *ibid.,* 99 (combmakers); *ibid.,* 347 (an oar factory).

[33] *Ibid.,* 97.

[34] R. Lopez, "Silk Industry in the Byzantine Empire," *Speculum* **XX.1** (January, 1945), 3–8 ff.

worm cocoons—to the finished, dyed, woven product. The raw-silk guild bought the stuff as it came into the market from "outsiders," who might be foreigners or provincials. The raw-silk guild also dominated the next step in production through their *de facto* control of the silk-spinners' (threadmakers') guild.[35] The spun silk was then sold to the weavers—*serikarioi*—who spun and dyed cloth. This was the guild most subject to minute regulation: what size and quality cloth they might make, what color they might dye it (never the "Imperial" shades of purple) and to whom they might sell it.[36] Two guilds were involved in the sale of silk garments, of which one (the *prandiopratai*) was involved in the importation and sale of Syrian (i.e., foreign) silks and silk garments.[37]

The *Book of the Prefect,* the invaluable if limited source for 10th-century Byzantine commercial activity in the city, leaves the impression of a tightly regulated textile industry in which the amount of cloth sold was a minor consideration. Anyone who had the price might buy "private" cloth—if he was a resident of the city. Most foreigners were under special regulations limiting their purchases, and so were provincials to an almost similar degree.[38] The city absorbed most of the cloth woven, and obviously its citizens had a double advantage—first in the fact that their standard of living, higher than elsewhere in the Empire, might allow them these sumptuary cloths; second, in that they were allowed to buy almost without restriction. The city was treated as an extraordinary market, where the richness of the dress of its citizens was meant to reflect the immeasurable force of concentrated wealth, the golden power, of the Center.

Thus the mercantile aspect of the making and selling of ordinary silks was to a considerable extent affected by noncommercial imperatives—imperatives that became absolute in the case of the so-called "forbidden" silks made up in the Imperial workshops by Imperial guildsmen, the workers one observer has called an "aristocracy of labor."[39] These guilds—purple-dyers, weavers

[35] Lopez, "Silk Industry," 18, 22.
[36] *Ibid.*, 19; "Book of the Prefect," 609, sect. VIII.
[37] Lopez, "Silk Industry," 19–20; "Book of the Prefect," 605, 606, sect. IV, V.
[38] Lopez, "Silk Industry," 22–23.
[39] *Ibid.*, 3–8.

and tailors, and gold embroiderers—produced silks and brocades that transcended *luxe* and were infused with a powerful and magical efflatus. The artisans were actually employees of the treasury *tou eidikou,* the Privy Purse, and worked in buildings in or by the Sacred Palace. Their products were regarded as treasure, not as commercial items or a resource in trade. They wove, embroidered, and tailored the state robes, which in their set variety of color and richness acted as the insignia of the Court, they produced robes and other garments for the ecclesiastical hierarchy, and they made the Imperial robes themselves, the glorious sheaths of gold and silver thread, multicolored silk, and set jewels which were both subtle and potent icons in their own essence.[40]

Precious garments of the sort worn by the highest in the land were of course "forbidden." All of the production of the Imperial silk guilds fell into this category, and because of the restrictions an artificial scarcity was created which moved these silks and brocades beyond price. Here they became an extension of Byzantine politics and of the art and science (or scientific art) of Byzantine diplomacy. Cloth that had passed through the hands of the Imperial purple-dyers, or the gold embroiderers, was a monopoly of the State, conceived in precisely the same terms as minted coin. Other fabrics might be "forbidden" as well (those valued, because of the fineness of weave, or size, above a certain set price) but the manufactures of the Imperial fabric guilds were invariably so. Their production was, in fact, caught up in the ritual gestures of the State, and the workers themselves were drawn into the processional declarations of universal harmony.[41]

Textiles of the highest grade of opulence and workmanship were sent off to the rulers of the peripheral world, either as gifts outright—proofs of the wonder-working artisanry of the city—or as "gifts," in a diplomatic usage which meant tribute. The few examples of the Macedonian period that survive in the West are of the first type.[42] The recorded treaties give examples of the

[40] *Ibid.,* 4.

[41] *De ceremoniis,* **II**, 725; Lopez; "Silk Industry," 5–6.

[42] Illustrated in O. von Falke, *Decorative Silks* (New York, 1936), 10–12, 25–28; Figs. 56, 77, 176, 177, 183, 186, 189. See also J. Ebersolt, *Les arts somptuaires de Byzance* (Paris, 1923).

latter. The Bulgars demanded "scarlet robes of honor" to the value of thirty gold pounds as part of the settlement of 814 A.D. which was reratified periodically throughout the 9th century: perhaps, however, this grant was a sort of export license.[43] Under the Tsar Simeon they demanded and received even more. The Pechenegs, barbarians who held the key to the south Russian steppes in the Byzantine diplomatic balance of the 10th century, received pieces of purple cloth (the *blattia* often mentioned in the ceremonies, meaning hanging cloths), silk ribbons and gold brocade, and "scarlet or 'Parthian' leather."[44]

The treatise *On the Administration of the Empire* compiled by the Emperor Constantine VII warns many times against the gross insatiability of the barbarians, and includes advice on how to lie, in a dignified fashion, to those Gentiles who demanded "Imperial vestures or diadems or state robes (*ek ton Basileion estheton e stemmaton e stolon*) in return for some service: the Emperor was to explain that the Holy Constantine, the sacred Founder, had been granted these objects "not made by the hands of men" and in his turn strictly forbade that they pass out of the Empire.[45] Actually regalian materials *were* sent out, in the form of robes and crowns, but Constantine VII seems to be trying to support the Imperial theory that this grant never had the form of a *quid pro quo,* but was a mysterious extension of sovereignty and brought vassalage in its wake. It is clear that the sacred fabrics, in their significant color and exquisite workmanship, bore a strong message; they strove to *épater le barbare,* but they also declared the existence of an inexhaustible treasure, from which the Emperor granted riches as he willed to those who recognized his central place.[46]

Closely associated with the Imperial artists in textiles were other craftsmen whose works were extensively used to support

[43] Theophanes, *Chronographia* (Ed. Bekker, Bonn, CSHB, 1839–41) 421 (Ed. de Boor, Leipzig, 1883), 273; Theophanes Cont., 357; George Cedrenus, II, 154; Lopez, "Silk Industry," 32.

[44] Constantine Porphyrogenitus, *De administrando imperio* (Ed. Moravcsik, transl. R. Jenkins, Budapest, 1949) 6/53.

[45] *Ibid.,* 13/67.

[46] For regalian materials sent to Smbat and Ashot of Armenia: Sebeos, *Histoire universelle* (Transl. F. Macler, Paris, 1904), 148.

diplomatic arrangements. The guild of jewelers (silversmiths and goldsmiths) were privileged to take part in ceremonies as the textile guildsmen were. Their most elaborate confections went into the Palace and the churches, and we have enough hints to show that they went abroad as well. The treasury of San Marco, filled by the pious rapacity of the Venetians, has some Byzantine lapidary and metalwork, not all of it stolen after 1204; other Western cathedral treasuries have or had objects easily identifiable as Byzantine, but a number are ivories, almost impossible to date exactly.[47] It goes without saying that the sumptuary artists of Constantinople were closely associated with the Palace, and the State had first call on their services as it did in the case of the Imperial guilds noted in the *Book of the Prefect* and elsewhere. There were goldsmiths, for example, who replaced the gold services given to the Russian party of the princess Olga in 959 A.D.[48] There were, as we know from the surviving materials and from the sources, Imperial craftsmen who specialized in the limning and the scripts of the sacred "writings" or *grammata*: Imperial documents such as chrysobulls and fine editions which were sent abroad as gifts or kept in the Imperial libraries. Even the containers in which the gifts were sent were finely worked and regarded as precious in their own right.[49]

Despite the existence of a significant sumptuary industry Constantinople was a consuming, not a producing, metropolis. The manufacturing described here had only a tangential relationship to the flow of goods and services to and from the city—to true economic interchange—since the market was only slightly involved. The specialized products—fabrics, fine metalwork, ivories, books or whatever—were exchanged more subtly, for "harmony" (that is, peace) or in order to secure a recognition of primacy that went beyond merely economic categories of wealth or the power of the marketplace. Byzantine sumptuary production made up an *oikosoekonomie,* in Weber's phrase, of a very limited but potent kind, precisely because of its separation from eco-

[47] For Venice: A. Pasini, *Il tesoro di San Marco* (Venice, 1889), 55, pl. XXXV.

[48] *De ceremoniis,* 570–580.

[49] Maqqari in A. A. Vasiliev, *Byzance et les Arabes.* 11ième partie: *La dynastie macédonienne* (Brussels, 1936), 266–267.

nomic determinatives. It was emphasized that the Emperor did not trade—or not directly—nor haggle over value given or received. There is an immense arrogance implicit in this view of economic man, and a curious parallel to the *potlatch* mentality of certain Amerindian tribes, in which status was judged by the amount of wealth distributed or destroyed rather than accumulated. On the other hand, the material object, the product of expert artisanry, seems to have been looked upon not as a beautiful thing which therefore was destined for the highest use, but as an object that was beautiful *because* it passed into the Emperor's possession. Like the icon, with which Constantine VII indirectly compares it, the robe of state was not made by hands, and its original creators, however they parallel in their organization the guilds of the West, had no creative craft status.[50] The great Byzantine fabric preserved at Aix-la-Chappelle is signed not by the designer but by the officials who oversaw the Imperial factory where it was made.[51]

Supply, Exchange, and Services

The *Book of the Prefect,* incomplete as it is, gives us most of what we know about the provisioning of the city and the services available there, especially those of immediate interest to the Prefect and thus to the Throne in whose name the Prefect acted and regulated. The principal provisioning guilds are here: victualers (*saldamarioi* or sausage-sellers: keepers of a general store), porkdealers, butchers (all animals but swine), fishmongers, bakers.[52] The number of minor guilds serving foodstuffs of some sort to the public must have been large, and also the number of guildless itinerant peddlers or truck farmers from the suburbs, though in all cases the officers of the guild and of the Prefecture were on the watch for those who trespassed on the competent area or responsibilities of the individual guilds. The *Book of the Prefect* also legislates on the tavernkeepers, whose wicked but necessary work of keeping the population well lubricated was hedged by a variety of temperance restrictions.[53] Two service

50 *De admin. imp.,* 13/67.
51 Lopez, "Silk Industry," 6 n. 1.
52 "Book of the Prefect," 613/XIII, 615/XV, XVI, 616/XVII, XVIII.
53 *Ibid.,* 617/XIX.

guilds are given special attention because of their obvious value in the smooth functioning of civic and economic life: the notaries, who were "writers of contracts" and therefore regulators of the nonfamilial or civic-legal relationships of the citizens, and the bankers, that is, money-changers, who could take deposits and could undertake to make loans as well, though no regulation of this activity is included in the *Book*.[54] The edict concludes with a catch-all ruling on the contractual obligations of "joiners, plasterers, marbleworkers, locksmiths, painters, and the rest"—in other words, the building trades.[55] The other guilds whose products were of interest and available to the mass of citizens were the soapmakers and the candlemakers, and the makers of straps—that is, harnessmakers.[56]

The provisioning guilds supplied most of the eatables of the city, with the exception of those items sold in the suburbs at local markets or in traveling markets within the city by the truck farmers themselves (probably poultry and eggs were also sold in this fashion by local poultry farmers).[57] The victualers dealt in the basics of the Constantinopolitan diet: meat (salted or pickled), "pickled fish, meal, cheese, honey, olive oil, green vegetables of all sorts, butter" as well as bulk products, pots, bottles, and nails.[58] The butchers bought, slaughtered, and sold—mostly, as their section of the regulations reads, sheep and lambs.[59] The porkdealers were subject to special sanitary regulations; perhaps because of the chancy edibility of unrefrigerated pork, or perhaps the remnants of older taboos kept the two guilds separate.[60] The fishmongers, like the porkdealers, had a separate market, in the *Megaloi Emboloi* or Great Porticos, presumably at the end nearest the Golden Horn.[61] The bakers were to furnish bread without interruption to the city, and bought their grain directly from the

54 *Ibid.*, 600–603/I, 605/III.
55 *Ibid.*, 619–20/XXII.
56 *Ibid.*, 612/XI, 613/XII, 614/XIV.
57 M. Ya. Syuzyumov, "Ekonomika prigorodov vizantiiskikh krupnikh gorodov," *Vizantiiskii Vremmenik* **XI** (1956), 74–75.
58 "Book of the Prefect," 614/XIII.
59 *Ibid.*, 615/XIV.
60 *Ibid.*, 616/XV.
61 *Ibid.*, 616/XVII.

stores accumulated by the Prefect.[62] In their case as in all others the hoarding of foodstuffs was carefully watched.

Of the two service guilds of the notaries and the bankers, the first occupied a prominent place in the city. The rules governing their recruitment, training, behavior, business practices, life (and death, when the whole guild paraded with the corpse) are particularly minute.[63] As in the case of the Imperial textile guilds and the workers in precious metals the notaries were to take a part in ceremonies and processions, and their own ceremony of installation is given in detail.[64] The notaries were elevated in importance because they were associated with the law; they were to "have by heart the forty titles of the *Manual of Law* and . . . the sixty books of the Basilika."[65] Their principal responsibility was the correct drawing-up of documents on "sales, marriage settlements, wills, and contracts," and they received a fee for each depending on the value of the matter at hand.[66] In a city of Constantinople's size their total in fees must have been considerable, for by law there could be only twenty-four of them.[67] They could hire secretaries to do the donkey-work of transcribing and drawing up documents, but the efficient or concluding formulas which validated the document had to be their own.[68] Closely associated with this guild were those of the "teachers of law and ordinary (*koinos*) teachers." An aspiring notary studied law, of course, as did others training for the bureaucracy, but according to the relevant sections of the *Book of the Prefect* these teachers had a position inferior to that of the notaries they trained.[69]

Another "intermediate" or service-liaison guild is mentioned in the *Book*; its position seems supernumary because one would expect the officers of the Prefect to have this as one of their

[62] *Ibid.*, 616/XVIII.
[63] *Ibid.*, 600–603/I.
[64] *Ibid.*, 601/I.
[65] *Ibid.*, 600/I.
[66] *Ibid.*, 603/I.
[67] *Ibid.*
[68] *Ibid.*, 602/I.
[69] *Ibid.*

responsibilities: this was the guild of cattlemarket inspectors, who made sure that buyers of cattle were aware of the defects "visible and concealed" of the animals they bought. Why minor officers of the Prefecture did not do this is unclear, unless the Prefect felt that the temptation to take bribes was too strong.[70]

The guilds supplying goods and services, and the provisioning and other guilds included with them in the *Book of the Prefect* form a small stratified commercial society, in which the strata are readable but only with careful and tentative reading. The Byzantine view of status was faceted; monetary reward was only one of the facets, and the relationship between honor in the society and remuneration might be unbalanced. All things being considered, the *Book* presents an upper-lower to upper-middle class spread, with the guild of notaries at the top, outranking the Imperial textile guilds. The primacy of the silk industry gave next place to the silk guilds, and within their ranks the raw-silk dealers and dealers in Syrian stuffs outweighed the clothiers, who were higher than the spinners and weavers. The jewelers, an important and a "ceremonial" guild, still admitted slaves and must have been classed with the clothiers. The perfumers enjoyed *éclat,* since their selling benches were by law immediately next to the main Palace gate, but they must have been a middling guild, perhaps a bit lower than the candlemakers but above the soapmakers who, again, might be slaves (which ordinarily lowered the status of the guild). The provisioning guilds were led by the bakers, whose importance had always been clear, then the butchers and fishmongers, then the porkdealers and last the victualers. The section of the *Book* dealing with the leathercutters' guild leaves the distinct impression that the leathercutters themselves, whose work was essential to the military posture of the State (they were harnessmakers and saddlers) were a guild in fairly high regard, as compared with the poorly considered skin-softeners and tanners, two subsidiary guilds. Tanners and tavernkeepers occupied a low social position, whatever their profits might be. Below all of these were the nonguild workmen and artisans.

[70] *Ibid.,* 617–618/XXI.

Controls: The Ritualized Economy

Government and guild monopolies. The intrusion of the State into commerce and manufacturing is common enough in all societies and polities. It may spring from the responsibility assumed by the State for its own defense: all armaments or materials necessary for war might be put under direct control, which of course impinges on the "right to bear arms" of the citizen and acts as a police regulation; in Constantinople only the Prefect's men and the Guards went armed, while the Arsenal of the Mangana, a factory and weapons store under the Curator of the Mangana, located close to the Palace precinct, was a necessary physical adjunct to the overawing moral power of the Throne.[71] The Byzantines kept the strictest security over their terrible secret weapon, the so-called Greek Fire; Constantine VII cautioned his son against letting any amount of it go to the barbarians. The formula, so far as we know, never passed out of Byzantine hands.[72]

Beyond these fundamental measures for ensuring the safety of the State and the power structure, a government might inject itself directly into the economy to any degree and for many reasons. The Hellenistic states from whom the Byzantine theory of governance descended used monopolies extensively: as all Ptolemaic Egypt was simply *gē basilikē,* the God-King's estate, and all economic activities were defined as "public," that is, every resource was directly controlled by the Two Crowns.[73] Rome, however, was not much concerned with state monopolies, and developed no pattern of interference in commerce which Byzantium can be said to follow, beyond the concept of liturgies and, to an extent, the silk monopoly.[74]

The Byzantine state monopoly of certain grades and types of silk cloth springs from the following objectives:

1. As an extension of sumptuary law: an attempt to harmonize or equalize private resources;

[71] For the Mangana, see Janin, *Constantinople,* 295–296.
[72] *De admin. imp.,* 13/69–71.
[73] See note 8 above.
[74] Lopez, "Silk Industry," 10, n. 4.

2. Depending partly from this, as an attempt to force a "hierarchy of dress"; a stratification of uniform or insigne within an identifiable "ritualized" group of citizens;

3. As a device for creating a scarcity profitable to the State;

4. As a device for assuring the accumulation of a "treasure," a resource whose value could not be measured merely by monetary worth;

5. As a necessary precondition to the maintenance of Imperial *regalian* rights, or at least state control of specially efflated or radiated materials that gave power or authority by contact.

Of all these possibilities the last two are of special interest. That view of the silk monopoly which treated a manufactured article as a treasure, not subject to purely economic definition, has been compared to the Imperial monopoly of the mint without the full significance of the comparison being drawn out.[75] The Byzantine state regarded the two monopolies as similar in type; this is clear from the identical punishment—amputation of the offending hand—which was dealt out to forgers or parers and to those who dyed cloth a forbidden color or made up forbidden garments.[76]

A state monopoly of the mint is still looked upon as an essential aspect of sovereignty, and in this Byzantium resembles all mature states.[77] It is notable that the Byzantines, some time in the cloudy centuries between Heraclius and the Macedonian dynasty, centralized their mint, moving all coining activities to Constantinople. More decisively important than this centralization, however (for some of the provincial mints were situated in captured cities and others were threatened by invasion), was the Byzantine reading or definition of the prime gold coin (*nomisma* or *solidus*) not simply as a token of exchange but as a sign of ultimate sovereignty. By coining—that is, imprinting his icon and name on a gold disk—an Emperor proclaimed his right to deal out the gold, the accumulated "light" or visible, concentrated treasure (wealth as the efficient aspect of pure power) of the State.[78]

[75] *Ibid.*, 7–8.

[76] "Book of the Prefect," 605/III, 609/VIII.

[77] Eisenstadt, *The Political Systems of Empires*, 126–127.

[78] On the mint: P. G. Grierson, "Coinage and Money in the Byzantine

There would always be a relationship between the amount of gold coming into the Imperial coffers—an amount consistent with the extractive skill of the taxing agencies, the relative prosperity of the land, and the availability of gold itself—and the minting of any Emperor, but since the act of minting carried other, non-economic imperatives an Emperor would proclaim himself, and broadcast his sacred images, even when the commercial use of, and need for, the *nomismata* had fallen off. This might help to explain why gold mintings, as we know from survivals (especially the discovery of hoards) maintain a reasonably consistent level during the centuries when we strongly suspect the commercial life of the Empire to have diminished.[79]

The *kekolymena* or forbidden fabrics, controlled and stored by the agency of the Privy Purse, made up part of the treasure of the State. They were monopolized as gold was monopolized, and were consciously kept free of the commercial stream and the contamination of the marketplace, or of commercial and economic definition. Their value was set beyond price, though the law had to classify some silks by price for clarity's sake.[80]

The regalian use or coloration of the forbidden materials again leads toward an examination of the Byzantine view toward trade and commerce and to the *exotikoi*—those outside the city, whether foreigners or provincials. Silk cloth, worked or unworked, was a prime item in trade, especially to the nations to the north and west, yet the Byzantines cut back its export far past the point where an artificial, and profitable, shortage occurred. The *kekolymena* could only be extracted from the guardian State by extraordinary means, such as diplomatic arrangements, but more: all silks were restricted, even those available to the city

Empire, 498—ca. 1090," *Moneta e Scambi nell' alto Medievo* (Centro Italiano de Studi sull'alto Medievo; Settimani di Studio VIII, Spoleto, 1961), 411–453.

[79] S. Vryonis, "An Attic Horde of Byzantine Gold Coins (668–741) From the Thomas Whittemore Collection and the Numismatic Evidence for the Urban History of Byzantium," *Mélanges G. Ostrogorskij* I (1963), 291–300; cf. A. Kazhdan, "Vizantiiskie goroda v VII–XI vv.", *Sovietskaya Arkheologiya* **21** (1954), 164–183.

[80] "Book of the Prefect," 606, 609.

populace. The Byzantine state monopoly effectively reserved the use of this cloth to the city, and to some other favored classes.[81]

All silk goods destined for export had to be marked by the office of the Prefect; all "strangers" had to declare their purchases; raw silk could not be taken abroad—that is, out of the city—and had to be sold openly not privately, so that the details of the sale might be supervised; no robe or garment costing more than ten *nomismata* could be sold to a foreigner; no expert worker ("slave, hired laborer, or overseer") could be sold to a foreigner.[82] From the treaties and other documents we know that the foreigner labored under other discriminatory regulations, some directed specifically at foreign merchants and others at all foreigners. At one point the *mitaton* or trading-post-*cum*-hostel which was reserved for Bulgar merchants was removed from Constantinople to Thessalonike, which was a *casus belli* as far as the Bulgars were concerned;[83] all foreigners were restricted to a three-month stay except the favored Syrian silk-merchants and, latterly, the Russians; even the Russians were housed outside the city, registered, and could enter the city only unarmed, escorted, and in groups of no more than 50.[84]

In its commerce with foreigners the Byzantine state intruded a monopoly based on its desire to maintain the noneconomic value of some items or materials. It also demanded restrictions that made trade of all sorts almost always a matter of state concern, to be overseen by officers of the Crown. Thus "free trade" was limited sharply, and commerce was allowed no separately valid existence: it was not regarded as harmonious within the fabric of society until it was regulated. The Byzantines did not, however, carry their policy of the control of commercial exchanges as far as the Ptolemies had, and in any case their motives in controlling commercial exchange were different: the Ptolemies wanted to

[81] Lopez, "Silk Industry," 2.
[82] "Book of the Prefect," 606–7/IV, 608/VI.
[83] See note 43 above.
[84] Lopez, "Silk Industry," 28, 30, 34–35; "Book of the Prefect," 617/XXI; for the Russians see Sorlin, *Les traités,* 458, 330, 459; also in *The Russian Primary Chronicle: Laurentian Text* (Ed. and transl. O. P. Sherbowitz-Wetzor and S. H. Cross, Cambridge, Mass., 1953), 65, 74–75.

maximize trade and extract every possible advantage from it, the Byzantine state was disinclined to even consider economic advantage.

Guild monopolies and harmony. The Proëm to the *Book of the Prefect* sets up the tonic dominant of this commercial law: the harmony of all tones is crucial. God had given "order and harmony to the Universe" and "engraved the Law on the tables" so that inequity and disharmony among men should not prevail, and "all things should be apportioned with just measure."[85] The *Book* was an attempt to enforce this divinely appointed harmony by recognizing and reinforcing the guild structure: the craft and occupational organizations. The crafts and occupations were first minutely described, and the intrusion of nonguild persons interdicted; both the members of the guilds and the officers of the Prefect were made responsible for seeing to this. Recruitment into the guilds was regulated: standards of proficiency (as in the case of the guild of notaries) and proof of good character (for bankers, clothiers, spinners, weavers, porkdealers) was demanded.[86] No one was to teach a trade without the knowledge and permission of the officers of the guild *and* the Prefect.[87] Once committed to a trade, the regulations forbade a guild member to practice another. Victualers were not to sell those goods restricted to the perfumers or the candlemakers; teachers of law were not to try to draw up the contracts whose arcane intricacies they taught; silkworkers were enjoined from crossing over, even to a minute extent, into another part of the trade; butchers were not to sell pork; harnessmakers were separated from skin-softeners and these from tanners.[88] In all these restrictions the Prefect, acting in the name of the State, spoke for "the very best order," the commercial harmony which was an absolute desideratum—even while he enforced the monopoly of each guild relative to the consumer.[89] Thus, while he stood behind the commercial regulations which were much to the advantage of the protected guilds, his place was still next to the Throne, and the Throne wanted

85 "Book of the Prefect," 600.
86 *Ibid.*, 600/I, 605/III, 608/VII, 609/VIII, 615/XVI.
87 *Ibid.*, passim.
88 *Ibid.*, 614/XIII, 602/I, 609/VIII, 615/XV, 614/XIV.
89 *Ibid.*, 616/XVIII.

commercial activity not only to be fitted to the needs of the populace, but responsive to the other, noneconomic imperatives which the State demanded.

Each commercial transaction was hedged with rules protecting the customer-consumer. The bankers (money-changers) had by law to guard against the circulation of counterfeit coins.[90] Those shops where goods were weighed out (perfumers, candlemakers, soapmakers, victualers, probably bakers) or measured out using liquid measures (tavernkeepers, victualers) had to have their balances, weights, or containers checked and stamped by the Prefect's men.[91] These rules extended from the State's monopoly of measurement, as ancient and necessary a part of its sovereignty as coining.

In regulating the place where a trade or service might be carried on the State reacted to a number of stimuli and from a complex set of assumptions. In some guilds or occupations there must have been a history of concentrated or *métier-quartier* location stretching back to the beginning of commerce in cities. The origins of the craft-street or quarter lie in the social cohesiveness felt within that craft, even in the solidarity of cult (which had passed from patron gods to patron saints), and social cohesion was supported by economic and technical advantages found in the craft-street, such as the solution or easing of problems of supply, and the high visibility of concentrated crafts that drew customers to the quarter, as well as a special view of competition. The competitive sense felt within the craft that is physically arranged in this mode is obviously of a distinct kind. However, there are also societal pressures, and pressures from the State, which act to concentrate the crafts and occupations or, conversely, try to separate and scatter them. These forces acting from outside the craft may move to the ends of social aid and availability, or simply see concentration as an aid to control or policing, or have other and wider aims.[92]

The *Book of the Prefect* shows a rich composite of all these

[90] *Ibid.*, 605/IV.

[91] *Ibid.*, 612/X, 612/XI, 613/XII, 614/XIII, 616/XVIII, 617/XIX.

[92] On the *métier-quartier* and its origins: see Adams, *The Evolution of Urban Society*, 83, 126–27, with emphasis on kin and cult ties.

possibilities. The cohesion of a guild is shown, for example, in the case of the Syrian-silk dealers, who are not only concentrated in their own section of the Embolé but who act in concert to buy the whole bulk of imported Syrian goods.[93] It appears that the linen merchants also bought the imported linen as a group, and both the butchers and the porkdealers had to make their purchases of animals on the hoof in the fora of the Strategion, the Tauros, or the Amastrianos and nowhere else, and they evidently butchered there as well, under the Prefect's eye.[94] Certain guilds on the other hand were commanded to locate themselves throughout the city, available to the wards and neighborhoods: the victualers were so ordered, and by inference the bankers and the bakers (who also had a special street).[95] With the exception of these high intensity, frequently used service-and-supply occupations, the guilds were concentrated. The notaries, as another exception, were each alloted a section of the city.[96]

The linen merchants could make up garments in their shops but, according to the regulations, could not sell them there; they had to go about porting their wares on their backs "and sell them on a day when the market is open"—that is, in the various neighborhoods.[97] The dealers in raw silk exercised their trade "in the place assigned to them," all of them together.[98] The shops of the candlemakers might have been made accessible in one neighborhood, but had to be physically separated from the others by a certain distance. By law this guild had to sell from their workshops, not on the street, probably to remove the sale of church candles as much as possible from the commercial taint.[99] The soapmakers too had their shops no nearer than "seven cubits and twelve feet" from each other; this, like the similar rule in the candlemakers' case and other laws concerning the bakers, was to

[93] "Book of the Prefect," 606–7/V.
[94] *Ibid.*, 615/XV, 615/XVI, 618/XXI.
[95] *Ibid.*, 613/XIII, 605/III, 616/XVIII; see also Janin, *Constantinople*, 95–96.
[96] See note 67 above.
[97] "Book of the Prefect," 611/VII.
[98] *Ibid.*, 607/VI.
[99] *Ibid.*, 612/XI.

lessen the danger of fire; for the same reason other industries were removed outside the walls entirely.[100] The fishmongers were to sell from the so-called Great Embolé only.[101] In addition, we know of the existence of other *métier quartier* markets or guild locations in the city, some already mentioned. There was a charcoal market in the city, a slave market near the Artopoleia (the Bakers' Street) called the "valley of weeping" (*koilas klaphthmonos*), and a barley market near the Sophian Harbor.[102]

The *Book* places several guilds in such locations as to create a mutually enhancing and reinforcing interaction of commerce and stronger considerations. The most open declaration of this interaction and effect is in the rule bearing on the perfumers, that they should display their aromatic wares immediately outside the main gate, the Chalké gate, of the Palace, to "send forth a savory aroma" befitting the royal precinct.[103] As an extension of this conceit all workers in "treasure" or items of *luxe* were concentrated high on the *Mesè*, as near the Palace as possible: jewelers, dealers in imported silks, and even furriers.[104] The Imperial silk guilds were, of course, actually located in the Palace itself. Here the element of control and protection, while present, cannot be as powerful as the desire to focus all elements of the treasure of the State, to make all elements of power act in concert with one another.

Competition: price, weight, measure. Of the principal guilds of the city—those the *Book of the Prefect* treats specifically and in detail—none was allowed to take an unregulated profit; more, no guildsman could act in such a competitive fashion that his profit was maximized either at the cost of the customer or of a fellow guild member. The minute rules that result from this consideration need not be repeated for each guild. We note that the notaries charged, by law, no less than half a *nomisma* for their work and no more than two; that the victualers were allowed a

100 *Ibid.*, 613/XII, 616/XVIII; compare Syuzyumov, "Ekonomika prigorodov," 66.
101 "Book of the Prefect," 616/XVII; compare Janin, *Constantinople,* 98.
102 Janin, *Constantinople,* 97, 98.
103 "Book of the Prefect," 611/X.
104 "Book of the Prefect," 604/III, 606/V; Janin, *Constantinople,* 98.

profit of "two *miliaresia* on the *nomisma*"—i.e., 17 percent—and the fishmongers a good deal less, while the bakers were allowed a clear profit of about 4 percent.[105] The regulations in most cases did not specify profits this closely, but insisted upon open, easily checked sales—*not* to foreigners (*exotikoi*) in secret, not at prices raised after a deposit was paid, nor to anyone not of the same guild for resale, nor in any dubious or dishonest fashion at all. Guild members were repeatedly warned against hoarding in order to create a false shortage and raise prices (as, perfume dealers, candlemakers, victualers, leathercutters, porkdealers, or anyone else the Prefect's *legatarios* discovers) and against forcing a competitor out of business by raising his rent—the most common prohibition of all.[106]

Competition and profit were further limited by rules based on religious prescription circumscribing trade at certain times: the familiar "blue law," with its long pedigree, closed taverns on "high festivals or on Sundays" as well as after 7 P.M.[107] Victualers, too, were forbidden to sell on Sunday "or on another Holy Day."[108] Soapmakers, who used animal fats in their work, could not make soap of these fats during Lent, and Lenten limitations also, naturally, bore on the butchers.[109]

Another limitation sprang from the same moral-religious base as the common "blue law," and ruled on the fitness of certain persons to carry out a trade or occupation. The good character of all prospective guildsmen had to be attested to before they might join the guild, but in the case of the silk-spinners' guild the interest of the policing authorities went so far as to demand that a spinner who was "gossiping, a boaster, troublesome, or noisy" be expelled from the guild "with blows and insults . . . ."[110] Silk spinners who were slaves also labored under the discrimination of being prevented from advancing themselves into the more élite raw-silk dealers' guild.[111] The fact of being a slave was not

[105] "Book of the Prefect," 614/XIII, 616/XVII, 616/XVIII.
[106] *Ibid.*, passim.
[107] *Ibid.*, 617/XIX.
[108] *Ibid.*, 614/XIII.
[109] *Ibid.*, 613/XII, 615/XV.
[110] *Ibid.*, 609/VII.
[111] *Ibid.*, 608/VII.

a bar to joining many guilds, but a goldsmith-slave, caught out in a shady practice, was confiscated by the State—a severe penalty, probably connected with the mutually antagonistic taboos that surrounded slavery and the precious metal; it is rather surprising that slaves were allowed to practice this craft at all.[112] Again, any banker who set his slave in his own place, so that the slave actually performed the act of exchange, could have his hand cut off as if he were a counterfeiter—the act was one of *lèse majesté.*[113]

The aim of the State, in promulgating and enforcing its guild regulations, was to provide a mercantile community in which service, not competition for profit, was the prime factor. Economic competition was viewed as pernicious at base, as tending to evil, and the directives of the *Book of the Eparch* are turned sternly against it. "Good business" was nearly an oxymoron in Byzantium, so far as the Emperor was concerned, and the businessman in his rôle as businessman was much distrusted. Thus the State went far beyond the normal desires of any guild to limit competition, in forcing its own limits. The fair price that might be generated from within the guild was braced up by government edicts, when the government had not already decided what that fair price should be, so that any sharp practice that might evade it was not only unethical but illegal. Economic harmony meant the manufacturing and exchange of goods, or the offering of services, in a balanced and regulated fashion; the "laws" of supply and demand had no accepted force, to say nothing of legal standing.

Unescapably, we have to ask how the severity of the intrusion of the State affected the formation of the commercial classes: if the denial of the "play" or competitive element in commerce drew men off into other areas where this element could work itself out. Probably, yes. The guilds were open; there was no hereditary limitation, except in the case of the Imperial guilds, the "aristocrats."[114] The ease with which a worker could gain membership in a guild can mean either that there was a plentiful supply of candidates (for when recruitment fell off the Roman Imperial

112 *Ibid.,* 604/II.
113 *Ibid.,* 605/III.
114 Lopez, "Silk Industry," 5, n. 1.

government had formed the guilds into hereditary corporations) or, with more likelihood, that recruitment was steady but that the guilds were not over popular. The fact that slaves were admitted into many guilds is a strong indication that free men were not taking up that particular craft or occupation.

The bias or set of the Byzantine state against commercial play or exchange might also explain the ambiguity expressed by the State toward the foreigner. In Byzantium he was strictly proscribed from dealing in certain tabooed commodities, isolated, suspected, guarded and in general treated as a social and cultural contaminant, but from the beginning of the 10th century foreigners were also granted trading and commercial rights which not only allowed him to compete with the native commercial community, but gave him a distinct advantage. The Russian merchants coming to Constantinople first enjoyed the profits of this turn in Byzantine policy, for despite the restrictions placed on them they were also freed from the payment of the *kommerkion,* the impost tax.[115] This tax was also lifted for foreigners coming into the city with raw silk, according to the *Book of the Prefect.*[116] The Venetians occupied a singular, and singularly profitable position, since they were tacitly counted among the vassals of the Emperor but fell under the protection of the Logothete of the Drome, the Foreign Minister, which freed them from the regular customs examination.[117]

Though it applied principally to import-export trade, the relaxation of commercial restrictions on foreigners showed that the Imperial bias was against commerce generally: to make or create was acceptable, particularly when the product was detached from the market, as were the Imperial fabrics. To sell or trade was suspect, even tainted; it was an exotic occupation truly fit for foreigners, who were already tainted.

Local and subeconomies. The details of economic life in Constantinople have a spurious clarity. Some areas such as the manufacturing controlled by the Imperial guilds are full described;

115 Sorlin, *Les traités,* 331; *Russian Primary Chronicle,* 65.
116 "Book of the Prefect," 607/VI.
117 Lopez, "Silk Industry," 39; Dolger, *Regesten* I, 781/100.

as is the production of the secondary guilds, and the trade in items protected by law—noneconomic production or circumscribed production. The *Book of the Prefect* gives us most of this material, while such documents as treaties, in their "commercial" section, provide a list of trade goods (though again in many cases such noneconomic motives as prestige are involved) and some manufactures. The nature and extent of the "neighborhood" economy, however, is really nonverifiable; we can guess, and we can extrapolate from parallel cultural situations. A great deal more remains unclear—for instance, where was the heavy industry (in the medieval sense or scope) that supported the mass economy of a large city like Constantinople? Mostly, it seems, it was located in the District (*ktima*) or suburbs.

Into the faubourgs, or "beyond-the-walls," were those enterprises that the city needed but would not or could not support within the walls. These fell into three types: (a) dangerous or noxious manufactures; (b) industries or enterprises that required more space than could be spared in the city proper, and those that needed special power sources not available in the city (such as mills); and (c) tabooed or ill-omened commerce.

(a) Dangerous manufacturing or that which had unpleasant effects or side-products included blacksmithing, possibly all metal crafts on a large scale (foundaries in the proper sense) and glassworks.[118] The main danger in these obviously came from fire. Charcoal burning had to be carried out reasonably close to the sources of supply and was no urban industry in any event; it was restricted to the Thracian suburbs.[119] The smokehouses producing the smoked meats of which the city was inordinately fond were also found here.[120] Tanning, most noxious of all industries, is in a special category.

(b) Space-consuming industries that could not be accommodated within the walls included brickmaking, with its large kilns and extensive storage areas. The Byzantines required brick in quantity at all times, since so much of their construction used it,

118 Syuzyumov, "Ekonomika prigorodov," 66.
119 *Ibid.*, 70–71.
120 *Ibid.*, 74.

and their brickyards must have been extensive.[121] Stoneworkers, with their space-consuming stock-in-trade, had to be beyond the walls as well.[122] Ropewalks, where the factory space necessary was considerable, went into the suburbs, certainly not far from the shore and probably near Marmora, to supply maritime needs.[123] Coopers, again needing plenty of storage space, were nearby.[124] Shipyards were the center of this pelagic subeconomy on the Marmoran shore, which included fisheries, cooping, ropemaking, probably fishcuring or smoking.[125]

Part of the silk industry, which needed fairly large buildings, may or may not have been sited in the faubourgs. The Imperial or "forbidden" silks and fine worked silks were produced inside the Palace precinct itself, but the factories where the lesser grades —the truly commercial grades—of cloth were woven are not readily identifiable.[126] It is no proof for a suburban location to connect the Jews to the silk industry, for Jews were allowed to work in the city but not (after the 7th century) to live there.[127] It may be that the gradual filling up of space within the walls, in Constantinople as elsewhere, forced silkmaking into the suburbs. The mulberry trees on whose leaves the worms fed must have always been there.

Water-powered mills, especially for grain, went into the Thracian suburbs for obvious reasons. These were the mills for mass production, since there were smaller mills in the city itself. Olive and wine presses were here, because there were local crops to process.[128]

(c) There were also unlucky enterprises, which went beyond the walls to avoid contaminating the protected enclosure. Among these the Byzantines included, for reasons obscure to us, the whole craft of ceramic-making. "The potters' trade was not considered honorable," and this goes far toward explaining the

[121] *Ibid.*, 67–68.
[122] *Ibid.*, 69.
[123] *Ibid.*, 78.
[124] *Ibid.*, 79.
[125] *Ibid.*
[126] *Ibid.*, 70.
[127] *Ibid.*, Janin, *Constantinople*, 260.
[128] Syuzyumov, "Ekonomika prigorodov," 71–72, 73.

general mediocrity of Byzantine ceramics.[129] The pots, once made, were sold by "general" merchants inside the city.[130]

A second trade, strongly tainted in both the physical and the spiritual-magical senses, was tanning—necessary and repulsive as it was and is. Where the tanneries of Constantinople were in the 10th century is not certain. They may not have been in the real faubourgs, however, but in a corner of the city that had its own special, unfortunate character: the extreme southwest section. In this locality, although it was dominated by the great Golden Gate, executed prisoners were buried, and this automatically marks off a distinct, negative precinct.[131] In this area may have been the quarter called Braka (Ebraika, the Jews' Quarter) otherwise unplaced.[132] The Jews supposedly lived in the Sykai (Galata) suburb, but at one time they had been associated with the trade of tanning by law if not by choice, and could have had business and residence in this tabooed quarter of the city.[133] The tanneries of modern Istanbul produce their great stink there; this is no final argument, but can at the least, using the idea of the persistence of an unlucky *topos*, point to where the Byzantine tanneries were likely to have been located.

129 *Ibid.*, 67–68; compare Suidas, *Suidae Lexikon* (Ed. A. Adler, Leipzig), s.v. *keramein.*

130 "Book of the Prefect," 614/XIII.

131 Janin, *Constantinople*, 405.

132 *Ibid.*, 327.

133 *Ibid.*, 260.

The extension of the Imperial Will, from the Skyllitzes Matritensis.
(Courtesy of Dr. S. Cirac Estopanan.)

THREE

The Bureaucracy

> Then the (old) man presents the wash-basin and jug, and the Emperor washes his hands and says to his minister: "Truly, I am innocent of the blood of all men: let not God make me responsible for their blood, for I put it upon your neck." Then he puts the clothes which he wears upon his minister, takes the inkstand of Pilate—this is the inkstand of the man who proclaimed himself innocent of the blood of Christ—may peace be upon him!—puts it upon the neck of the minister, and says to him: "Rule justly as Pilate ruled justly." Then they bring him about over the squares of Constantinople and proclaim: "Rule justly, as the Emperor has placed you in charge of the people's matters."
>
> Harun-Ibn-Yahya, in ibn-Rosteh, *Kitāb al-a'lāq al-nafīsa.*

THE BUREAUCRACY IN THE CITY

The Imperial city, in its operations and self-maintenance, cannot be separated from the services of an hierarchic bureaucracy; nor can this bureaucracy, redefined, be separated from the myths that nourish the city. If the Emperor creates, his servants must prolong and continually reify the act of creation: they must administer. Within the Imperial tradition the fact of urban life in its complexity, and of bureaucratic control and proliferation, seem to make each the cause of the other. In Constantinople's instance, the shapes of life in the city were influenced by the presence and the actions of the civil servants—in the directions they gave to political action; in the resources they commanded; in the demands they made for working space and durable signs of control; in the mental sets they displayed—their biases, training, morale, aims, and purposes. And, in Constantinople, the dominant status of the bureaucratic structure was even more solidly conceived because vital currents within the society itself were channeled through it in a manner nearly incomprehensible to us. It would seem, for example, that the concern for economic aggrandizement, for gain—the urge to compete in the marketplace—which we would call, however mistakenly, invincibly human, could not operate in Constantinople, and was shunted off into the "game" or *agon* of competition for honors among the administrators. And, the definition of the nature of nobility, insofar as the Emperor could exercise his will over it, was involved in the body, if not the discrete functions, of officials of the State.

History

The Byzantine bureaucracy of the 9th and 10th centuries, in the perfection of its effective form and in the balanced intricacy of its relations to the Emperor, to the people, and to other centers of political force, had reached almost precisely the same point in development as the city which was its great headquarters. It was large, it was powerful, and it was aware of is power, but it was controlled, and it was not yet sclerotic.

Its history as an organism follows the great themes of Byzantine self-definition. Up to the disrupting crisis of the late 6th and early 7th centuries it was a civil service in the late, "lower" Roman mold. Its nomenclature and titlature were vaguely reminiscent of the Julio-Claudians, but its heart, mass, and directive instincts belonged to the period after Diocletian, when the Emperor's office and the supporting administrative organs climbed together, to the cost of the old forms.[1] By Justinian's reign it had achieved a degree of self-direction and a toponymy that advanced its chief bureaucrats to nearly autonomous positions within the State. The Justinianic civil service was an elaborate double pyramid, descending from two great officers of state, the Master of Offices and the Praetorian Prefect. Rank and function were conjoined. The bureaucracy was still marked with a strong *Roma-*

[1] A. E. R. Boak, *The Master of Offices in the Later Roman and Byzantine Empires*, in *Two Studies in Later Roman and Byzantine Administration* (New York, 1924), 19 ff.

nitas both in language, traditions, and structure, and had reached a plateau of predictable efficiency and internalized control. It was rigorously separated from the military, another arm of state service—in this period, almost entirely mercenary.[2]

The perfected Justinianic bureaucratic machine did not survive the 6th century intact. It was strained by the whole range of troubles that came after the great "Romanizing" Emperor's death, and it was broken and reformed in the terrible years when the Empire shuddered under the strokes of the advancing Slavs and the Avar-Turk barbarians and entered its last great contest with Persia.

The Persian war and its aftermath must be marked as a watershed in the history of a steadily more "Byzantine" empire, though certain individual responses (such as the reform of provincial government) were deep rooted. The aftermath of that war, so far as the external relations of East Rome were concerned, was a galloping irony. Under a soldier-emperor of genius, Heraclius, the Byzantines finally hammered Persia to pieces, and then when the old rival—the "Sun" to Rome's "Moon"—was dead, a howling tide of Arabs, armed with a new name of God, swept the victory away. Syria and Palestine and vassal Persia fell, Egypt fell, Cyrenaica, all of North Africa. The line of the Taurus barely held and great *razzias* made it semifictional, while the Eastern Mediterranean was seamed by Arab fleets. For two hundred years Byzantium would try merely to survive the perennial and endemic enmity of Islam and the vigorous encroachments of new Slav and Turkic hordes from beyond its shrinking European borders.

The Arab assault had been called the Orient's revenge on Rome, or on Alexander, but before Islam's outburst East Rome had begun to both look and feel more "Eastern."[3] Its administrative machine was naturally caught up in the changes this new look and feel portended. "Eastern" in this context is more than ordinarily confusing; it signifies a strong and permanently effective turn in the directions that had been outlined in the policies of the Greek or Greco-Hellenistic superstates that appeared in the Near East after the Alexandrian conquests. This meant:

[2] *Ibid.*, 51 ff.
[3] Zakythinos, "Étatisme byzantine," 678–679.

(a) An increasingly manifest autocracy, with the Persian Empire, and all its traditions of kingship in the Mesopotamian mold, used as a paradigm. Actually the "orientalizing" of the Court and the Emperor's person, the dissolution of intermediary powers, the emphasis on the iconic and viceregal aspect of the *Basileus/Autokrator* went well beyond the limits Sassanid Persia had achieved, and referred to Greek Hellenistic models and to the Roman—especially post-Constantinian Roman—experience and experiment as well. The dramatic aspect of the overwhelming of Persia had clouded this fact.[4]

(b) The creation of a crisis or siege-state, powerfully centralized on the one hand both in theory and in physical actuality, with a new degree and type of rationalization of manpower and resources, yet with the reorganized provincial governments given the autonomy of beleaguered fortresses under a single military governor. The state, now directed toward brute survival, became thoroughly permeated with military assumptions and attributes.[5]

(c) Almost as an afterthought, but a vigorous one, came a refocusing of and concentration on Hellenic—Greek—culture in both its pagan and Christian forms. This cultural redirection was made simpler because the subcultures (we can count the Western-Latin among them for the present) had been peeled away or had seceded, but there was a visibly *positive* drive to create a Greek cultural matrix, a cultural citizenship, in what was left.[6]

(d) Finally, and always to be considered, the state-under-siege found itself pressed by economic stringency. From the time that Egypt and Syria, richest of the provinces, were torn from the Byzantine grip, the Empire had to accustom itself to a shortage-economy, an economic situation where resources were drastically limited and had to be drastically apportioned and controlled. The resulting strain never subsided; it was felt both in the capital,

[4] *Ibid.*, 667–669.

[5] On the siege-state, see Teall's discussion of conditions in the city in the 7th and 8th centuries: "Grain Supply," 100–102, 103–105.

[6] See N. Baynes, "*The Hellenistic Civilization and East Rome* (Cambridge, 1956), 37–38; Zakythinos, "Étatisme byzantine," 679; N. Iorga, *Histoire de la vie byzantine. Empire et civilisation, d'après les sources, illustrée par les monnaies* II (Bucharest, 1934), 94.

which had been heretofore fed from the magnificent Egyptian granaries, and in the smallest of the remaining provinces, which had to bear the burden of taxation and the responsibility for providing basic resources and military manpower as well.[7]

All of these factors impinged on and formed the post-Heraclian bureaucracy, or so we assume, since the history of the Byzantine civil administration in the period 650–800 A.D. is as problematical as other political-governmental developments. Vital social and economic rearrangements in this period are no clearer. The Empire slides behind a great historical occlusion, yet from the fragmented hints left to us we have the impression not of a society battered or traumatized into silence, but one in which frantic and creative energy was absorbed in moving and making for survival, in a concern for existential process rather than logical-historical analysis.[8]

What happened to the service organs—the bureaucracy—of the Byzantine Empire in its "Middle Age," during more than a hundred and fifty years of conflict and fertile and confused growth, was approximately this:

(a) It was drastically reduced in size, obviously, as the Empire shrank. It was, furthermore, concentrated in the cities and especially in the City, as effective administration of the embattled theme-provinces passed into military hands; it never, however, abdicated all responsibilities in the provinces.[9]

(b) Its Justinianic or, more precisely, its Constantinian-Theodosian character as a perfected Late Roman organization, dissolved. The most apparent change in detail was the loss of a Latin or heavily Latinized official terminology. More important:

(1) The successful concentration of all the forms and permutations of authority into the figure of the Emperor had drastic effects on the apparatus of State. The hierarchic officialdom which had peaked in the superministers, the Prefect and the Master of Offices, was fragmented and its compo-

[7] Rouillard, *La vie rurale,* 175, 178, 181 ff.

[8] The lack of historical self-examination during these centuries is only one indication of the state of crisis.

[9] Dendias, "Études," 137; Glykatzi-Ahrweiler, "Recherches," 42–44.

nents were leveled. Graded decision making, the creation of chains-of-command, and rules for advancement or failure, were all shifted from within the structure of the civil service to become, in theory, the sole domain of the Autokrator-Sovereign.[10]

The Emperor's powerful intrusion into the quondam autonomy of the bureaus of State was reinforced by new controlling definitions of those bureaus. In their new "leveled" or equalized status the heads of the various departments, about sixty in all, were made responsible to, and reported directly to the Emperor. The intermediary advisory or responsible controlling board, the *Silention* or Kitchen Cabinet (which had to exist), was made up of a shifting membership; its powers, though great, were unstructured and almost covert. The old equation between function and rank, the predictable tie between "office" and "honor" was theoretically broken; this meant that any patent of nobility through service to the State was put directly into the Emperor's hands. And, as in all professional bureaucracies, the salaries and perquisites that rewarded service were controlled and dispensed by the Throne.[11]

(2) The modular structure of the bureaucracy was reshaped, and new or previously less important posts come into significant being or visibility. One of these was the Eparch or Prefect of the City, whose responsibilities within the capital were now sharpened and broadened as the city concentrated more power within itself.[12] Another group of posts, the *logothetai* or Treasurers, came forward to meet the new problems of the allocation of scarce resources.[13] One of these, the Logothete of the Drome, moved beyond his financial responsibility (for the *Dromos* or Public Post, the principle means of Imperial communication); he eventually assumed

[10] Boak, *Master of Offices*, 49–50 ff; Bury, *Imperial Administrative System*, 19–20.

[11] R. Guilland, "Venalité et favoritisme à Byzance," *Revue des Études Byzantines* X (1952), 35–46.

[12] Bury, *Imperial Administrative System*, 69–73.

[13] Zakythinos, "Étatisme byzantine," 675; Bury, *Imperial Administrative System*, 86–91, 98–100; Dölger, *Finanzverwaltung*, 13–14.

control of the machinery of diplomatic relations, but in its technical, not policy-making aspects.[14] Instances can be multiplied, but the point here is that the bureaucracy took its new toponymy, with all the new nodes and foci of responsibility, from an environment of endemic crisis.

(c) A reinforced Hellenism, the "new" cultural orientation of the Empire, affected and in turn was affected by the "new" bureaucracy. This culture was intensely megalopolitan, not merely urban, in feeling, and in its Byzantine form it continued the established Hellenistic patterns of conservatism, a strong bent toward encyclopaedism, rhetoric, and the thesauric tradition.[15] Its creativity, in other words, would have to be of a very special and derivative sort. The Byzantine bureaucracy, with its own strong urges toward well-defined pattern and conservative style, seems inevitably to have been drawn into a pact of mutual comfort and reinforcement with the culture of Constantinople. This would be particularly noticeable in the middle and upper strata of Byzantine officialdom. Thus the bureaucracy, though it undoubtedly served as a channel for social mobility and cross-class interplay, also maintained the cultural rigidity and mandarin taste that is part of Hellenistic classicism and also part of the "renaissance" mentality which, from time to time, revived that classicism in Byzantium as elsewhere.

By the time the Empire emerged from its stormy, and undoubtedly fertile, middle age, the administrative organs of the State had taken on the structural characteristics that I mean to examine in detail.

This administrative structure was to move and be articulated in an environment which had itself been shaped in the internal and external struggles—physical, moral, doctrinal—of the 7–9th centuries. The central fact of that environment was the dominance of the King-Emperor in his city, with the appearance of the great radial lines of force that were meant to hold all, convince

[14] Bury, *Imperial Administrative System,* 91; see also D. A. Miller, "The Logothete of the Drome in the Middle Byzantine Period," *Byzantion* **36** (1966, II), 438–439.

[15] Baynes, *The Hellenistic Civilization,* 22; Zakythinos, "Étatisme byzantine," 679.

all—and serve all. The bureaucracy, in theory, took its place only along these lines of force. At the same time the civil officers of the State had to, and did, make moves to oppose this theory, and to separate themselves, to become a distinct entity with underivative powers, and a consciousness both of service and of right.[16] This consciousness grew sharper because of the appearance of another power, an aristocracy with dangerous attributes: cohesion through blood, name, dynasty; a base on the land (a primary resource); a claim to political consideration because of military service and especially military leadership, and a monopoly of administrative effectiveness in the provinces. This aristocracy had as well a *mythos* of caste that rejected, in effect, the city and its works, and the Byzantine bureaucracy was more and more strongly of the city.[17]

The Emperor and the Administrative Organism

To understand the massive bureaucratic structure that found its true home in the city, we must push out of the way or satisfactorily explain another Byzantine paradox. In this paradox the administrative machinery, on the one hand, is recognized as "Byzantine"—that is, complex, highly specialized, thoroughly hierarchized, and in a sort of super-Parkinsonian way hypnotized by an ideal of stasis, by the passing of endless papers from the Byzantine version of desk to desk. On the other hand, the weight of actual information we have reflects the bureaucracy not in its function as an administrative machine but as a Court, a huge ceremonial appendix in which the placing and spacing of the ranks of nobles had, again in theory, nothing to do with offices occupied and jobs done. This latter was the view from the Emperor's side.[18]

The natural self-defined shape of the Byzantine—or any—bureaucracy has a strong resemblance to the first image. In this self-definition the great services—finance, communications (the chancery), legal problems and decisions, policing and security—as well as the subbureaus of every sort moved in a sealed

[16] Eisenstadt, *Political Systems of Empires,* 157 ff, 160 ff.
[17] See Chapt. 5, footnotes 47 and 49.
[18] Eisenstadt, *Political Systems of Empires,* 132 ff.

world where administration became an end in itself. Here the professional found that his own *raison d'être* was also the Final Cause of the state. The society existed not to be ruled, but to be administered. In this image the Emperor was not a magician, but was that necessary finial to the whole elaborate construction—the Bureaucrat-in-Chief. Competition, and the consequent rise or fall or stagnation of the individual official, was governed by interservice rules of the most minute particularity, rules by which the Emperor should abide as well as every other civil servant.[19]

The resources that the bureaus extracted from the producers in the society should go, according to a fixed scale, to pay for the continuation of those bureaus as a matter of course. Finally, the society itself had to be subject to the extended perfection of rule or regulation: the Rule of Law. It would be not only the legal officers of the hierarchy who would insist on this devotion to legality—and insist that the Emperor insist as well—but all who felt themselves servants of the highest good, which was order.

There are any number of logical and practical flaws in this dream of order. The ground rules for bureaucratic procedure (especially advancement), for instance, may have no resemblance at all to what the Emperor might conceive as the perfect image of Law; they might even be illegal. If we take for granted that *something* like this service mentality existed in Byzantium, however, flawed or not, we are on fairly firm ground. Yet the weight of evidence is on the other side, because of the fortuitous survival of the great handbooks of ceremonial—the culminating expression of the Imperial theory of the service organisms. In these handbooks the separate realm, the Peaceable Kingdom of the bureaucracy, is replaced by another Eden; the rule by which men serve is dissolved in an efflux of magic.

THE STRUCTURE OF THE BUREAUCRACY

The Byzantine bureaucracy, important a fact of the civilization as it was, has not revealed too many of its secrets to us yet. The general outlines of structure and operation are probably as clear

[19] See Michael Psellos on the bureaucratic reaction to those who were loyal to the Emperor alone: *Chronographia* II.3.

as they ever will be, but the complex permutations of the two modes by which the Byzantines defined their administration—honor and function—are not clear at all. Analysts of this administrative system have the problem of reconstructing an exotic and subtle system—and a large one—with a multiplicity of differentiations and gradations, and to perform this miracle of resuscitation they must use data that are rich but scattered, historically disjunct, and worse, not really applicable to a structural analysis. One major source, the 10th-century *Book of Ceremonies,* is an omnium-gatherum of the rituals of state that arranges the bureaucracy in that magical order which transforms them from a working apparatus to a Sacred Hierarchy.[20] The treatise *On the Administration of the Empire* does not describe the administration of the Empire except in terms of the highest range of policy, though it contains, by happenstance, some other nuggets of useful information.[21] The *Kleterologion* of the Master of Ceremonies, Philotheus, is designed as just that: a Dining List or ceremonial notebook for the great Imperial banquets, with interpolated appendices, the whole compiled from older lists and sources, though fortunately some of these sources were actual lists of chains of subordination and command.[22] There are also fragmentary *taktika* or compilations of ranks, and, of course, the remarks of chronographers and historians, correspondents and legists, tourists and hagiographers. Out of the whole mass we can extract no identifiable Table of Organization, no clear and precise descriptions of function. What we do have has to be laboriously conned, and equally laboriously rearranged. The structure that does emerge from all this is, however, worth taking pains over, for it is all we can know of the operative and effective administrative arm of this Imperial state—a state in which a main form of political behavior was cast in the bureaucratic mold.

The Imperial bureaucracy can be arranged according to two scales of activity and visibility. Rank or title gave access to the ceremonial Sacred Hierarchy, but there were certainly masses of lesser officials who never attained even the lowest rank in it.

[20] Proem to the *De ceremoniis,* 3–5; translated in Barker, *Social and Political Thought,* 103–104.

[21] See the General Introduction to the *De administrando imperio,* II (*Commentary,* edited by R. Jenkins, London, 1962), 1–9.

[22] Bury, *Imperial Administrative System,* 7–18.

The hierarchy, which was made up of eighteen or nineteen grades, was also broken down: the highest four were reserved to the Imperial family itself (or whoever might be coöpted into it), while the ranks below were divided into a "military" series—titles specifically drawn from military or quasimilitary occupations such as *spatharios*—"swordsman," or "guardsman"—and a "senatorial" (*synkletikos*) series. The difference between the two seems not to have been one of residual function but of ceremonial place: the *synkletikoi* were of the "stabilized" ranks, who appeared in the set-piece ceremonies; the military titles were processional, and their holders appeared in the *proeleusis* or Imperial cortège. Each of the dignities was differentiated by insigne (*brabeion*: the hierarchy of rank is officially termed "those honored by insigne"—*ai dia brabeiou axiai*), and it is clear that the table of ranks was in the process of being gradually inflated in the 10th century, with more frequent promotions to the highest dignities (especially Patrician) seen.[23]

The second scale, that of function or office, placed the bureaucrat in his proper working rôle. Since our sources are seriously biased toward the ceremonial scale, or toward the highest strata of officeholders, we have only the most casual data on the functionary mass, the clerks or *notarioi* who filled up the individual bureaus. These were called, in general terms, either *thematic, tagmatic,* or *synkletic,* depending on whether they worked in the thematic provinces, under the tagmatic chiefs (commanders of the Palace troops), or in any of the civil bureaus properly speaking. Higher functionaries were divided, according to the indefatigable compiler Philotheus, into seven types.[24]

(a) *Strategoi.* The viceroy-generals of the various *themes,* here (in theory) regarded as military functionaries. There was also a *strategos ek prosopou,* a "personal appointee" of the Emperor, assigned, evidently, to new themes.

(b) *Domestics.* These were the chiefs of the tagmatic or

[23] *Ibid.*, 20–36; Guilland, "Etudes sur l'histoire administrative de Byzance," *Byzantina-Metabyzantina* I (I) (1946), 176.

[24] Bury, *Imperial Administrative System,* 36–39, 39–119. For modern works on individual offices see the Bibliography in Vol. IV, *The Cambridge Medieval History,* part II: (Cambridge, 1967), 403–408, and especially the listed studies of Guilland.

Household troops. One, the Domestic of the Schools or Scholarians, was Commander-in-Chief of the field army. Three more—the Domestics of the Excubitors, the Arithmoi, and the Hikanatoi—were rated nearly as highly, and their regiments, too, were regarded as élite troops.

(c) "Judges" (*kritai*). With these officials begins the civilian bureaucracy properly speaking, though the provincial Strategoi commanded numbers of civil employees as well as the military ranks. The *kritai* included such important officers of state as the Prefect of the City, the Quaestor (who had a wide judicial function), and a judge who examined petitions.

(d) *Secretikoi.* In this category, defined usually as Treasurers, were included the Sakellarios or Comptroller General, the two operative treasurers of the realm (one overseeing taxation, one overseeing the military chest), a Logothete (or treasurer) who was not involved in finance at all but served as Foreign Minister (the Logothete of the Drome), various *chartularii* or high-ranking clerks, and the Imperial Secretary (*Protoasecretes*). There were also two Curators, one supervising the arsenal and workshops of the Mangana, and the Orphanotropos, who oversaw the Great Orphanage of Constantinople.

(e) *Demokratoi.* The two Demarchs, bureaucratic supervisors of the Green and Blue demes.

(f) *Stratarchs.* These were the chiefs of the foreign bodyguards, the Lord High Admiral (*Drungarios tou ploimou*), an official who supervised the cavalry remounts, another who headed a *taxis* or office of special emissaries (*basilikoi*), and the Count of the Stables.

(g) *Various.* The most important of these extraneous offices was that of the Rector, the chief of the household, the Synkellos, an ecclesiastic who was appointed by the Emperor and acted as liaison between Emperor and Patriarch, and a Master of Ceremonies.

The number of high-ranking officers in these seven more or less arbitrary divisions totaled about sixty. In theory each of them was responsible directly to the Throne: there were no intermediary superministries or pyramidal interpolations between the Emperor and his highest functionaries, a purposeful arrangement which obviously put a tremendous strain on the Emperor, and which was in fact necessarily amended by the existence of an informal council of state. The titles of these officers merely emphasize the breadth of Byzantine bureaucratic jurisdiction, and give no idea of the functioning of the bureaus that labored under them. To move past the point of casual identification it must be necessary to examine a *taxis* or bureaucratic section in some detail.

The *taxis* of the misnamed Logothete of the Drome was concerned with all the technical aspects of Byzantine diplomacy and with some subsidiary areas.[25] Its chief had his origin in the *dēmosios dromos* or Public Post, the network of roads, way-stations, and remount-depots which was the principal communications channel of the government. From Treasurer of the Post the Logothete gradually became head not only of its communicative machinery but of peripheral areas. The fact that the Post was an extensive or outward-vectored instrument, and especially the fact that all diplomatic missions moved along its routes, eventually seems to have converted the Logothete as chief of the Post to a specialist in "foreign affairs," in every technical aspect of the conduct of diplomacy.

The Logothete continued to head up the Public Post, with its staff of couriers, *mandatores,* and inspectors, probably supervised by a *chartularius* or Chief Clerk. Another subsection, whose responsibilities can only be inferred from scattered information, was an Office for Barbarians (a continuation of a section so named which is last identified in the 6th century), with a chief called "the one concerned with barbarians" (*o epi ton barbaron*) of fairly high rank, and below him several more *chartularii,* the Warden (*curator*) of the Envoys' Quarters, and possibly a peculiar figure called the First Clerk (*protonotarios*) of the Drome. Below *these* intermediate civil servants were more clerks, inspectors, and guards, all concerned in the care, feeding, and quarantine of foreign diplomats in the city. A third subsection, even less well defined than the others, was the corps of interpreters so necessary to the ongoing business of diplomacy, and including every level of linguistic skill and responsibility. Some

[25] Bury, *Imperial Administrative System,* 91–93; Miller, "Logothete," 438–470.

interpreters mentioned by name in our sources for the 10th century were of high rank (one, a Krinites, of the Armenian family, was a *protospather*—the 11th rank, immediately below Patrician) but there must have been dozens of lesser fry, available for the ordinary contacts with foreigners or even, in the late 10th century, attached for convenience to the Varangian Guard.[26]

The *taxis* of the Logothete of the Drome was involved in that most vital of Byzantine acts of state, the defense of the realm by diplomatic means, and yet our reconstruction is lamentably full of gaps, holes, and mooted conclusions. The subsection for barbarian affairs *probably* existed in the form described; the interpreters *probably* fell under the Logothete: they had been under the old Office for Barbarian Affairs in the 6th century, and in the 10th century seem to be on their way to becoming the separate office they were in the 12th, under a Great Interpreter.[27] In addition we know that some bureau gathered and collated intelligence from abroad—accumulated the files, for example, which were used by the Emperor Constantine VII in compiling some of the more technically detailed chapters in this treatise *De administrando imperio.* Certainly this collection and collation fell into the province of the Logothete, and it would be pleasant to have a description of the department designated "Records," presided over by a wizened *chartularius* with forty years' service. This description, of course, does not exist. We do know that another function, that of protecting the internal security of the state, fell in part to the Logothete, because we have been left hints that the Logothete not only "ran" or controlled agents in foreign countries, but cooperated with whatever official dealt with subversion within the Empire—especially the subversion undertaken by Anatolian magnates who were in the habit of traitorously negotiating with Syrian Emirs or with Baghdad itself.[27a] The machinery for protecting the internal security of the

[26] Miller, "Logothete," 449–458, for the corps of interpreters; 444–449, for the Office for Barbarians.

[27] Miller, "Logothete," 452, for the Great Interpreter; E. Stein, *Untersuchungen zur spatbyzantinischen Verfassungs- und Wirtschaftsgeschichte* (Hanover, 1925), 36–37.

[27a] Miller, "Logothete," 468, n. 1 for the cooperating director of "active" counterespionage; see also Jenkins, "The Flight of Samonas," 217–235.

state is not usually open to detailed scrutiny even in modern times, but in the Byzantine instance almost every other function of the bureaucracy is questionable as well. We can recapitulate little more than the outer shell of the bureaucratic maze.

The Logothete himself was—again with the usual caveats—a member of another aspect or division of the Byzantine administrative machine: the informal Council of State or *Synkletos* (another meaning of this term) which served the Emperor as his highest advisory body.[27b] Membership in this group shifted, but ordinarily the Logothete must have been involved, because he had so much information in hand. The rest of the council's membership is hinted at from time to time: in terms of common sense it would have included the First Secretary, the Eparch of the City, the *paracoimomenos* or whichever of the eunuch officers of the bedchamber was particularly influential, and the Domestic of the Schools. The Rector came into real prominence in the 10th century and may have been coopted into this intimate circle. Sure indications of membership in the *Synkletos* are not easy to find, though councils of regency—as after the death of the Emperor Alexander in 913—were likely to have been made up of ex-*Synkletikoi*.[27c] The officials chosen by the Emperor to conduct affairs while the Emperor was on campaign must also be highly rated—three eunuchs were so designated in the late 9th and 10th century: the *prepositos* Baanes, the *paracoimomenos* Basil, and Joseph Bringas, also *paracoimomenos*.[27d]

The eunuch bureaucracy makes up a special category of the generalized bureaucratic function. The prominence of the "beardless" in the Byzantine hierarchy still prejudices casual observers against the Empire, but the Byzantines themselves were not overly fond of the eunuch-bureaucrats: those who had real power were all the more feared because of their mysterious and taboo-laden infirmity, while the ordinary eunuchs were resented and

[27b] Bury, *Imperial Administrative System*, 37.

[27c] Ostrogorsky, *History of the Byzantine State* (New Brunswick, N.J., 1957), 231–235.

[27d] R. Guilland, "Les eunuques dans l'empire byzantin: Étude de titulature et de prosopographie byzantine," *Revue des Études Byzantines* I (1943), 221, 223–227.

mocked, even by the Emperors who used them. They had, one Emperor said:

> . . . an effeminate soul, perverse by natural inclination, quick to invent all sorts of mischiefs and to execute them . . . they are instruments of turpitude, guides to illicit arts and receptacles of vice.[27e]

They were reportedly more venal, more thirsty for power, vengeful, immoral. Nevertheless they were useful, and not only were certain offices assigned to none but eunuchs, but in the ritual hierarchy they played a vital part, representing "a celestial power on earth"—the power of the angelic host. "Like the angels, they surrounded the *basileus,* who represented God on earth. Like the seraphim, the eunuchs drew near the *basileus,* with their faces hidden behind their white hands."[27f] So far as function was concerned, the eunuchs were extensively employed in the intimate household of the Emperor, where by the 10th century ten posts were invariably occupied by them; the most important of these were the *paracoimomenos,* or Chief Gentleman of the Bedchamber, and the *protovestiarios* or Chief of the Palace Wardrobe, which contained treasures other than state robes.[27g] The usefulness of eunuchs in these sensitive positions was regarded as self-evident, since no eunuch could himself plot to seize the Imperial throne. Eunuchs were not limited to Palace service, however, but found employment throughout the bureaucracy. Only three offices were officially closed to them: Eparch of the City, Quaestor, and Domestic of the Schools—and eunuchs were in fact given the latter post or entrusted with other high military commands.[27h] They were as successful, on the average, as other generals, though none managed to equal the fame of Justinian's great eunuch general, Narses.

The titlature of eunuch officials made up a separate list, with the titles drawn from what had obviously at one time been simple functions, such as *nipsistiarios* or "bathing attendant." At the top

[27e] *Ibid.,* 235.
[27f] *Ibid.,* 201.
[27g] Bury, *Imperial Administrative System,* 125.
[27h] Guilland, "Fonctions et dignités des Eunuques," *Revue des Études Byzantines* II (1944), 185–186.

of the range of eunuch dignities were two which were common to both eunuchs and their bearded brethren: *protospatharios* and patrician. *Magister* seems to have been interdicted, as were the "consular" ranks—*hypatos, dishypatos,* and *anthypatos*.[27i]

The eunuch officers made up, in theory, that part of the bureaucracy that was most rarified, most closely attached to the Imperial view of what a bureaucracy should be. They were separated from the instinct of the ordinary bureaucrat to perpetuate his post dynastically, and should have been the most Imperially-oriented servants of the state—as in fact most of them were. We can expect that there was no love lost between the ordinary bureaucracy and the favored eunuch ranks.

Recruitment and Training

Though the Byzantine civil service was concentrated in the capital, and had a *morale* that was intensely urban, its period of greatest growth and balance was marked by the presence of a strong magnetic power extending into the countryside. It was one of the most successful modes for mobilization of certain strata outside the city, setting up a linkage connecting the central government with, especially, that group whose allegiance was sought by other means as well: the rural middle class.

That this class, in Byzantium as in other Imperial societies, was drawn to take service is clear but still conjectural as to cause. In East Rome it was a class nurtured and protected by Imperial legislation from the 7th century on; the Emperor's concern and protective arm was visible until other forces intervened in the 10th century. Certainly this protection was clear enough to the protected class, and it was also obvious that the bureaucracy served the Emperor along lines familiar to them; it was not yet a rival.[28] At the same time, the civil service perpetuated a kind of tradition-in-service, a sobriety and solidity that must have appealed to the squirearchic mentality. The bureaucracy served as an acceptable arena for competitive and ambitious minds—especially since mercantile activity was so strongly limited. Finally, the bureaucracy stood against a class with which the rural middle

[27i] *Ibid.*, 187 ff.

[28] Rouillard, *La vie rurale,* 90, 106.

class felt itself very nearly at war—the "powerful" on the land, the magnate families, the aristocracy.

In the correct balance of things the bureaucracy would be recruited from those elements friendly to the Imperial idea—to the maintenance of a strongly centralized power—and to the Imperial figure who could demand and receive ritual and material obedience and support. These elements would include certain urban classes, both native to the city and drawn from other cities: the professionals, the remnants of the old curial class (in the smaller cities) and the literati—if they can be separately considered.[29] I have emphasized the connective links to the countryside to provide some counterweight to my image of the city as a ritual-fortress: that it was, but not to the exclusion of other possibilities. In the official terminology of the Court, in the 10th century, *paganos* had no connotation of "pagan" nor even of "rural"; it could mean "common" or a "private" citizen (compared with the ancient Greek *idiotikos*) but more, it had assumed the meaning of *functionless*—without an office, even without a use.[30]

So far as the recruitment of successive generations of civil servants was concerned, we can see or deduce a constant confrontation between two ideals or, more pointedly, between the Imperial desire and human nature. The Emperor wanted to keep every channel of mobility free, on the one hand, to allow his own inscrutable will room to act, to reward or punish any of his instruments. The bureaucracy itself, and especially the upper levels (*spatharocandidatus* and higher, that is), though its members may themselves have benefited from free channels and open opportunities, moved as much as they dared toward closing them off, especially in favor of their own family, friends, and allies.[31]

There are arguments for and against this human tendency to protect one's own. A "dynastic" bureaucracy or civil service, in a complex polity, has much to recommend it, since it ensures a steady base of recruitment, and can also show a tradition of ser-

[29] Eisenstadt, *Political Systems of Empires,* 284.

[30] Guilland, "Études sur l'histoire," (*Byzantina-Metabyzantina*) 167.

[31] Eisenstadt, *Political Systems of Empires,* 280; Guilland, "Venalité et favoritisme," 35–36.

vice, a continued acceptance of patterns of training, *ethos* and behavior—generally speaking, a professional outlook. Danger comes from the tendency for the upper reaches of the bureaucracy to try to aristocratize themselves; to try to convert that *noblesse* that the Emperor granted, independent of function, to a hierarchized, solidified power—allied, in fact, to the new threatening power of the provincial gentry, true dynasts and wielders of great localized strength.[32] Certainly a movement in this direction had begun in the 9th century, a movement that cast its shadow into the careers of the emperors of the Amorian house. The evidence for this movement is not only the appearance through the years of the same family names in the higher ranks of officialdom, or the casual notation by a chronicler of service by both a father and a son. The continuity or inheritance of position must be noted, the marriage alliances made between bureaucratic families, the nobility professed and defended. It seems likely in fact that the advent of the Macedonian dynasty scotched, but only for a time, a vigorous push in the direction of bureaucratic dynasticism.[33]

Basil I put into effect several policies designed to offset the greedier ambitions of a civil service set on aristocratizing itself. The peculiarly popular tenor which his house liked to display, and the propaganda of concealed nobility-under-poverty (the so-called Legend of Basil, in which the founder of the dynasty became a Byzantine Dick Whittington) was supported by very positive action.[34] Basil's elimination of the Caesar Bardas even before he had taken the throne is a hint, for Bardas was certainly an aristocrat. After Basil had come to power certain high posts were rapidly downgraded, among them the office of Logothete of the Drome. Under the Macedonians new men or, in truth, unknown men from the provinces or even from beyond the borders appear in numbers, and under Basil's successors we seem to see more and more friction between parvenues in the bureaucracy and the more established families.

32 See especially the case of Leo Choerosphactes given below.
33 Miller, "Logothete," 464–468; H.-G. Beck, "Der byzantinische 'Ministerpräsident'," *Byzantinische Zeitschrift* 48 (1955), 330.
34 Vogt et Hausherr, *Oraison funèbre,* 51 ff.

One of the most singular servants of Leo VI was the faithful, sinister, Levantine figure of the Syrian eunuch, Samonas, *cubicularius* (Gentleman of the Bedchamber) and certainly director of the internal security forces of the state—an abomination to the aristocracy and its allies.[35] Romanus Lecapenus, an Armenian peasant risen to the throne, was another example of the type. As a contrast to these, and showing in his career the sort of ambitions the Imperial house had to guard against, we have the career of the "Magister, Proconsul, and Patrician" Leo Choerosphactes, himself a country boy but founder of a bureaucratic dynasty, a litterateur and stylist, related widely to other high officials (and to the Imperial house)—and finally implicated in a plot by the purely aristocratic house of Ducas to overthrow the Macedonians.[36]

There were pressures, then, not fierce but continuous, to distort the original Imperial idea of what a bureaucracy should be and do. The power of the Emperor as directing figure to withstand these pressures was not always certain. There was a control and a complication in the fact that the recruitment of functionaries was intricately involved with the needs of the treasury. *Titles*—not offices—were bought outright and openly; their sacred insigne were sold by the Emperor according to a more or less fixed tariff, though the highest orders of nobility had no set price.[37] Evidently the title-holder paid an additional sum as an investment, in order to secure the small salary that went with each title, and also paid out a kind of initiation fee that went to the other dignitaries of the court. Then, having given with one hand, the new noble retook with the other. It is notable that his salary was small, salary being the set and predictable sums paid out to him as both a noble and a functionary (for he collected both, unless he happened to be "simple"—i.e., either untitled or having no function).[38] The major part of a dignitary's income came directly from the Emperor or, in the official terminology, from Heaven. It included largesses distributed on ritual occasions: before Easter,

[35] *Vita Euthemii,* 54–55, 74–75; Jenkins, "The Flight of Samonas," 217–235. On Romanus Lecapenus; Runciman, *Romanus Lecapenus,* 63–65.
[36] Kolias, *Léon Choerosphactès,* 16–54.
[37] R. Guilland, "Venalité et favoritisme," 37, 38–39.
[38] *Ibid.,* 42–44.

at the Brumalia, and on the anniversaries of coronation or birth. More, there were arbitrary distributions of such luxury items as state robes, and outright gifts of land, mansions, and other property.[39] The informality of these generosities is remarkable, and they must be regarded as a means of control, a purposeful avoidance of predictable channels of reward.

This was the official pattern by which one bought office and entered the favored service. The question remains as to just how deeply *private* venality ate into the bureaucratic structure. We know that the granting of titles could be deputized, that intermediaries acting in the sovereign's name might make their own private arrangements before a title was granted.[40] The private sale of offices was quite illegal, and yet offices were sold—given the peculiar nature of the highest administrative élite serving the Throne, this was inevitable.

The inner circle, the handful of ministers who provided the necessary mediation between the Emperor and the mass of officials, had great but ill-defined powers. Their position in regard to the monarch might be open, recognized or constitutional, functional and official—this was true in the case of the Eparch of the City, for example, or in that of the Rector. Other members of this inner council had positions, or ties to the Imperial figure, which were extra-official and personal. Into this category go such shadowy and intriguing figures as the "Agarene" *cubicularius*—the well-hated Samonas.

The venality of someone like Samonas was taken for granted by the witnesses of the time. This venality, however, served in its own way as a counterweight to other influences working against the Emperor. Through someone like Samonas, a commoner, an "outsider," a channel for advancement was kept open that avoided the coral-like accumulation of aristocratic tendencies in the establishment, the bureaucratic nobility, and counteracted their traditional dynasticism and inclination to nepotistic favoritism.

Recruitment and advancement in the Byzantine civil service, insofar as it can be reconstructed, involved any one or a combination of the following factors:

[39] *Ibid.*, 46 ff.
[40] *Ibid.*, 40, 41.

(a) There *was* advancement by merit and skill, a measured progression from lower responsibilities to higher, with rank won by persistence.[41]

(b) There was the use of family and personal allegiances, a reliance on a dynastic tradition of service. This need not necessarily be in opposition to the goals of the Chief Bureaucrat, since he occasionally made arrangements himself for the well-being and advancement of the sons of his servants.[42]

(c) There was the use of wealth to gain higher honors, either openly or through more discreet channels.[43]

(d) There was pure chance, a working of the inscrutable Imperial will.

(e) There was, also, an element that makes the Byzantine bureaucrat of the upper levels (those on whom we have most information) so particularly Byzantine: the working out of a *cultural* code, the showing of merit through a display of the educational and intellectual ideals of the Hellenistic-Byzantine culture. The bureaucracy of the 9th-11th centuries was thus caught up in the problems of defining and maintaining the inherited matrix; in its own mentality it showed all the faults and all the derivative but solid achievements of Byzantine education.

The Bureaucracy and the Literate Culture

The recruitment of functionaries was firmly tied to Byzantium's cultural inheritance in a number of complex ways. Young brains were not funneled directly from the institutions of higher education (that is, the University of Constantinople) into public service; this is understandable in modern terms but was not the Byzantine style—partly because the University had an erratic and intermittent existence, though the bureaucracy did not.[44]

The University had its uses, and more will be said about it. It had been reformed or refounded by Basil I with an eye to the

[41] See the early example of John Lydus, in Barker, *Social and Political Thought,* 77–80.

[42] F. Dvornik, *Les Légendes de Constantin et de Méthode: vues de Byzance* (*Byzantinoslavica* Suppl. 1) (Prague, 1933), 37.

[43] Guilland, "Venalite," passim; Dendias, "Etudes," 138–139.

[44] Dvornik, *Les légendes,* 27–28, n. 5.

training of officials, and it continued to be useful here, especially the Faculty of Law.[45] But technical training was not the aim of the University nor of Byzantine education in general, though the technical manuals and memorabilia of Hellenistic science might be studied in passing, and certain habits of observation and organization must have been valuable to learn. The technical skills of the civil servant were most often learned on the job, although occasionally when a young man was destined for a "family" post he might be privately educated with that post in view.[46]

The education of a young Byzantine involved exposure to, and then immersement in, the literate heritage, through a number of formal and informal means. Actually we know very little about Byzantine higher education, and a good deal less about primary and secondary education, if these modern categories apply at all. The great mass of personal data that survives from this period is not biographical but hagiographical, and the attitude of a saintly figure's biographer toward secular learning was likely to be at least cautious and possibly antagonistic. One of our most valuable sources for the education of the time, for example, the *Vita* of St. John the Psichaite, tells us in vituperative detail all the profane knowledge that the saint did *not* learn.[47]

Yet even the sternest saint who ever rejected Homer in favor of the Scriptures had to be taught to read, and simple literacy was available almost anywhere in the Empire—available, that is, to those who sought it out: the rural and small-town middle class would be the lowest level likely to do this.[48] Women, if educated, were taught at home by tutors, which obviously raises a class or economic barrier.[49] Studies, at any rate, began at the age of 6 or 7, consisted primarily of grammar (elementary, *empeiria*), and

[45] See footnote 55 of this chapter.

[46] Da Costa-Louillet, "Saintes de Constantinople aux VIIIe, IXe et Xe siècles," *Byzantion* **24** (1954), 231–232: the example is that of St. Plato of Sakkoudios.

[47] Da Costa-Louillet, "Saintes" 259.

[48] Dvornik, *Les légendes,* 25–26.

[49] Example of St. Theophano (Da Costa-Louillet, "Saintes de Constantinople" (II) *Byzantion* **25** (1955), 827.

probably were directed by individual priests, unless a child's own family was prepared to undertake the task.[50]

Anyone with ambition, either in the civil service or otherwise, would have to move past simple literacy. There were, we know, teachers called *koinos* or "common" who taught the next degree of general culture.[51] "Secondary" education, which lasted until 17 or 18 years, was evidently subvented by monasteries. Part of it was devoted to Scripture and the rudiments of theology, and it is clear that this reflected a real bifurcation in the culture, a separation of two "sciences."[52] Whether or not a pupil could obtain a secular education at this point may have depended on whether there was a master available; some young men migrated to Constantinople at just this point in their education, others seem to have been well enough trained in the provinces to enable them to move on to the capital later.[53]

There is a gap between what we can guess of the education of the larger number of young men entering the bureaucracy and moving up to higher levels of responsibility, and what we know of the training that a few, comparatively, received beyond the "secondary" stage. The secondary stage included more complex grammar, poetics, some literature—especially Homer, possibly dialectic, geometry.[54] The third stage might be called a "university" education, except that it could be received privately, from one master. If there was no state-supported higher school in Constantinople, and for long periods this was the case, there *was* always advanced schooling in the profane sciences, schooling which followed the Hellenistic pattern—meaning that rhetoric and all its permutations was closely regarded, together with the *quadrivium* of arithmetic, astronomy, geometry, and music.[55]

[50] Dvornik, *Les légendes,* 25.
[51] "Book of the Prefect," 602, sect. I.
[52] Dvornik, *Les légendes,* 26, 28.
[53] *Ibid.,* 31–32.
[54] *Ibid.,* 30; J. Hussey, *Church and Learning in the Byzantine Empire: 867–1185* (Oxford, 1937), 23.
[55] The question of the University is complicated both by lack of data between 726 and 830 A.D.) and various interpretations of what the University was: L. Brehier, "Notes sur l'histoire de l'enseignement supérieur à Constantinople," *Byzantion* III (1926), 81, states that higher education vanished during this period; Dvornik (*Les légendes,* 82) denies this.

The Bureaucrat in Arts and Letters

The bureaucratic style. There is no doubt about the effectiveness of the Byzantine bureaucracy—especially when it was firmly directed and frequently flushed out with "new men" from lower strata. Obviously the Empire's very name depended on its effective administration, on all the departments acting as extensions of the Imperial right arm. If this perfection was the dream of the Chief Bureaucrat, it was a dream never fulfilled, for in the very act of fully articulating a mature bureaucracy the direction of that organism from above was put in peril.

Three countervailing currents can be discerned which, running together, rendered the Byzantine civil service an uncertain instrument. One was the interior patterning of the bureaucracy itself; its tendency to jell, to firm up around the imperative notions of predictability, hierarchy, internal logic—and most particularly dependence on the written record, the document, the paper chain of command.[56] The second was Hellenisticism, the civilization of culture. As I have noted, its traditions fed into the recruiting program of the bureaucracy, and proficiency in its categories was the invariable mark of an educated official. Its structure was closed but comprehensive and, again, predictable and in one sense Aristotelian. Its commanding image was that of the museum. The third was the influence of the city itself. The city, to its administrators, was the place of undeniably solid accomplishment, the material crux where Man the Administrator acted and where the acts had, always, a visible effect and reality. The power of the city was nearly a perceptible corona over the architectural masses, instantly recognizable, where that power was generated as if independently of man. Outside the city's walls, who could say what unintelligible and inchoate nonsense went on?

The effect of these currents on the mature bureaucracy was to produce a bureaucratic style or mode, almost a way of life. This style shapes so much of what we have left of the personal data describing Byzantine civil servants that it tends to overpower what we know to have been the genuine administrative talent and productivity of this group, and the subtle, agelessly effective

[56] Eisenstadt, *Political Systems of Empires,* 280.

extension it made of the business of ruling an Empire. We have to call the style Alexandrian, not Augustan, but it has no mystery to it, and within its patterned coils men act as dancers on a stage that never changes, and their steps are clear, codified, efficient, but totally predictable. Its confidence, the persistent control of its images, is sometimes intimidating and sometimes simply exasperating, and exasperation is liable to divert our judgment of individuals and events.

There are individuals who serve as referents for the juncture of style and service in the Byzantine bureaucracy. Leo Choerosphactes, who flourished in the late 9th and early 10th centuries, was a highly educated, ambitious, and productive civil servant. He held the chancery office of *epi tou kanikleiou* under Basil the Macedonian; under Leo the Wise he carried out diplomatic assignments of stupifying complexity. He negotiated with the Caliphate, but his most difficult task was to try to deal with the Bulgarian Tsar, Simeon, at the height of Simeon's power and arrogance. Leo's correspondence with Simeon survives, and in it we see the Byzantine playing the Bulgar as if he were a large, dangerous, intelligent bull—with a penknife. The tone of Leo's letters is masterly: graceful yet persistent, supple, minatory, lively. Leo was anything but a fool, but eventually he committed enough errors of judgment to find himself in exile.[57]

In his private correspondence and especially in the letters from exile Leo uses every weapon in the considerable armory of the well-taught Byzantine. In one letter of the several addressed to the Emperor Leo himself, he shows a perfect grasp of Imperial political theology: he "like a virtuous disciple of Christ and of the anointed of the Lord" (a neat display of turns: *os chresto to Christou mathete kai kechrismeno para Christou*) knows "that I will be purified . . . I will be saved, and that I will enter into your royal house as into the temple of God."[58] In the next he is the perfect classicist, with a quote from Simonides, another from Plato's *Phaedrus,* a comparison of himself to Sisyphus. His rock (Petra, where he spent his exile) is like that of Euripides' (actually Aeschylus') *Prometheus.* May his accusers perish, they, more

[57] Kolias, *Léon Choerosphactès,* see Introduction.
[58] *Ibid.,* lettre XX (XV).

perverse than the sorcerer Telchines; madmen who need hellebore—not the ordinary, but that of Phocis (a reference to a treatise of Dioscorides). His wife is ill and he has not seen her for six years, and he suffers "like the sister of Orestes for her brother, or like Hecuba and Priam for Cassandra." He follows with some Pindar, a Biblical image or two, and "Aristides also went into exile, but he returned; and Xenophon, but he was saved; Themistocles was in strange lands but was honored the more, and Demosthenes—but envy was the cause." He knows that his sufferings were sharper than those of Callisthenes, Zeno, and Philoctetes, and ends by asking if he might not return like the swallow in spring, making beautiful music; "My love, as I name my master, I am thy faithful servant, and my faith will save me."[59]

Another letter is completely Biblical: the first part drawn mostly from the Psalms, the second from the Gospels, as first David the King speaks for him, and then Christ, who is of the line of David. A third in the sequence deserts both pagan rhetoric and Christian homiletics and deals matter-of-factly with the services Leo had performed for his Imperial master. But it ends: "Save me, rescue me, and I will dance the satyr-dance like Skirtos, or like the comic-dancer who dances the cordax." "Smile upon me, O my Sun, yes, smile; smile, and I will laugh." This is pathetic and pretentious after a dignified beginning.[60]

The last letter recorded as sent to the Emperor Leo has an abrupt and impatient tone; perhaps the civil servant felt at last that he had nothing to lose: "When, O despot, did you prefer the company of pigs and not of men?" The pigs are his accusers, of course. He adds a final, withering blast of classicized proverbs—let his master save him, condemned to the wild beasts of Libya, the evils of Lemnos, and so forth and so on.[61] There is some humanity here, submerged in a welter of cutout, preassembled reactions. Since he is an exile he is self-cast for the classical role of the exile: the figures and tropes are all too ready to hand. Genuine loneliness, real anguish of spirit, are sunk into a syrupy

59 *Ibid.*, lettre XXI (XVI).
60 *Ibid.*, lettre XXIII (XVIII).
61 *Ibid.*, lettre XXIV (XIX).

lake of learning. His undoubted skill with words allows him to sculpt the sentences that do not convince—or do not convince us. There is a tone, the unmistakable dissonance in humanism, which degrades men rather than raising them. Leo is, in his misfortune, a recognizable renaissance man.

Once we have identified Leo his quirks are more understandable. He was a great pursuer of power—delegated power, which adorned him like a ceremonial robe. He was a collector and encyclopaedist of renascent classicism; classicism that had always been current in Byzantium but that emerged into its own in the wealthier, slightly less warlike setting of the late 9th century. He was a bookman, a quoter, a stylist of the true bureaucratic style. He was an egoist, whose loyalties were liable to swerve according to his personal advantage, and what sent him into exile was his involvement in an abortive plot against the dynasty. The best explanation for this contretemps is that Leo, a noble of the "service" nobility (though his family evidently was of the gentry) in time grew away from the Imperial hand that had created him, and looked for an alliance with the landed aristocracy.

At the same time that Leo served as an efficient civil servant and expressed himself as a classicizing litterateur, he directed a great part of his undeniable talent toward religion and this is, again, much in the pattern of the Byzantine literati. Of his poetry much is religious, including troparia for various feasts of the church. His prose writings include commentaries on the Old Testament and the Evangels, discourses on homiletic subjects and other writings on the minutiae of Orthodox dogma.[62] In the great quarrel—fiercer than the iconoclastic controversy—which sprang from the old question as to how Athens and Jerusalem could possibly both contain the elect of God, Leo was a typical moderate. The pagans, to him, blended into and reinforced the Epiphany; he refused to set them apart. Like most of the higher bureaucracy his education made him naturally sympathetic to the *politiques,* the clergy who accommodated learning to piety, and who among the Fathers of the Church followed the great Gregory Nazianzenos.[63]

[62] *Ibid.,* 71.

[63] Jenkins, *Byzantium: The Imperial Centuries,* 96–97; see C. Mango's introduction to *The Homilies of Photius* (Cambridge, Mass., 1958).

Leo flourished at the beginning of the 10th century; Michael Psellos decorated its end—the end, at least, of that harmony the Macedonian dynasty had tried to induce. The two men are very passable mirrors for their time, and struck from the same mental mold.

Michael—born Constantine—Psellos was a native-born Constantinopolitan of the upper middle class. His early years were spent training a considerable intelligence and mounting the first steps in the *cursus honorum*.[64] In both he had success. Like Leo Choerosphactes he pursued a chancery career, where the written and stabilized word was strongest; he was first secretary to a provincial judge (John Vestis) in Mesopotamia, Thrace and Macedonia, then secretary to the *protoasecretis* Philaretos, and eventually *protoasecretis* himself, then Vestarch, and at the peak of his career *paradynasteion* or "Imperial Friend" to the Emperor, and a mover and shaker in the highest administrative circles.[65] He married well (evidently into the Argyros clan) and his orbit of intellectual friends included the most talented minds of the time.[66] His circle of enemies was also large.

Psellos is the highest expression and nearly the terminal point of the type sketched in Leo. He is also much more visible, in every sense, than Leo. Psellos' literary and, with emphasis, philosophical ambitions were stronger, and the picture we have of him is dimensionalized by his own history, a book that succeeds in setting Psellos himself into a frame of time, and that involves his massive ego in the solvent of historicity. As a historian Psellos is of great interest, but it must be remembered that he was a civil servant first.

He regarded himself as the perfect civil servant. Unable to separate any fiber of his life from those surrounding it, in his own eyes, he flowed like honey. He was, as was natural to him, a trusted aid to distinguished, discerning, and occasionally disarmed monarchs. Unlike Leo, he never seriously involved himself in an unsuccessful backroom intrigue and never, therefore, suffered the consequences as Leo did, but he spent some time in a

[64] E. Renauld, ed. *Michael Psellos Chronographie, ou Histoire d'un siècle de Byzance,* I (Paris, 1926), ix.

[65] P. Joannou, "Psellos et le monastère Τὰ Ναρσοῦ," *Byzantinische Zeitschrift* 44 (1951), 283–284.

[66] *Ibid.*

monastery out of prudence and a pious curiosity, and some time a bit later under surveillance.[67] He held higher posts than Leo and stayed closer to the fount of power, and through all of his career he was supported by what he cheerfully admitted to be extraordinary brilliance and exceptional skill as an orator—a skill which he never turned up to its full voltage, since at that point he could convince anyone of anything . . .[68]

Psellos' antique egotism, to us, makes him more of a character, an individual—less the servant of power. His individuality was, however, an extension of the patterns into which his class and the bureaucracy set him. His social attitudes are static but nervous: we note his fierce distrust of new men, parvenues, the lower classes, and foreigners (has hatred of "Masedonians" evidently sprang from the time he spent among them in his early years).[69] His learning was undoubtedly vast, his scope so encyclopaedic that one scholar has put him into the same category with Pliny the Elder and Pico della Mirandola.[70] These are in fact good parallels: the Roman collector and Hellenizer, the Italian *philosophe,* are both cut similarly from the strange, productive but self-centered and psychologically inept fabric called humanism. Psellos himself wanted to be remembered as the refounder of philosophy in the civilized world, and especially as the Philosopher who recovered Plato and struck down the ignorant, but his surviving work includes great slabs of theology, rhetorical exercises and orations, mathematical explorations, and demonology.[71] *De omnifaria doctrina* is an indicative title in his total body of work.[72]

He was a casual believer, safely skeptical, and yet rather hurt that his more committed friends could question his piety and his oaths by "the God whom philosophy reverses."[73] He was especially hurt that his vows to take up the monastic life could be turned against him, and that he might (and did) find himself

67 *Ibid.,* 286–287.
68 Psellos, *Chronographia,* VI.94, VI.176, VI.191.
69 *Ibid.,* VI.102.
70 Renauld, *Michael Psellos Chronographie,* xv.
71 *Ibid.,* xviii–xlvii.
72 *De omnifaria doctrina,* ed. L. Westerink (Utrecht, 1948), cap. 120 ff.
73 Psellos, Chronography, VII (Eudokia-Romanus), 14.

popped back into a monastery with "rustic and gross" and "uncultured" monks.[74]

It must be asked how far we can trust or generalize from Psellos' data because of the advertisements for himself that create within it the tone of ego and even of autobiography. We may be tempted to take him from under the "Byzantine" rubric entirely, since in the ordinary view to be Byzantine means to accept the occlusion of individuality behind the theocratic State. Now, Psellos is undoubtedly an individual; his *Chronography* has a good deal in it that resembles autobiography (there is more here than in his letters). He has something more than the Hellenistic "character." But he is not *sui generis*, and through his predecessor, the Patrician, Magister, and Anthypatos Leo Choerosphactes we see just how Byzantine Michael was, and how close he held to a particular bureaucratic mold.

The Byzantine bureaucracy has been urged both through its own developing consciousness of service and through the actions of the Macedonian Imperial house toward a grasp of secular effectiveness and mediation. It was supported in this by the tradition of learning and education in Byzantium, a tradition whose currents quickened from time to time as they did in the 9th century. This tradition was powerfully classicist—that is, it looked at the cultural heritage as essentially stable and free of history, and with all its spaces safely filled in.[75] Its view of man was individualistic and humanistic, but only as man was isolated and recognizable in and through the heritage. Man as a psychological being was poorly defined—sketched is the better verb. The character of man was its focus, and this was a sculptural concept, rounded and three-dimensional but without environment either internally or externally.

Both Leo Choeresphactes and Michael Psellos took their education and their cultural sets from a "renaissance" classicism, and expressed themselves within its broad but shallow vocabulary (although each had a deeper vocabulary that was theological and

[74] Joannou, "Psellos," 287. He also called the monks "true Scyths and Bohemians."

[75] Compare N. Baynes, *The Hellenistic Civilization and East Rome*, 8–9, 22.

philosophical). As bureaucrats their egos were built and supported by service, by the manipulation rather than the ordering or creation of power. Eventually the individual acts and manipulations they performed gathered enough weight that, in their own minds, they could cut themselves free from the power that stood behind them, created them, and was expressed through them. Power seemed then to be strictly manipulative, invariably visible, the sum of all its parts or acts. Within the bureaucratic framework of other states this could merely lead to an exaggerated "civil servant" mentality resembling that celebrated by C. Northcote Parkinson, but in Byzantium it could work out in intervention by the bureaucracy in the political matter of the succession to the throne and other high-level political decisions. Loyalty had a peculiarly restricted sense in East Rome in any case, since the devolution of the highest office rested with an inscrutable God, but the bureaucrat began to add an element nearly Macchiavellian in its realism. In the crisis of the 11th century a triumphant bureaucracy, acting from the best of self-generated motives, would do great and permanent harm.

The bureaucratic style: art. The history of the high art of Byzantium is both clarified and addled by the interruption we call the iconoclastic quarrel. That history is made clearer because iconoclasm seems to intrude as a hard-edged caesura, after which the major art of Byzantium—religious art, church art—strengthened, with all the traceable elements intact, reappears, but reappears as self-conscious and even organized as uniquely Byzantine.[76] Opposition, clearly, made for an art that defined itself in defense and became both more creative and more recognizable or understandable as a cultural expression. At the same time we have to know that the iconographic aspect of iconoclasm has never really been searched to its roots, and the simplicities that have been repeated about it have made for further confusion.[77] The confrontation between Imperial power and other segments of the polity (or of the *oecumene*, more properly)—especially a

[76] See A. Grabar, *Byzantine Painting* (Skira, 1953), 87 ff; D. Mathew, *Byzantine Aesthetics* (London, 1963), 100.

[77] A. Grabar, *L'iconoclasme byzantine: dossier archéologique* (Paris, 1957), 47–76, 115–142.

monastic Church Militant—is still a puzzle. So is what we can see of the popular reaction to the series of Imperial acts called "icon-breaking," and the argument or hypothesis based on geography, which makes the East (puritanical? authoritarian? infected by Islam or by the nonfiguring Orient?) seek to put down the West ("Hellenic," democratic and anti-Imperial, orthodox in the traditional sense) has serious flaws, not least of which is the assumption that iconoclasm was always supported by the Anatolian regiments who were, to a man, howling image-smashers, proto-Cromwellians.[78] What finally appears *after* iconoclasm dies is, in the realm of art, all we can go on: a revectored art with its patterns and rules, lines and tints, made more visible by novelty and forced contrast. What, if anything, did the Byzantine civil service have to do with any of these problems?

Little attention has been paid to the parellelism and even the conjunction of two movements in the Empire of the early 9th century: iconoclasm in its second, less fervid phase—its "administered" phase—and the growing power and self-consciousness of a highly articulated and specialized, highly *successful* bureaucracy. It can be said that in the course of time the bureaucracy liquidated iconoclasm and went on, after the return of orthodoxy, to new successes. This development, which thrust certain prepotent Grand Ministers forward and upward as heads of a vast new pyramid of civil servants, was cut short and rerouted by the Macedonian dynasty, which also moved to turn to its advantage the rediscovered culture into which the bureaucracy was dipping. In this, at least, they were only partially successful.

It seems that the bureaucracy used, captured, or absorbed the vitality of iconoclasm in the early 9th century, converting iconoclasm's remaining energy—a power and purity of concept, and a strong secularism—to its own uses. At the same time, the bureaucracy began more and more to emphasize a cultural orientation, an organization of all human cultural creativity transmitted intact from the past, a classicism that, as it was revived, renovated the entire society of culture to which the bureaucracy's

[78] W. Kaegi, "The Byzantine Army and Iconoclasm," *Byzantinoslavica* XXVII/I (1966): 48–70.

status (they hoped) accredited them.[79] As they did all this they met and to their own satisfaction threw down some old enemies: the mossbacked zealots in the monasteries, who had bawled against the secular and Imperial power that supported the civil service, and who continued to oppose the secular learning that enriched it.

As the bureaucracy of the 9th century was rooted in the traumatic rearrangements of the late 7th and 8th centuries, which demanded and produced a rationalized, trusted mediatory bureaucratic structure as a necessity for the continued life of the Empire, so the "new" art of the posticonoclastic century was rooted in iconoclasm itself, in a refiguration, revitalizing, reradiation of the old balance between material and immaterial, between man's work and God's will. We can even say that, guided by the bureaucracy, the material and the human found new expressions in Byzantium.

The Byzantine art of the new era is a distinguished art in all respects, though it found different modes that are not in this discussion, especially in the primitivist "spiritual" art of some of the provinces. The prime characteristics of this bureaucratic art are highly visible: a rich recovery of the shapes of Hellenistic illusionism, and its graceful vocabulary of perceptible form and even of emotive expression; a strict isolation and organization of theme; a new richness of color, and nearly an obsession with harmony and balance.[80] The art of Constantinople is very much of the city—the city where the vast flux of Christian mystery was caught, and form induced in and from it, and where the icon's meaning was made broad enough to include the cosmos. The great church art (of which only a few examples have survived in the capital itself) triumphantly asserted not the victory of the icon alone, but the victory of the classical inheritance too: the victory of beauty and character christened and transmuted.

Beauty and character—harmonius form and acceptible individuation—were placed in an architectural mode fitted closely to their nature. Effective visibility and a special intelligibility were arranged for, even as the size of the framework—the church it-

79 Matthew, *Byzantine Aesthetics,* 122–127.
80 *Ibid.*

self—was less massive, less Imperial. The interior organization of theme and effect emphasized the prime rule of an ordered universe, with its sacred hierarchy that arranges all matter and all spirit. The *cursus honorum* ascended on the walls from the sainted human to the ineffable Divine: Christ All-Ruler, carrying in His hand the Law.[81] In these churches, with the curved and closed micro-world barely marked by icon-overpowered walls, men are surely put in their place. The elaborately calculated series of visual pressure-points, based on the optical theories of the great Hellenistic scientists, were designed to net and yet to move the worshipper, whose sense of sight was almost overworked.[82]

The Byzantine bureaucracy did not, at this time, build major churches: this cosmomimetic art was still in Imperial hands. A direct influence by them on artistic themes and settings has to be doubted. The conjunction of ideas and ideals which suggests a "bureaucratic art," however, makes the best of sense. The city style, the art of the Center, was an art whose affects met every criterion the Sacred Hierarchy could set. The major art of the 10th and 11th centuries, the art called Macedonian which was created in the Capital and exported from there (eventually as far as the cathedrals of Sicily in one direction and those of Kiev in another) was an art in which the hieratic and the hierarchic fused.

This was an art of barely-controlled luxury in texture, yet with its lines drawn both gracefully and powerfully: the great *Theotokos* of Ha. Sophia must be one of its earliest triumphs, and she has her antecedents in pose and iconographic detail, but her limpid strength is both new and a recollection of the oldest goddesses. Again, this art can break clear into narrative, yet it encapsulates the great mysteries of the Christian faith in a golden calm. It is an art that an official, a noble of the robe-of-office, could trust and revere because it was truly *his*. This identification is especially clear because the upsurge of classicized learning and the freshly cleared currents of the Hellenistic heritage simply fed into this art, transfusing and reforming it in the act. The

[81] O. Demus, *Byzantine Mosaic Decoration* (London, 1948), 16–29.
[82] Mathew, *Byzantine Aesthetics*, 118.

stiffened mystery and obscure experimentation of the 6th and 7th centuries had been broken by Imperial order. Now the bureaucrats, who were creations of the necessities of the Imperial posture, saw their own place in society buttressed by the forms of art, graceful as a rhetorical trope, swung in a field of gold. The art however was not reminiscential but truly renascent; confidence and clarity shone wherever the artists worked, and even the new and vibrant colors fed every instinct of a rising class.

The people in the Hippodrome, from the Skyllitzes Matritensis. (Courtesy of Dr. S. Cirac Estopanan.)

FOUR

The Common Life

> One day before the day of assembly, a proclamation is made in the town that the Basileus intends to visit the Hippodrome. The people hasten thither for the spectacle and jostle in throngs and in the morning the king comes with his intimates and servants, all of them dressed in red. He sits on an eminence overlooking the place and there appears his wife called *dizbuna* with her servants and intimates, all of them dressed in green, and she sits in a place opposite the king. Then arrive the entertainers and players of string instruments and begin their performance.
>
> Marvazi, *Tabā'i al-ḥayawān*

THE COMMON LIFE

The Setting of Daily Life

Streets, crowding, patterns of life. Constantinople's citizens, important or unimportant, moved in the same cityscape, were subject to the same physical and emotional pressures coming from the shape and "grain" of the city, and from each other. Except for the few who lived in the Palace precincts, or the monks slightly separated in their own enclaves, the citizenry took potluck together. Economic advantage might be displayed in the private spaces of individual houses, in furnishing or decoration or cubic feet of elbowroom, but beyond the doorways were the same streets and communicating spaces—the artificially widened and directed "sacred" streets and the other ritual *grossraumen,* and the utility streets, with their peculiar patterns of use, construction, direction and internal cohesion and predictability.[1]

[1] K. Lynch, "The Form of Cities," 57–58.

In a city of Constantinople's type the residential street *occurs* in that space left from other concerns. This space was not limitless; it ended at the wall-circuit, and it was heavily cut up by public uses and spaces. It was a living-space as well which was earnestly competed for, because the population of Constantinople never fell permanently to the point where pressure was not felt. There had been traumatic drops in the population as a result of epidemic or civil disturbance; there were periods when the attractive power of the city was not at its height and the flow to it was slack: this happened in the 7th and 8th centuries when the energies of the Empire shifted outward to the threatened provinces. Even then refugees from embattled or overrun provinces obviously had the incentive to move inward to the Center. It was also not to the sovereign's advantage to allow his capital to be drastically depopulated, if only because of the needs of defense, and migration to the city could be and was forced.[2] Certainly by the end of the 9th century any significant absolute loss in the population of the city (using the population of the early Justinianic capital as par) must have been recouped.[3]

The assembled citizens, with exceptions, had to seek living and working space *in* the city: the suburbs were important, but not, in the 10th century, as a residential area. "Beyond the walls"—the faubourg—was too vulnerable to attack, and it was also beyond the prophylactic guardianship of the more than physical forces that were concentrated in the city. The sanctified walls, guarded of God, held off other than mortal enemies. Constantinopolitans lived in their city, and by the act of living in it they formed it by the mass of their subjective reactions; yet they were subjected to the material and emotional patterns left by the generations before them. The *street*, especially, obtruded itself on them as a force.

The Constantinopolitan street pattern seems to have shown a Near Eastern or organically Mediterranean substratum under a

[2] P. Charanis, "The Transfer of Population as a Policy in the Byzantine Empire," *Comparative Studies in Society and History* **III** (2) (January, 1961), 144, 149–150.

[3] A. Andreadès, "De la population de Constantinoples sous les empereurs byzantins," *Metron* **I**, 2 (1920), 38 ff.

Hellenistic overlay. The aspect of plan, directed from above, cut the wedge-shaped city into smaller wedges, demarcated by the defenses, the sacralized ways, the specialized commercial streets or *emboloi,* and the concentrative spaces. Out of and into the artificially-broadened superstreets led the neighborhood ways. They were narrow, both for reasons of scarcity of space and as a protective feature—from climate, both heat and cold, and from the flow of intrusive power outside; they were tortuous, because they served the residences of the neighborhood, with their variety of age and type of construction, rather than imposing a grid pattern on them. The streets formed a communicative network which was slow-paced, "private" and specialized, requiring a private knowledge only the neighborhood gave, obstructive to the stranger and the outsider. Deeply shadowed during the day, this sort of street was practically useless at night except in grave emergency or possibly at festival time.[4]

Such a street system—which is no system—creates a "grain" worth observing closely. A relatively large number of people were concentrated and served at once, since the reaction to scarce land, in Constantinople as elsewhere, was to build vertically to the limit of the building technology of the time and the available materials. Actual population density is almost impossible to calculate precisely, but it must have been as high or slightly higher than in the poorer sections of modern Istanbul. The "neighborhood" was a dense, compacted mixture; it was also a rich mixture. It included the full range of economic and class divisions as these were expressed in Byzantium: day laborers, small shopkeepers serving the local market on its most basic level, artisans who did not "live in" behind or above their shops in another quarter (or who worked in the Palace workshops), bureaucrats of all ranks and offices. There were no aristocratic residential quarters and no slums, properly speaking. Residential streets were heterogeneous in composition, and the view and impression from inside them was of openness (to the native), availability, predictability; the "grain" was small, narrowly segmented, irregular, sensuous. The rhythm of life was ordinarily commanded by the sun, since

[4] Lynch, "The Form of Cities," 62–63; Lynch, *The Image of the City* (Cambridge, Mass., 1960), 46–117.

artificial lighting could not carry many activities far beyond sundown. The pace of life had to be adjusted to the human step—rapid progress to or from was impossible here, because of both street pattern and congestion.

Housing. Of all human activities, day-to-day life is most difficult to reconstruct; of all human artifacts the buildings in which most human activity takes place are (especially in a site still occupied) most difficult to resurrect. Dwellings are used, abused, burnt, torn down, renovated, and redecorated; even when they are built of durable materials all the accidents of time concentrate on them. If they do survive, they may or may not be recognizable. The Byzantine "city" house of the 9th and 10th centuries is certainly not with us, and yet its appearance and many of the details of life in it are not totally beyond recovery, principally by analogy and parallel.

Outside Constantinople, archaeological exploration has turned up Byzantine residential remains; these are mainly of the 12th century, dating from the reflorescence of small-city life in the Empire. In Athens and in Old Corinth enough Byzantine foundations have been uncovered to give a glimpse into the formation of a small neighborhood. Soviet researchers have done the same for Byzantine Cherson, in the Crimea.[5] In these instances, however, the residential and residential-commercial plats uncovered consisted of one-story buildings—no press of population or exigency of space forced these cities to imitate the true urban tenement. Byzantine cities outside of Constantinople do not yield enough information, then, and we must look to common type rather than to direct survival.

A scholar early in this century believed that the Byzantine house, especially the tenement or narrow, multistory house, came from Syria, imported during the 6th century along with other "Asiatic" architectural modes such as those which were drawn on in raising Haghia Sophia.[6] Probably other traditions were used as

[5] Henry S. Robinson and Saul S. Weinberg, "Excavations at Corinth: 1959," *Hesperia* **XXIX**, 3 (July-September, 1960), 225–253; H. S. Robinson, "Excavations at Corinth, 1960," *Hesperia* **XXXI**, 2 (April-June, 1962), 95–133; A. L. Yakobson, "O chislennosti naseleniya srednovekovogo Cheronesa," *Vizantiiskii Vremmenik* **19** (1961), 154–165.

[6] L. de Beylie, *L'Habitation byzantine: (Recherches sur l'architecture civile des Byzantins et son influence en Europe* (Grenoble-Paris, 1902), 30–31.

well, but long before the 10th century whatever Roman appearance Constantinople had boasted had disappeared—so far as its domestic architecture was concerned—with the last of the *domi*. The *domus*, or townhouse of the nobility, used too much lateral space with its single-storied rooms clustered around a central *atrium*. Variations on it survived in the countryside, but in Constantinople it vanished—probably by the mid-7th century. A traveler of that century described the capital as looking "just like Rome"—he was bemused, probably, by the Roman flourishes in the form of public building left over from Constantine's time.[7] On the other hand, Rome for its commons *was* a Rome of tenements.

Constantinople was a Hellenistic city (as Rome had finally become one), most closely allied to the *megalopoleis* of the great Greek dispersal and their descendants of the Near and Middle East. Constantinople of the 10th century can be best evoked by studying Baghdad, Ottoman Brussa, or certain Iraqi cities, but many of the keys to its appearance are still present in Istanbul.[8] The ordinary city dwelling was of stone, brick, or wood, and in all cases the outline would be similar: three stories or possibly more, with a top-heavy air given by the encorbelments, enclosed balconies, and other protuberances from the upper stories.[9] These, of course, increased the room available on the second and succeeding stories. These additions are mentioned in the late 9th century *Novellae* of Leo VI as possible fire-hazards, they are plentifully illustrated in the invaluable Skylitzes manuscript of the 10th century, and they endure to this day in any closely built-up "oriental" city or city with medieval quarters where the street plan insists on them, as in Istanbul.[10] In Constantinople the more durable constructions—stone and brick or both—probably outnumbered the wooden, with wooden superstructures often built up on a brick or rubble base.

In these houses, families had as much space as their means permitted. The wealthy might occupy an entire building, with storage space on the first (ground) floor and living quarters

[7] Arculfus, *The Pilgrimage of Arculfus* (Palestine Pilgrim Text Society, 3; London, 1897), 53.

[8] E. Gerland, "Das Wohnhaus der byzantiner," *Burgwart* **16** (1915), 10 ff.

[9] de Beylie, *L'Habitation byzantine*, 30.

[10] Leo VI, Novel 113, in Noailles et Dain, *Les novelles de Léon VI le Sage* (Paris, 1944), 372–375.

above. Apartment life, however, was the norm. Separate quarters for men and women were more likely seen than special rooms for sleeping or cooking. If possible, the house was turned inward, away from the street, and was deep, with an arcaded courtyard.[11] So far as comforts were concerned, the residential quarters that adjoined the great aqueduct were best off for water, though there were cisterns of all sizes everywhere.[12] For heat and cooking there was wood and especially charcoal, brought in from the suburbs. For light there were the small bronze and clay lamps which have been found in such numbers, filled with olive oil or grease—or, for the élite, candelabra, on state occasions.

No matter how poorly a family might be housed, there were those worse off, who slept in the streets. Actually they were to be found in the "public" parts of the city; there were complaints of them in the porticoes and on church porches.[13] They were certainly recent arrivals, in the main, like Basil the Macedonian himself who, according to his legend, came into the city and fell asleep in the Church of St. Diomedes.[14] These migrants made up an ever-shifting population, since no one could sleep in the streets of Constantinople through the year; sturdy beggars there always were, but it would take a phenomenally sturdy specimen to spend many winter nights out-of-doors.

Some other features of life in the streets and houses need to be examined, such as what we know of the pattern of migration to the city. Actually we know very little. Under ordinary circumstances, however, the peasant migrant protects himself in his encounter with the indifferent city by seeking out those who had gone before—relatives, friends, fellow-villagers.[15] In Constantinople the recent arrivals, especially those of the lower classes, were likely to coalesce into tightly-knit neighborhood fragments.

[11] C. Texier and H. P. Pullen, *Byzantine Architecture* (London, 1864), 141, plate XXVII; Gerland, "Das Wohnhaus," 18–19; de Beylie, *L'Habitation byzantine,* 73.

[12] Janin, *Constantinople,* 201–215.

[13] A. Kazhdan, "Sotsial'nii sostav," 87.

[14] A. Vogt et I. Hausherr, eds., *Oraison funèbre de Basile Ie par son fils Léon VI le Sage* (*Orientalia Christiana,* **26.1** (April, 1932), 51 ff.

[15] This is the "barrio" mentality noted in modern industrial cities; cf. R. Redfield, *Peasant Society and Culture* (Chicago, 1956), 47.

These transplanted village-neighborhoods provided a necessarily quick schooling in the ways of the city, together with economic aid and possibly employment, but most of all they padded the new arrival against the shocks of transition.

The location of these "subquarters" would naturally shift in the course of the years (if we could locate them at all). There were certain exotic groups that were segregated by Imperial command: Armenians, Jews, Moslems (probably including the Moslem Syrian merchants in silk).[16] Each of these segregated groups—isolated because of their heretical faith and the risk of contamination, not because of "race" or nationality—was centered on its appropriate church, synagogue, or mosque. It seems natural that at least in the case of the numerous Armenians the core of newly arrived and unassimilated immigrants was surrounded by a larger group of the more successful and the fully or partially assimilated, who still chose to live where there was community of language and a continuation of their subculture—particular folkways, *gemeinschaftlichheit,* even special foodstuffs and festivals. However, where the emigrants from Thrace or Hellas, or the Bithynians, or the villagers from Cappadocia were likely to congregate, isn't clear, though the likelihood of their forming village-neighborhoods is clear enough. Individuals from higher social strata who came to the city with better expectations might join relatives there, unless they were entering a monastery or had some other form of protection such as from the Orphanotrophos (who protected the orphans of high state officials as an expression of Imperial "provision" or *sophrosyne*).[17]

In the neighborhoods, small shops served the local needs of the residents, though evidently Constantinopolitans liked to go out into the suburbs to buy fresh produce.[18] Meat was available in the large markets set aside for its sale (the Amastrian Forum and and the Forum of Beef) or, presumably, from neighborhood butchers.[19] Other goods and services came into the streets on the

[16] See Chapt. 1, footnote 37.

[17] See F. Dvornik, *Les Légendes de Constantin et de Méthode: Vues de Byzance* (*Byzantinoslavica*, Suppl. I; Prague, 1933), for the case of Constantin-Cyril, the future missionary-saint.

[18] Syuzyumov, "Ekonomika prigorodov," 71.

[19] Janin, *Constantinople,* 68–70.

backs of itinerant tradesmen and artisans—the essential repairmen, for instance, in a society where nothing could be wasted. Such artisans as the tinkers lived in the faubourgs and plied their trade in the streets and ways.[20] Charcoal and other bulk necessities were as likely to be carried in by men as by beasts.

Insofar as shopping is concerned, a class line is clear between the families with at least one servant and those with none, where the women of the household had to go into the streets. In Byzantium, as in most traditional societies, women were secluded, but only in those class strata where seclusion was (a) feasible, and (b) where the economic solidarity and well-being of the family was involved. These strata would be, predictably, the urban and rural upper and middle classes, who gathered into the "extended-family" unit, protected their womenfolk before marriage to secure their marketable value, and after marriage to protect an investment. The lower classes had little family property to bargain with, and no servants to release their women from chores.[21]

Food and drink. The absolute basics of the Byzantine diet, bread and olive oil, came into the city in quantities, and at a price protected and subvented by the State.[22] The major part of the grain was ground at waterpowered mills outside the walls; the olive crops of Korkyra, Kos, Chios, the coasts of Asia Minor and Macedonia, plus olives from orchards around the city itself, were pressed for oil.[23] A meal with meat must have been very occasional for most of the citizenry, though every family had to have at least its Paschal lamb. Mutton and pork were in greatest supply, then veal (often disguised as beef).[24] Fish was a good

[20] Syuzyumov, "Ekonomika prigorodov," 67.

[21] On a parallel in Indian "traditional" civilization, see K. W. Kapadia, *Marriage and Family in India* (Oxford, 1958), 204–243. See G. Da Costa-Louillet, "Les Saints de Constantinople," *Byzantion* **24** (1954), 235; L. Bréhier, "La femme dans la famille à Byzance," *Mélanges Grégoire* I (Annuaire de l'institut de philologie et d'histoire orientales et slaves, **IX**; Brussels, 1949), 105–108.

[22] Teale, "Grain Supply," 75; Liutprand of Cremona, *Legatio*, in *The Works of Liutprand of Cremona* (Transl. F. Wright, London, 1930), **XLIV**; Ph. Koukoules, βυζαντινῶν βίος καὶ Πολιτισμός **V** (Athenai, 1954), 12.

[23] G. Rouillard, *La vie rurale dans l'empire byzantine* (Paris, 1953), 177; Syuzyumov, "Ekonomika prigorodov," 72–73.

[24] Koukoules, βυζαντινῶν βίος καὶ Πολιτισμός **V** 90 ff.

deal more plentiful; there were fishing communities in *ktima* or "District" of Constantinople, along the Sea of Marmora.[25] For that matter, fish can be taken from the Golden Horn at need, and still are. Chicken and other fowl were available, raised in the suburbs. Cheeses were processed locally and probably imported as well, and other milk products were available.[26]

The District of Constantinople—the suburban theme that stretched as far as the Long Walls (40 km from the city) raised a vast amount of garden truck, and from the planting schedule which has fortunately survived we can guess at what was, at least, for sale in season. Course vegetables could be had early in the year: beets, turnips ("head" and "field" turnips), two kinds of cabbage, an endive called "Brumalian," and some lettuces. Slightly later the lettuces came into their own—"two-hearted," Phrygian, "cold," bitter, branched lettuce, "country" lettuce, "forced" lettuce, and more. Carrots, onions, beetroot, mallow, and radishes were grown. There were flavoring herbs: cardamon, coriander, *euxòmon* (eruca sativa). There was a kind of very popular green called, simply, "green" (prasos). There were vegetables we can no longer identify.[27] All that seems to be missing from this list are the bean family and other legumes, but we know that they were part of the diet from other sources. The Constantinopolitan diet undoubtedly included other foodstuffs, which came into the city from considerable distances, but the list given does show which eatables were in good supply, therefore cheap, therefore likely to be part of the daily menu.

The residents of the city drank wine, unless they belonged to some obscure minority of beer- or mead-drinkers. There was a *vin du pays* from the vineyards in the District, and wine was imported from some of the old, select island vineyards, like Chios, and from Crete, Lemnos, the Pelopponessos, the Black Sea coast, and Macedonia.[28]

[25] Syuzyumov, "Ekonomika prigorodov," 75.
[26] *Ibid.*, 76.
[27] H. Beckh, ed. *Geoponica sive Cassieni Bassi Scholastici de re rustica eclogae* (Bibl. Tuebner; Lipsiae, 1895), Book XII; 347–349. See also E. Lipshitz, "K izucheniya ekonomiki prigorodov Konstantinopolya v X v.," *Vizantiiskii Vremmenik* **XIV** (1958), 81–85.
[28] Rouillard, *La vie rurale*, 177.

Entertainment, recreation, leisure. In a metaphor-creating culture such as that of Byzantium, we have the problem not only of recognizing the creation of metaphoric sets as an act of intellect, the reaction of a "self-consciously communal, rule-making, consolidating" society or social élite, but of reconstructing the lower or broader forms of metaphoric thought devised by the common people, their crossing or confusing of what we would call categories, such as "work" or "duty" and "play" or "leisure," and consolidating all of these across a horizontal metaphoric nexus.[29] The act of experiencing the celebration of the Eucharist, as an example, on the Lord's Days and feast days, was a duty entwined with the good of the soul, which was to be bathed in the eternal miracle; yet, obviously, the aesthetic sense was bathed as well, and in addition there was a social experience, the "play" of dress and costume, the small neighborhood rituals and—eternal as the Eucharist—gossip.

As he moved from his own locality, the citizen had a wider opportunity to move in a multileveled experience that was "recreational," which is to say, play on a low level, together with other possibilities. In the massive secular and secular-sacred processional occasions he was drawn in, he partook, with the rest of the *laos,* in the antiphonic ritual lauds, and thereby he became an instrument of divine praise.[30] His voice carried, in a true sense, "many years" to the chosen Sovereign. In addition he saw the great ways and squares filled with all the evidence of pride and power—the Sacred Hierarchy marshaled in order, their ceremonial robes glittering like dawn and sunset, titles and offices reverberating in the smoky air, while the barbarian soldiers of the Bodyguard clanked along suspiciously in the midst of the armored glory of the Household regiments, and the Emperor commanded all to be. This is very high-grade theater, in which the plot of the play concerns the Imperial mastery of all the perceptible world, while the Emperor's Christ-imitating essence extends the image of mastery into the realm of eternality.[31]

[29] For the possibilities of metaphor I am indebted to R. J. Kaufmann, and especially to his unpublished study on "Metaphor and Historical Methodology."

[30] Treitinger, *Kaiser-und Reichsidee,* 71–83.

[31] As in the "Adventus"; see E. Kantorowicz, *Selected Studies* (Locust Valley, New York, 1966), 44 ff.

Even when the man of the commons moved to the Hippodrome, which was indubitably *his* place, the *topos* where his power was freer and stronger, he did not go only to be entertained. In the months of January and February the new year was inaugurated with a series of "courses" or races that were invested with powerful metaphoric resonances, for in them the playing out of Fortune, the ludic element, was made universal. A metaphoric bridge was built before the spectators: the chariot driven to victory was made the sun-chariot driven by the creator of all life, Helios become Christ, while victory itself was crossed with the images of eternal Chance and eternal Victory, the charioteer as Emperor-Christ.[32] All courses were capable of eliciting these images, but the "solemn" courses were as charged as true ritual. "Solemn" courses were defined as those "with the obeisance"—*to hippikon to hippodromion proskynesimon,* and in these the Emperor's place was raised and isolated by means of the abject *proskynesis* and by seating most of the high officers with the Demes or "factions."[33] Priests, ordinarily forbidden to attend the games, could appear at the "solemn" courses, as is understandable.

The superefficient races once out of the way, the people had a whole series of ordinary—*paganos*—courses to attend, some sponsored by the Emperor, some by the Demes themselves, arranged in advance with the proper authorities.[34] The great enthusiasm of the Byzantines was for chariot-racing, although they enjoyed flat-races and even the occasional footrace (archaic and ceremonial), and the great Hippodrome was the place to see all of them.[35] At the same time, the people in the Hippodrome might have their choice of a considerable variety of exhibitions and events falling more clearly into the area of straight entertainment. There were athletic exhibitions and contests, including boxing of the Classical or murderous variety. There were "circus" shows, with displays of wild animals, freaks, and natural and unnatural oddities. There were games that began to recall the *ludi* of Old Rome, including combats between wild animals and mock-hunts. During the inter-

[32] R. Guilland, "Études sur l'Hippodrome de Byzance," *Byzantinoslavica* **XXVII** (2/1966), 37; Grabar, *L'Empereur dans l'art byzantine*, 85.
[33] *De ceremoniis,* 73, 367.
[34] Guilland, "Etudes sur l'Hippodrome," 2, 36.
[35] *Ibid.,* 26–27.

missions in the courses tension was relieved by an assortment of clowns, jugglers, acrobats, mimes, makers of dramatic speeches, and musicians. Dramatic scenes were also staged by troupes of actors.[36]

The Hippodrome was the setting for at least two other forms of theater-ritual having no connection with the racecourse. One was the Triumph play, in which the victorious Emperor displayed captives and booty; the other was the public display of criminals, and their execution or some lesser punishment. The Hippodrome was reserved for the highest class of criminal, those the Imperial authority thought worth paying this sort of attention; the lesser were likely to be found in the Amastrian Forum or along the Mese.[37] The most notable criminal was the unsuccessful plotter against the Emperor's majesty, and these were displayed frequently enough. The rebel had, in the Byzantine view, put himself outside the ordained and harmonious polity, and so might have his "otherness" underscored in a number of ways: his very nature as a man might be denied by exposing him in women's clothes, which is more than humiliation.[38] A kind of contemptuous reversal of roles was also shown in the "dishonorable" (*atimo*) monastic tonsure, which put a man outside the secular community by force, and which was often accompanied by exile.[39] Mutilation, piously substituted for more extreme penalties, must be a gesture at least as magical as punitive.

Execution must be seen as the final and total rejection of a criminal by his society, and in Byzantium, a strongly traditional society, the aspect of rejection as well as that of punishment is represented in the forms of execution favored. Thus the rebel who was exposed to beasts in the arena while the citizenry looked on was literally thrown into the "wild," the inhuman and unordered darkness.[40] Beheading or impalement, using a human

[36] R. Guilland, "Études sur l'Hippodrome de Byzance," *Byzantinoslavica* **XXVII** (1/1966), 289–301.
[37] *Ibid.,* 302.
[38] *Ibid.,* 304.
[39] "Book of the Prefect," 611/X; 614/XIII; 616–617/XVII; 619/XXII; See Leo VI, *Novel* 34, 105 (Noialles et Dain, *Les Novelles,* 136–139, 342–347.
[40] See plate 486, *Skyllitzes Matritensis:* t. 1, *Reproduciones y miniatures* (Barcelona-Madrid, 1965).

agency to inflict death, would actually be less severe (however this might impress the condemned). In any event, the observation of punishment by the people had a complicated purpose. It served *pour encourager les autres.* It made the people, by their presence, a part of the act of rejection. It was as well a powerful theatrical and ritual event—and even entertainment.

The theater as a separate and developed art did not exist in Constantinople of the 10th century, though the physical equipment, left by the Romans and the Constantinids, had not disappeared.[41] The *literati* of the city could quote (and misquote) Euripides, but they knew him only from the page; their Euripides was completely visual-verbal, not theatrical—there was no "play" to him.[42] There were both actors and mimes in Byzantium, and here as elsewhere they had a dubious, taboo-laden place in the society. Actors were presumed to be infected by their work—no longer possessed by the gods, possibly now possessed by demons—but they did perform "scenes" in the Hippodrome.[43] Presumably professional actors had no part in the "mystery" plays, which came out of the liturgy and had dialogue freely adapted from the great events of the Christian passion; a few of these have been left to us.[44] Liutprand of Cremona says that the Constantinopolitans celebrated the ascension of the Prophet Elijah, on the 20th of July, with stage-plays, and for all we know these were a type intermediate between the secular "scene" and the playlet-mystery.[45] There were Palace mimes, who served in the indispensable place of the Court Fool and as such had extraordinary freedom of speech; there were certainly popular mimes as well.[46] All in all, however, the theatrical sense—the "necessary unreality" in a culture, and the urge to metaphorize and "play" of the Byzantines was thoroughly served without a theater.

[41] Bréhier, *La civilisation byzantine,* 104–105.

[42] Leo Choerosphactes; in G. Kolias, *Léon Choerosphactès, Magistre Proconsul et Patrice* (*Texte und Forschungen zur Byzantinisch-neugriechischen Philologie,* no. 31) (Athens, 1939); lettre XVII/92, XXI/98–100.

[43] Guilland, "Études sur l'Hippodrome" 1, 300.

[44] A. Vogt, "Études sur le théâtre byzantin," *Byzantion* VI (1931): 37–74, 623–40.

[45] Liutprand, *Legatio,* **XXXI.**

[46] Guilland, "Études sur l'Hippodrome," 1, 292–293.

It amazes us how much time a medieval population seems to have had to spare for state and religious occasions and celebrations. In Constantinople's case the low, rather uneasy harmonic of the life of the commons was frequently made tonally more rich by resonances from the Acropolis—from Palace, Hippodrome, and Great Cathedral. Still, week by week, the leisure time of the citizenry was taken up in pastimes that concentrated in the neighborhood or the parish. Three are especially prominent—partly because of the monotonous regularity with which the clergy denounced them; we know from these denunciations that the Byzantines enjoyed life in the bath, life in the tavern, and the Sporting Life.

The massive baths of the Hellenistic city were not lacking in Constantinople, but a change seems to occur in the 9th century and later, with the construction of numbers of smaller *thermae*.[47] As a measure for improving health and sanitation the bath was imperative, but it served as well as a social mixer and focus. To the church it was a prime symbol of the lingering paganism of the body, but the only morally prophylactic measure that could be enforced was the separation of men and women. New baths were built in the city as late as the 11th century; their plan was simplified, a hot room and one less hot, with a room in which to recover. The general idea passed on to the succeeding Turks. To the Byzantines, like the Turks, the bath was the project of a full day for both men and women.[48]

The tavern was suspected by both secular and sacred authority; it was the place of contact between the common male citizen and the underlife of the city.[49] There social drinking went on, and the attendant assaults, batteries, and breaches of the Imperial peace; there the prostitutes spread their nets; there entertainment of a low and fascinating kind was seen—and there the Byzantine might indulge himself in his favorite vice, which was gambling.

[47] Janin, *Constantinople,* 216–224; T. Praeger, ed., *Pseudo-Codinus origines continuens; adiecta est forma urbis Constantinopolis,* Fasc. Alter of *Scriptores originem Constantinopolitanarum* (Bibl. Tuebner, Lipsiae, 1901–1907), **III**, 221 ff; Ph. Koukoules, "Τὰ λουτρά των βυζαντινῶν" *Epiteiris Eteiris Byzantinon Spoudon* **XI** (1935); 192–238.

[48] Koukoules, "Τὰ λουτρά," 201.

[49] "Book of the Prefect," 617/XIX.

Because of the static sets of a traditional society, one in which mobility is inhibited as much by a shortage of resources as by any true system of caste, gambling is almost always present. It serves a whole host of psycho-social functions: giving the player the opportunity for the opening "out," or for a private play or drama, but especially giving the illusion of the possibility of control over fate. Thus gambling is always connected with magic and superstition, for at base it depends for its impact on the players' conviction that Fortune is stronger than Nature, that the constrictions of circumstance can be made to give way. The true gambler has no truck with the purely aleatory, no matter how long he has known the dice.[50]

The dice dominated the Byzantine gambling scheme; in a primitive form ("bones"), in dice games of various sorts and names, in backgammon, in a kind of miniature hippodrome called "wooden horse" (*xylinon hippikon*).[51] Small devices for mechanically throwing the dice were known.[52] After the dice, checkers or draughts were important and chess was known, but the passion of the Constantinopolitans was for some game depending on chance.[53] Naturally the superstitions that clustered around gambling brought the church down against it (these superstitions were older than the Christian faith), and the Canons were relentlessly opposed to gambling. Priests were of course forbidden to involve themselves.[54] Probably the church argued as vainly in the case of its own priesthood as in the case of the population at large.

THE COMMON LIFE

The Citizen

The constitutional people: the Deme. The Byzantine state was an absolute monarchy, as everyone knows. In no Byzantine theory of polity and politics, no matter how archaic, was sovereignty derived from the *populus*. *Demokratia* to the Byzantines was

[50] Ph. Koukoules, βυζαντινῶν βίος καὶ Πολιτισμός I (Athena, 1948), 186 ff.
[51] *Ibid.*, 200–218.
[52] *Ibid.*, 203; see plate T′.
[53] *Ibid.*, 220 ff.
[54] Leo VI, *Novel* 87 (Noailles et Dain, *Les Novelles*, 290–293).

synonymous with mass rebellion—as *tyrannos* meant an individual rebel (whose "unsuccessful" rebellion was taken for granted, since successful rebellion was not rebellion at all, but meant the creation of the state anew under a new divine mandate).[55] The sword-authority of the *autokrator,* as well as the magical ambiances of the *basileus,* derived from the choice of God.[56] Yet the people—the *laos*—had certain powers from God as well, of which the most potent was the "institutionalized revolutionary" power of acclaiming (that is, naming) the Emperor, while other powers were resident in the privileges accorded the so-called Demes or factions.[57]

What was the Deme of the 10th century? The root word is of course "people," and probably meant the people attached to residential wards or quarters.[58] *Quarter* is of ancient significance, since the four colors belonging to the four quarters describe either the four cardinal points or the four elements—in any case symbolizing the totality of the ordered universe; i.e., that universe whose prime refraction is the city.[59] We assume that the conversion of the constitutionally effective People, with their organization based on residence and civil or military service, into the "circus factions" was a Hellenistic development. This development substituted an artificial, or better a ritual, opposition of one "sporting" faction to another for the old game of politics. As such it was an extension of megalopolis and the new politics of megalopolis, and understandable both from the point of view of the ruler and from that of the ruled.[60]

The Deme as so-called circus faction, however, kept a certain capability for political action. The ritualized competition of the racecourse proved easy to divert into more serious channels. "Democracy" could metastasize, escaping its ritual bounds, and in 6th century Byzantium it reached a point where open social

[55] L. Bratianu, *Études byzantines d'histoire économique et sociale* (*Universitea Mihaĭleana din Iasi,* **IV** (Paris, 1938), 97.
[56] Bury, *The Constitution of the Later Roman Empire,* 20–21.
[57] *Ibid.,* 9.
[58] Manojlovic, "Peuple de Constantinople," 631, 634 ff.
[59] Müller, *Heilige Stadt,* 9–51; for Byzantine "colors" see John Malalas, *Chronographia* (Ed. Dindorf, CSHB, Bonn, 1831), 175–176.
[60] Manojlovic regards the *deme* as an Hellenic survival in any case: "Peuple de Constantinople," 668, 692; Zakythinos, "Étatisme byzantin," 670–671.

warfare between classes was imminent, and the power of the Emperor to contain this warfare was in question. A popular movement challenged the Imperial power at its core as strongly as the Persians or the Arabs did, and in the next century one sign of the intensification of Byzantine *étatisme*—the concentration of power at the center—was the emasculation of the Demes.[61]

By the 10th century—actually before the 8th—the Demes had lost certain potentialities, but had gained—or kept—others, often camouflaged and confused by Byzantine political onomastics. The Demes had been obliged to give up their pretension to self-generated political power—forced to give up, in other words, their movement toward becoming political parties, with their own interior organization and their own goals within the state.[62] They were continued as sporting associations or clubs, signed by the four colors—Blue, White, Green, Red—as semiconstitutional channels for the approach of the People to the Sovereign; however, Green and Blue were paramount. Their chiefs, the Demarchs, were officials of the Throne, part of the Sacred Hierarchy, occasionally superceded by *demokritai* who were even higher-ranking military officers, and the denaturing of any democratic essence in them would seem to have been complete.[63] In Byzantine terminology *laos*—the People—equalled *Demoi*—the Deme organizations, plural but circumscribed. The singular *Demos* was a term of suspicion, signifying the anarchic mass. Yet a "democracy" remained.[64]

The constitutional people: rights. A series of responsibilities devolved on the Deme organization and intrinsic in these responsibilities was the idea that the People, properly identified, should cooperate in the harmonious functioning of the State in the following ways:

(a) The attendance of the Demes in the Hippodrome when the "solemn" games were held was a ritual witnessing, proper to

61 Bratianu, *Études byzantins,* 118 ff; Manojlovic, "Peuple de Constantinople," 634 ff.

62 F. Dvornik, "The Circus Parties in Byzantium," *Byzantina-Metabyzantina* I (1946), 1, 129–133.

63 J. B. Bury, *The Imperial Administrative System in the Ninth Century,* 105; but see *De ceremoniis,* 8.

64 Manojlovic, "Peuple de Constantinople," 631, 670–671.

the reverification of the place of the Empire in the turning universe. These courses were not at all involved in sport.[65]

(b) The ceremonial acclamations of the two factions, on whatever occasion, were more than a choral rendition of convoluted and banal or obscure phrases that wearily supported the political *status quo.* The acclamations were seen instead as distinct elements in the joining of the temporal-punctual act of a particular ruler to eternal patterns. The recognized structural People created a constitution, a polity, by voice.[66]

(c) The act of acclaiming a new ruler was in a separate, higher category of significance. It might be done by the Army, acting as a representative fragment or synecdoche of the People, and in this case a ratification by the People should follow, with the end that popular acclamation or "naming" "gives directions for the establishment of a new power without actually choosing that individual."[67] We recall that the assumption of Imperial power was not a single act but a series of acts, with different parts of the polity represented in each step. The coronation itself was divided into parts, each cementing the new monarch more firmly into place at the highest point in the *oecumene.* Before coronation, the name of the Emperor had to be recognized and verified by the People—not to establish the delegation of authority or sovereignty, but to demonstrate that they as living cells in the divine polity supported the will of God. The acclamation was not factitious or redundant; it expressed reality in the fashion most comfortable to the Byzantines—as ritual.[68]

(d) The Demes in the Hippodrome had other rights. They controlled the approach to the throne: the public petition *viva voce* was in their right. On these occasions the phrase "to convoke a Hippodrome" was used, and the racecourse became almost a popular assembly, in that the elaborate fence of protocol that ordinarily shielded the Emperor was eliminated, and direct access to the ruler was made possible.[69] This reversal or release is the more necessary the tighter and more hierarchized the monarchy

[65] Guilland, "Études sur l'Hippodrome," 2, 37; *De ceremoniis,* 73, 367.
[66] Treitinger, *Kaiser- und Reichsidee,* 81 ff.
[67] Bury, *Constitution of the Later Roman Empire,* 9.
[68] Hocart, *Kingship,* 89 ff; *De ceremoniis,* 92, 96; Manojlovic, "Peuple de Constantinople," 695.
[69] Manojlovic, "Peuple de Constantinople," 693.

is; a pendular movement relieves tensions that otherwise would fracture the society. The accessibility of the Emperor on chosen occasions is the direct correlate of his profession of *philanthropia* as well as power, of magical mercy as the twin of justice in law. The traditional society must open a sector of its rigid framework in this fashion, as it opens and renews the structure of time itself in the ceremonies of New Year, releasing all inhibitions and categories.

(e) The Demes as civic organizations held two privileges, both involving some cost to themselves: they could present a certain number of Hippodrome courses per year, and they had the right (or responsibility?) of repairing the city's walls.[70] It is not clear how the funds to pay for these civic activities were found: were dues levied or a subscription raised at need? Or, did the Emperor release money through the Demarch?

(f) The Demes, finally, kept from their ancient "Hellenic" rights some remnant of the privilege of standing in arms to defend the state. This is a singular power to leave in the hands of ordinary citizens, and all observers are not in agreement as to how much real military strength the Demes were allowed to muster after their 6th century outbreaks and the repression that certainly followed. The existence of a true citizen militia (this is the third meaning of *Demos*) is authenticated as late as 717 A.D., and this *Demos* may have been a militia in formations firm and well-equipped enough to fight outside the walls.[71]

After this date the only clouded reference to a citizen militia is by the acidulated bishop Liutprand of Cremona in the 10th century, and he seems to have observed a ceremonial escort produced on state occasions.[72] Yet the military aspect of the Deme was recalled in various ways; we have noted that the officers who served as ritual chiefs of the factions—the *demokritai*—were commanders of the *tagmata* or Guards regiments: the Domestic of the Schools was *demokrites* of the Blues; the Excubitor, of the Greens.[73]

[70] Guilland, "Études sur l'Hippodrome," 2, 36; Manojlovic, "Peuple de Constantinople," 621 ff.

[71] *Ibid.*, 632.

[72] Liutprand, *Legatio,* 1.

[73] See n. 63 above; also Manojlovic, "Peuple de Constantinople," 622; Bratianu, *Études byzantines,* 119; *De ceremoniis,* 8.

The constitutional people: controls. It is somewhat surprising to see a state as powerfully autocratic as Byzantium allow even a residual fragment of armed force to remain in the hands of the people of the city; it is certain that the city militia had little real military weight. The Demes were, in fact, carefully pruned and controlled "popular" organizations.

(a) The Deme-commander or Demarch, who had once been a military officer (albeit in the militia) and even boasted some political gravity, was by the 10th century no more than the bureaucratic watchdog and honorary chieftain of the Deme: a controlling element in it rather than a representative of it.[74] His under-officers were also bureaucrats: keepers of records and sergeants-at-arms. His effectiveness within the Deme, however, did have some relation to the cooperation he might receive from below, especially from the intermediate, true representatives of the Deme—its noncommissioned officers, as it were.[75]

(b) The composition of the Deme itself was not completely free or open; it was an organization that reached down into the proletariat but did not include all of it.

The class-structure of Constantinople in the 10th century is not easy to analyze, though the analysis is often attempted; it is clear that the lowest stratum of free residents, the homeless and the semiemployed, were not included in the Deme organization. On the other hand, almost everyone else *was* included. Nor is there any conclusive proof that the factions differed in their social composition, with the Blues holding a higher place than the Greens. If this was true for the 6th century, and this is not unquestioned, it wasn't true for the 10th.[76] Byzantine political commentators are not often helpful in clarifying social questions, since their aim is the description of a balanced, theoretically bombproof polity, not the analysis of shadings of class antagonisms. They use such terms as *plethes*—the "many"—but have no precise class reference in mind; nor do they refer to exactly defined class lines when they contrast *okhlos*—the mob—with *laos*

[74] Manojlovic, "Peuple de Constantinople," 630.
[75] Manojlovic, "Peuple de Constantinople," 682.
[76] *Ibid.*, 642; see *De ceremoniis*, 590.

—the People.[77] This is one of the typically Byzantine representative images, contrasting the idea of plurality (*plethe, okhlos*) with order, harmony, unity (*laos*). In the same way the central, singular and paramount *laos* was, in its external relations, compared with the disparate, plural, therefore inferior *ethnoi*—the nations or Gentiles.[78]

(c) A third mode of control or influence is actually a pivoting concept, depending not on a definition of the people by the ruling élites, but on the people's definition of where it itself stood and within what myths it was prepared to work or live.

The Empire presented to its main urban concentration, in Constantinople, several central or commanding myths. It had no guarantee that they would be accepted (without resorting to totally repressive force) and no guarantee that they would not be transmuted in the process of acceptance, if they were accepted at all. In the 10th century *both* the degree of acceptance of certain politically resonant myths by the *populus*, and the degree of transmutation of the basic myth, changed. The "popular" propaganda of the Macedonian dynasty, which was built up of an amount of honest, traditional superstition and some purposive manipulation, seems to have had the wrong kind of success.[79] If it had been expected to draw the masses irrevocably into support of the ruling dynasty and all its works and instruments, it failed. The imagination of the urban mass and the peasantry was caught just as much by the élan and the rebellious pride of the great magnate families, caught by the idea and by the actuality of aristocratic opposition to the Throne. This is clear enough in the popular reaction that accompanied and followed the rebellion of the Ducades in 913, a rebellion that struck into the imagination of the people, becoming the germ of cycles of legends.[80] In the legends, which proliferated in balladic form, the aristocrat—the knight—becomes an epic and even tragic hero, done down by malign forces. The Emperor himself is not so much opposed to

77 Despite Kazhdan, "Sotsial'nii sostav," 90.

78 See the *De administrando imperio, Proem,* line 8. "Peoples" here are plural; see line 62, p. 112 for *laos* as "folk" or "a people" like *ethnos.*

79 Vogt et Hausherr, *Oraison funèbre,* 45–67.

80 Kazhdan, "Sotsial'nii sostav," 90 ff; H. Grégoire, "L'âge héroique de Byzance," *Mélanges offert à M. Nicholas Iorga* (Paris, 1933), 390–393.

the hero as he is a representation of a neutral figure: malignity is represented by Evil Counselors; in other words, by the bureaucrats.[81]

The people rallied behind the Macedonian dynasty on two occasions: against the conspiracy of the sons of Romanus Lecapenus (945) and against Michael V Caliphates' attempt to dislodge the Empresses Zoë and Theodora. In both instances the popular feeling stood for the dynasty against usurpers, usurpers whose origins were nonaristocratic. It is not at all clear what the dynasty seemed to represent in these confrontations, but it seems to have been accepted as fortunate—possessors of a fortune that inhered in its blood line. The Macedonians, in fact, were accepted as a great House—in other words, as aristocrats, whose position and dynastic rights might be endangered by upstarts. In confrontations, on the other hand, between the Imperial house and the dynasts, popular feeling was likely to be neutral or to support the dynasts, and in the case of a quarrel between a dynast and a great bureaucrat for supremacy (as between Nicephoras Phocas and the *paracoimomenos* Joseph Bringas, after the death of Romanus II in 963) the lower classes swung sharply over to Nicephoras.[82]

(d) The urban population might or might not be "controlled" by force or persuasion. It seems to be a truism that neither would have had effectiveness if the political *Urmythos* of the State was totally rejected.

Persuasion included a number of techniques that can be regarded skeptically, as bait for a parasitic class, or, as the fully-developed Imperial theory protested, as evidence for the essential *philanthropia* of the ruler-magician. Some of these devices have already been noted in other contexts. There was the controlled grain price and all the economic protectionism that was to the advantage of the mass of consumers; the socially ameliatory machinery—homes for the aged, orphanages, hospitals, hostels,

[81] The figure of the Emperor withdraws from later epic material in a fashion parallel to the tendency in Western medieval chivalric literature, from the Roland poems through the *Pèlerinage de Charlemagne* and on to Christian de Troyes.

[82] Cedrenus I, 345–348; Kazhdan, "Sotsial'nii sostav," 90.

and indiscriminate charities;[83] the free distribution of money or of booty; the favored tax situation in the city; the setting aside of minor offices to be filled by Constantinopolitans only; entertainment (when that, and not a ritual purpose, was the object).[84] Taken in their bulk these provisions aim at an ambiance of paradise, a civic environment where citizenship had a passive, receptive connotation.

The State's own survival, however, its right to defend itself, is accepted as the basis for its police power, the force that complements persuasion. In Constantinople the "police" were of several varieties and had varying responsibilities. There was a market police to enforce economic regulations and a closely related force that handled the waterfront, i.e., supervision and coast-guarding.[85] All these were under the Eparch of the City, who as senior police officer was ultimately responsible for ordinary security within the city.[86] He had no jurisdiction over the secret security forces controlled from the Palace, and of course in extreme emergencies the city would be put under the swords of the Household Regiments and their commanding officers. The Eparch's competence did not extend to certain foreigners in the city, such as those with diplomatic status, who were supervised or warded by the minions of an under-officer of the Logothete of the Drome (the Foreign Minister).[87] Policing the city during the day called mainly for inspectors and bumbailiffs of one sort or another, but at night the task grew more difficult. After sunset the streets of the city were in effect placed under martial law; a permanent curfew was enforced by armed men stationed at cross streets and in squares—"places where two, three, or four roads meet."[88] The nightwatch had the job of detaining and questioning anyone who moved after dark. No force of police, however, could be expected

[83] H. Monnier, *Les Novelles de Léon le Sage* (Bordeaux, 1923), 43.

[84] Kazhdan, "Sotsial'nii sostav," 88–89; *De ceremoniis,* 699; Hobsbawm, *Primitive Rebels,* 118–122.

[85] Dölger, *Regesten* I, 781/100.

[86] Bury, *Imperial Administrative System,* 69–70.

[87] *Ibid.,* 93, for the Warden of the Envoy's Quarters. See the complaints of the envoys Amalarius of Metz (*Versus Marini,* in *Monumenta Germaniae Historiae,* PLAC I, 427, 1.38–40); and Liutprand, *Legatio* I.

[88] Liutprand, *Antapodosis,* 2.XI.

to keep order in the obscurity of the side streets and alleyways, and the guardposts were only a reasonable compromise.

The Eparch thus enforced the law directly on the citizens; his men apprehended evildoers and guarded them in the public prisons; his men also carried out the sentences passed by the Imperial magistrates and performed the scourgings, the blindings, and other mutilations (except possibly in the case of the crime of rebellion, and tonsure was performed by an ecclesiastic) and the ultimate penalties—death by the sword, by hanging, by burning alive. His headquarters, the Praetorion, must have loomed grimly and heavily in the eyes of the citizens, as it coalesced the repressive power of the State into a material form. The Eparch, in the Praetorion, was the arm of chastisement; in an extraordinary illustration from the 11th century Scyllitzes manuscript he is shown bowing as the Emperor gives a command, and then commanding the executioner with the identical Imperial gesture: the upraised "hand of effective power."[89]

Classes and divisions. In discussing the Deme organizations, I left the purposeful impression that we aren't terribly confident about the social composition of these organizations. The "people" is extremely difficult to keep in steady focus when it moves from the ceremonial to the constitutional role, or when subjective social or class opinions are displayed. The people as ceremonial abstract was the *laos*; the people as a twinned, antiphonal ritual body was caught in the *demoi: laos* and *demoi* were very nearly identical but not quite so. Again, the ceremonial stress was always on unity and singularity or, in the case of the Demes, on the harmony of two perfectly tuned instruments, in a musical sense.

If the Demes were not all-inclusive, they did include strata that were much depressed in the economic scale; this is seen in their constitutional configuration, in which they are equated with the third of the triad of supporting elements in the *formulation* (not the continued existence) of an Imperial government or reign: this triad is the Army, the Senatorial order, and the *demotikon plethes*—i.e., the "popular mass."[90] This appears to

[89] See plate 101, *Skyllitzes Matritensis.* (Fig. 15 in this book).

[90] As seen in Michael Psellos, *Chronographia*, VII.1.

mean everyone below the senatorial rank, but probably has the more limited meaning of middle and lower classes, excluding the bureaucracy of all ranks. Since the Demes were heterogeneous socially, there were pressures that could split them along class-social fracture lines, but here again any intent to achieve a precise social-economic analysis of the Demes is blocked by extremely ambiguous terms and vague definitions, both by the Byzantines and on our part.

Plethes when used alone is normally derogatory: the plural, many-headed, anarchic, or ignorant mob. *Okhlos* is a much stronger term for the same mass. Yet a writer like Psellos will use *plethes* as "mob" but *demotikon plethes* as, approximately, *populus Romanum.*[91] He will also use *demos* in the mass-sense—as mob, conglomerate—and as a synonym for *everyone*—a unified People.[92] At one point he uses both *plethes* and *demos* in one context, and in such a fashion that the former must be the mob and the latter the organic citizenry.[93] Terms extracted or extended from the Roman political vocabulary (or the Marxist canon) make further confusion. The best example is *plebs,* which is not the Byzantine *okhlos,* nor is the reverse true; neither, as an additional point, is equal to a proletariat.

The powerful force of subjective opinion plays over the terminology like a balefire: one man's *okhlos* is another's *laos* or *demos.* Psellos, who combined intelligence, ego, and middle-class prejudices in about equal proportions, objected to the introduction by Constantine IX Monomachus of newly recruited officials into the *cursus honorum*: these men were "vagabonds of the market" (*tōn agoraion kai agyrten dēmōn*).[94] In fact the new officers were unlikely to have been vagabonds; they were probably lower-middle class in origin and merchants or artisan-merchants by original trade. The "people of the marketplace" are particularly noxious to Psellos even when they appear in a good or legitimate cause. His biases are shot through with the elementary assumption of the bureaucrat that almost anything is preferable to

[91] *Ibid.*
[92] *Ibid.*, V.37.
[93] *Ibid.*, VI.106.
[94] *Ibid.*, VI.29.

disorder, especially popular disorder. This view is visible in other observers, and the People, either as a self-conscious but amorphous political voice or in the organized Demes, does not identify itself. The literate upper and middle classes are our witnesses, and they are quick to use the word "mob." The literate minority may also separate out of the mass below them that portion whose behavior and affiliations are most acceptable: these are the *khrēsimoi* and *gnosimoi politai*, the "propertied" and "respected" citizens, from whom the lower bureaucratic ranks were often filled (these may have been Psellos' "market-place vagabonds").[95] When the choral people in the ceremonies referred to themselves it was as *laos*, naturally: "O God, Hear Thy People" is an example.[96] In other instances, either one or the other of the two Demes refers to itself as "the Blues," or "the Greens." The choral people also refer in their responses to the political or ecumenical abstractions of which they were a part: the *politeia*, the *Basileia*, the *orthodoxon kratos*.[97] It would be useful to know how the members of the Demes referred to themselves outside the ceremonial occasions, or what collective noun was used at the mass meetings of which Psellos speaks with suspicion.

It is clear, if anything is, that the Byzantines used as normal descriptive referents the *occupations* of its citizens. More comprehensive than these terms were social-economic categories that might be merely descriptive such as "merchant" or "artisans," or might carry pejorative significance: "street-people," "marketplace people." The largest category had two valences: the *constitutional*, in which the necessary third element in the original authentication of a new reign was the *demotikon plethes*, and the *ceremonial*, in which the synechdochal Demes or the singular *laos* stood for all. At all times the idea of singularity is superior to any concept of mass: the mere gross weight of numbers of individuals is not accepted as significant or politically valid, nor does the idea of a majority have force.

[95] Kazhdan, "Sotsial'nii sostav," 90; R. Karlin-Hayter, transl., "Vita s. Euthemii," *Byzantion* **25–27** (1955–57), 96.

[96] *De ceremoniis*, 332, 333.

[97] *De ceremoniis*, 357, 359.

THE POPULAR SPIRIT

Relations with the Nonurban

The countryside: ebb and flow. The ordinary relationship of any sizable city to its hinterland population is briefly put: the city pulls the young from the land because it offers more than the land can; the city loses the mature, who go back to the land as an investment or as an escape from the civic neuroses: work, service, duty, artificial distinctions.

When all the appendices and exceptions are added this sketch holds true, in its outlines, for Constantinople. The relationship between the man of the hinterland—the peasant—and his city is, as Redfield has suggested, a symbiotic one or, more precisely, the peasant way of life and mode of thought and reaction is really created by the city, which describes him at the same time that it describes its own citizens.[98] Even if the peasant stays on the land and is never seen within the walls, the city is perpetually on his mental and emotional horizon. It reaches out for him: his livelihood is affected by its taxes, its levies of manpower or service, its demands for specified products. Its magnetic materiality brings evil on him: enemies terrorize him as a subject of the city, he meets both the enmity of the attacker and the carelessness or greed of the defender. It has the appetite of a living organism for men: they disappear into it, and are changèd, bewitched. The city becomes a matter for legend, but its ordinary effect is to elicit that peasant response which is most familiar—the desire to be left severely alone, to be left in peace. The mentality of the peasant never loses this reactive tic.[99]

The city in its turn manufactures contrasting images. The plowed lands and the pastures, because they are beyond the wall, are beyond everything that is enclosed in the wall. They become esoteric and with this, "funny," in both the English senses of that word. The earth-traditions of the peasant are made ludicrous, his closeness (real or imagined) to basic urges becomes simple, the

[98] Redfield, *The Primitive World and Its Transformations,* 31 ff.

[99] See Hobsbawm's chapter on peasant anarchists, with examples from Spain and the Ukraine, in *Primitive Rebels,* 74–92, 183–186.

sign of the hick, yokel, bumpkin. Fear is barely masked in the laughter, for what makes the countryman strange also makes him powerful; the life of the soil must be perpetually either a contest or a union with daemonic powers—the powers of the wild beyond the sacred boundary.

In a healthy state these two polar, exaggerated attitudes cannot mutually isolate country and city. The vision of the city as the locus of order refers to the hinterland not as qualitatively, but as quantitatively different: a place with a lower degree of order, or where *cosmesis* is diluted or denatured. The actuality, the symbiotic necessity is not forgotten. In 10th century Byzantium the city was separated from its hinterland by a ritual definition, but this definition made the city only an icon of perfection, not perfection itself, and thus only a material projection in three dimensions of qualities that the entire God-guarded Empire possessed. If the city was different, it was because the perceptible world had to have a center; in terms of ritual metaphor the center could and did stand for all. However, the lapidary perfection of this system, the very act of defining it, seemed to show that it was ready to be broken, and broken it was, pushed by forces that on the one hand identified themselves with the noncivic and even the nonpolitical, and on the other, by superurban forces that isolated themselves *in* the city.[100] The 10th century capital invites a mixture of attitudes, and in these attitudes are a threatening number of hints pointing to the fracture lines of the future.

(a) The city continued to recruit from the countryside. Rather more of the recruits came from the European themes than had been seen earlier—at least this is the impression the hagiographies and such evidence as place-name surnames give.[101] The reason for the increase in cityward movement from the West may have been that the 8th and 9th century seeding of these lands, the forced shifts of population, and the successful *reconquista* of the Peloponnesus and the absorption of Slavic migrants had finally stabilized the area and produced an exportable surplus of manpower. Anatolia continued to send its sons to the city, but the strong flow from the Armenian lands was slightly diverted and

[100] See the *Epilog* at the end of the book.
[101] Kolias, *Léon Choerosphactès,* 16, 17 n. 2.

we assume that with the collapse of iconoclasm the Easterners found less welcome, but this is extremely uncertain.[102] Anatolia remained the richest and most populous part of the Empire, but other influences were at work there, tending toward decentralization.

(b) The modes of intercourse and interchange between country and city populations continued along approximately the same lines as before. The same currents tended to move through both —especially the strong currents that religion engendered. The attraction of the monastic life moved innumerable men (and women) in both directions—some to the great monastic establishments in Constantinople which, though separated, lay in the urban environment and served to a degree as training centers for the clerical bureaucracy and as nodes of theological learning (if not speculation); others moved out, especially late in life, to the isolation and fiercer *ascesis* of the monasteries of the hinterland—Athos, for example, founded in the last quarter of this century.[103]

We know that the land itself, its cultivation and the old rural patterns, were familiar in the city. Constantinopolitans were used to moving freely into the semirural *ktima* for marketing, and some actually owned land there, though it isn't clear how much of the truck-gardening near the city was conducted on a large-scale, tenant-farmed basis and how much land in the District was privately owned, and not in the category of glebe-land of the great city monasteries or part of the Imperial estates.[104] Beyond the *ktima*, land, as an investment, was drawing an increasing amount of attention on the part of such city dwellers as the successful bureaucrat and even the successful merchant, and this would bring its own problems. The strongest tie with the land was of course between the lowest stratum of immigrants and their recently left farms; these were peasants who had obeyed the magnetic call of the city, but whose lives were still vitally affected by the solid traditions of the countryside.

(c) Though the symbiotic mutual reliance of Center and

[102] Kaegi, "The Byzantine Army and Iconoclasm,"48–70.

[103] On monasticism, see Ch. V, "Byzantine Monasticism," by H. Delahaye, in N. Baynes and H. S. B. Moss, *Byzantium* (Oxford, 1948), 136–165; also Ch. XXV in *CMH,* IV.2., by J. Hussey.

[104] Syuzyumov, "Ekonomika prigorodov," 55–65, 80.

hinterland still existed and was recognized, a serious polarization and sclerosis of attitude had begun to appear. The proper functioning of the administrative tentacles that stretched out into the countryside depended on, among other factors, the attitude of the administrator to his responsibilities, and there are signs that part of the bureaucracy was losing its concern for mediation in or service to the hinterland. By the end of the century, when the ideas of such men as Michael Psellos were forming, some of the civil service was conceiving of itself as completely "civil"—as fully visible and effective only in the all-important city—and the country, to it, had become both uninteresting and alien. Psellos, the true bourgeois in every sense but the intellectual, cannot speak for any of the population below himself, but his opinions are still valuable. Psellos is a thoroughly citified individual; the idea of rural origin and rural tastes repels him. He reports that the Emperor Michael Caliphates' father came from "some totally desolate country place; some sort of Endsville" (*ek panēremou tinos agrou e tinos allēs eschatias*).[105] Caliphates' father was also landless, but Psellos' tone is noticeably contemptuous toward *place.* Outsiders were of several kinds to him, and one kind was the countryman of his own nation.

To match or overmatch this centripetal tendency, there was a centrifugal pressure. The reaction of the urban middle class was met by a reaction against the city as an ideal construct on the part of the peasants and peasant-soldiers of the provinces and the lower strata of Constantinople itself. The latter showed this in their behavior as early as 913 A.D., when the aristocratic rebel Constantine Ducas was their hero, and again in 963, when they helped to bring down the great official Joseph Bringas by opting for the soldier-aristocrat, Nicephoras Phocas.[106]

To summarize: the city was not yet, in the 10th century, self-isolated or totally disjunct from the matrix of the land. Its élites, however, especially the bureaucratic élite, were turning their natural urbanism into something harder and less flexible; were beginning to conceive of their peculiar order as cut off not only from interference from above, from the monarch, but also as

[105] Psellos, *Chronographia,* IV.26.
[106] See above, notes 80, 82.

closed to penetration from below. This sclerosis followed on other social changes, particularly the ominous new strength of the country gentry and the support which was either coming voluntarily or being demanded by them from the peasantry. The Imperial house, which stood for an adhesive and homogeneous, ritualized rather than socialized order, was finding it difficult to hold this order together. The radiating streams of power that ought to flow from the city were being interrupted and deflected.

The foreigner. The prerequisites for citizenship in the Empire, or membership in the *oecumene*, were: acceptance of the Imperial idea, reception of orthodoxy, and adherence to the Greek-Hellenistic cultural heritage, which was naturally expressed in Greek. Broadly diffused in the Empire, these prerequisites were concentrated and most visible in the city, and there deviation from them was more noticeable and more dangerous. The Imperial administration had its own ways of containing and restricting foreigners or exotic elements, and this negative quarantine, based on religious heterodoxy, not ethnic origin or race, was sometimes supported by positive measures based on cultural definitions: on two occasions in Byzantine history the capital was so disastrously emptied that the government had to repeople it, and in both cases it chose to recruit Greek-speaking, even "Helladic" elements: in 755 from "the islands and Greece," and after 1270 from Laconia.[107] But official attitudes are one thing; the views of the ordinary citizens—the *agoraioi*—on those from outside the compass of the Empire are another matter.

Whether a Constantinopolitan encountered foreigners at all, and in what numbers, and the nature of the contact, depended on his status, his job, probably the quarter in which he lived or worked as well. Unfortunately the social and psychological reactions of the commoners to an intrusive foreign element are almost impossible to reconstruct until they become "mass" or "mob" in character, affecting historically perceptible numbers of the populace.[108] The foreigners we know were present. They came into the city in significant numbers as commercial or business agents, and some were allowed to take up residence there. There

[107] Charanis, "Transfer of Population," 144, 149.
[108] See above, note 84.

were also the diplomatic visitors, and those outsiders who had a special military status. Tourists, however, would be few, though they give us our best views of Constantinople from the other, non-Byzantine point of view.

The number of foreigners attracted to the capital for commercial purposes was always large, and would be even larger after the commercial reflorescence that occurred in Byzantium at the turn of the 9th century.[109] Of these there would invariably be a sprinkling of true exotics: half-Arabs from the Emirate of Cordova, strange varieties of Turk or even Mongolian from the Transcaspian or from Central Asia, a rare black African from the Upper Nile, and the odd Frank. The foreign trading colonies of significant size have already been mentioned: Bulgars, Russians, Syrians, and the Italians, who were officially vassals of the Empire.[110] Except for the Syrians these colonies were not integrated into the commercial and business life of Constantinople—that is, did not compete—until late in the 10th century, when the first discriminatory regulations favoring the Italians went into effect.[111] From the date these first edicts appeared to the fatal riots against the Venetians in the 12th century is, emotionally, a very short step.

We accept that counterpressure builds against the foreigner when he moves into competition (more particularly successful competition) with the native: the Italians came to be the objects of this counterpressure, and possibly the Armenians as well, with whom the citizens of Greek culture competed in a different, noncommercial fashion. In Constantinople there also was a special feeling of contempt for the Bulgars, who came to the city (in peacetime) strictly as noncompeting import-export merchants; the Bulgars seem to have been regarded as the archetypal barbarians: brutal and incorrigible though Christian.[112] The Jews, though isolated by Imperial command, were never faced in Byzantium with the insanity with which medieval Europe was infected towards them, but Byzantium worked out the *agon* of its

109 E. Frances, "L'Empereur Nicéphore Ier et le commerce maritime byzantin," *Byzantinoslavica* **XXVII/1** (1966), 41–47.

110 See Chapt. 1, footnotes 37 and 38; Chapt. 2, footnote 117.

111 For the "Venetian edict" see Dölger, *Regesten* **1**, 710/111.

112 Nicephoras' remarks are repeated in Cedrenus **II**, 372.

neuroses elsewhere. Nor was there the excuse, in East Rome, of the usurious Jew, since moneylending was a sufficiently respected guild occupation, and the Imperial house itself was known to lend a *nomisma* or two.[113] The Moslems in the city were quartered near the Pratorion for more complete security, and this quarter was safe even during the height of the Arab wars.[114]

Superficially it would appear that the foreigners most in the eye of the common citizen must be the barbaric aliens of the Bodyguard, and that their commanding position must have been correspondingly resented. The view the citizens took of these privileged mercenaries cannot be known. The use, by the divine ruler or autocrat, of a barbarian lifeguard (as differentiated from a mercenary army) was a tradition of long standing, however, and it is likely that the troopers of the Guard were viewed not as high-class policemen, but as a barely human barrier, as tamed wild animals, between the Emperor and his enemies. The total number of foreigners in the *Hetairea* was not large, up to the time when Basil II recruited the Varangians in 988 A.D. Up until the advent of the Varangian *druzhina* (Scandinavian-Slavic in composition) most of the Guardsmen were Turkic: Ferghanese and Khazars predominating.[115] The Varangians would bring other problems, of course, relating to the changed character of the Byzantine army itself.[116]

The reaction of a city against the foreigners within it is conditioned by the entire shape and tone of its civilization, not just by individual economic incidents or the accidents of war. Outbreaks by the commons against foreigners, whatever the cause or excuse, are not really likely unless the State is willing to forego its responsibility to keep order or has lost the power to keep order. Historically, these outbreaks are also the invariable product of the most severe civic psychoses, the product of all the fears which end by striking out at the dangerous Outsider, the ill-wishing guest-enemy within the gates. These phenomena are true

113 "Book of the Prefect," 605/III.

114 Janin, *Constantinople,* 257–259.

115 See G. Moravcsik, *Byzantinoturcica,* II (Berlin, 1958), 335; for the Ferghanese see *De ceremoniis* 693, 697, 698, 749.

116 V. G. Vasilievskii, "Varyago-russkaya i varyago-angliiskaya druzhina v Konstantinopolye XI i XII vv.," in his *Trudy,* I (St. Petersburg, 1908).

defensive wars, declared by the frustrated mass when the apparatus of state refuses to "seek the accursed thing" and eject the scapegoat. Byzantium would have its share of such violence, especially after the decline of the Empire had set in.

More important than these mass irrationalities in determining how a foreigner is regarded, is that shape and tone I have mentioned; the whole complex of "national" attitudes toward those outside. In Byzantium, an Imperial state but the heir of classical formulae, the outsider was a refraction of the concept of the Barbarian.[117] *This* idea went deep into all strata.

The barbarian might be defined, as anciently, in terms of language and resultant culture. He might have an imperfect Christianity, which was quite as bad as having none at all. His manners might be uncouth. Or, he might merely be an unknown quality, a stranger. For a bureaucrat and litterateur from the middle class like Michael Psellos the term "barbarian" rolls off the tongue almost too easily. Constantine VIII, the brother and briefly the successor of Basil II, he accuses of bringing "barbarians and heathens"—"neither of noble birth or even free-born"—into the Sacred Hierarchy.[118] Many were castrated, which exaggerated their separateness. This sort of shotgun denigration is typical of Psellos, the urban bourgeois, when his own status in the hierarchy is threatened or impinged on (the "aged Michael"—Michael the Paphlagonian—also broke the *cursus honorum* and so did Constantine IX Monomachus; this is one of the most serious charges Psellos can bring against a sovereign).[119] As to the truth of the particular allegation against Constantine, the new men he introduced may have been foreigners by birth or extraction, but they were unlikely to have been heathen; this was accepted in the Bodyguard but not in either the regular—the "bearded"—or the eunuch ranks or offices. Eunuchhood was viewed ambiguously in Byzantium; there were posts open only

[117] For concepts of the "barbarian" see J. A. K. Thomson, *Greeks and Barbarians* (New York, 1921); for the Byzantine reaction, K. Lechner, "Hellenen und Barbaren im Weltbild der Byzantiner. Die alten Bezeichnungen als Ausdruck eines neuen Kulturbewützseins." Dissert. München, 1954.

[118] Psellos, *Chronographia*, **II**.3.

[119] *Ibid.*, **VI**. 29, **VII**.2.

to eunuchs and some of these were very high posts indeed, but in the 10th and 11th centuries the loss of manhood was often regarded as an adjunct of "foreignness."[120] It was used by the bureaucratic-aristocratic party (Leo Choerosphactes and his circle) as another stick with which to beat the Syrian Samonas, at the end of Leo VI's reign, and at other times was made synonymous with a lack of individuality or will.[121] Psellos insists that the "barbarians and heathens" were loyal only to the Emperor himself, i.e., had no bureaucratic consciousness.[122]

For the lower classes and the commoners of Constantinople the foreigner presented a different problem. As some sense of the cohesiveness and massive power of the Empire-in-the-City filtered down to them, their pride in "their" city engendered an offhand contempt for those unlucky enough to have been excluded. A visitor like Liutprand of Cremona seems to see the arrogance of Byzantium widely dispersed throughout the population, and he is enraged. The commoners he encountered as wardens were at least as contemptuously hostile as the high officers of state and the Emperor himself.[123] Liutprand's evidence is important, idiosyncratic and tetchy as he was. Liutprand had a monumental *amour-propre* and an adder's tongue, but he was also powerfully attracted to the radiative idea of Byzantium (this explains his violent about-face in the *Legatio* as contrasted with the earlier *Antapodosis*) and he was a realist. He came to Constantinople from Italy, where the Byzantine system, now based on false estimates of power and outmoded concepts of authority, backed by insufficient force, was in the process of foundering. He found in the capital no willingness to recognize a changed situation, but instead what he in his frustration had to see as archaic and nonsensical habits of domination, and the pride of the devil. In Liutprand's case the irascible pride of the Emperor, an Anatolian aristocrat who once called Bulgarian emissaries "leather-eaters" and "slaves" to their faces, was reinforced by the generalized arrogance and Cockney self-confidence of urban Byzantines of all

[120] See also Chapt. 3, footnote 27[e].
[121] Karlin-Heyter, ed., *Vita Euthemii*, 54, 74–75, 98–99.
[122] Psellos, *Chronographia*, **II**.3.
[123] Liutprand, *Legatio*, **I**.

ranks. Liutprand's reaction, his spite, his attempts to picture the whole of the Byzantine polity as motheaten but ludicrously pretentious, are peculiarly his own, and yet significant for what they reflect about the closing mind of Byzantium, the fossilizing of formerly creative instincts.

The Spiritual Life of the People

Popular religion and superstition. In their religious attitudes the city-folk of Constantinople were united to the rest of orthodoxy by the oldest and most potent ties, ties that were stronger than any specifically urban variations or influences. In the city a special religiosity might be fostered by the mass and number of religious structures, by some sense of the continuation and rhythm of liturgies, by knowledge of the reinforcing rituals of the State, or even by the larger idea of the God-guarded universal center where a counterpoise to the power of darkness existed, but the strongest evidence is that on the popular level Byzantine Christianity unified country and city. It was a faith characterized by all the features that appear to identify a "peasant" religion, but which in fact describe religion as a general, urban and rural, phenomenon within a traditional society.

The best and the most revealing sources for this popular Christianity are the *Lives* of the saints who came out of the mass and reflected its version of Christianity; *Lives* that are formularistic, naive, repetitious (judged as literature, that is, which they are not) and always worth careful reading. A number of hints and indirect data come from general histories and more official documents. Insights into pattern and structure can be drawn from both theoretical and field anthropology, and comparisons can be taken from the growing (and not well disciplined) collections of folkloric materials. Greek popular religion of the modern period has been examined by scholars as well, with an eye to establishing strands of continuity—the irreducible continuity of a primitive-peasant *cultus*.

"Popular Christianity" has enough of an invidious ring to demand correction or explanation. In Byzantium's case, the religion of the intellectual élites of the society differed from this popular cult only in detail and degree, not in kind. The intellectuals might deal in more rarified theological concepts and discuss them with a broader vocabulary and more acuity—but, on the one hand, these concepts were knowledgeably discussed on many, and lower, levels in Byzantium, and on the other, the best-educated men also accepted the mix of elements in the Christianity of their time and place.

The characteristics of this mix are:

(a) The survival in some form of pre-Christian cult-forms and beliefs. These could be as complex as the Orphic and other soteric juxtapositions and substitutions made to fill out the myth of Christ to a more richly rounded form, or thc ancient controls on time shown in the sacred year's round, with its crises and renewals. They might also involve the simple transference of myths and divine or semidivine personalities: the Byzantine calendar of saints was a gaudy tapestry, much rewoven and seldom rechecked or canonically drycleaned. The saint as a mediatory or intercessory figure had been proceeded by the Hero, and in a number of cases Christianity brought a new name (sometimes not even that) but no radical difference so far as the common believer was concerned.

(b) For the Byzantine faithful the liturgical structure was understood and emotionally and psychologically digested in a manner at the same time highly sensitized, open, and free of external censors, and yet literal, almost stodgy. The "experience" of the liturgy was highly potent, yet its content tended to be limited because its forms were sealed off from tampering. The intricate artistic formulae of this liturgy, the icons viewed as *acheiropoeitos* —"made without hands"—in more than just the simple matter of inspiration and creation, had little human depth or experiential development—in Byzantium, they could not. The extension of Byzantine man into the mysteries was made on several separated and exclusive levels, and this produced both a lack of tension and a loss of spiritual creativity. The iconoclastic troubles of the 7th to 9th centuries themselves were to a large degree a mask or external affect of a deeper crisis, which involved more than the opposition of the monks to churchmen allied with the State. The latter, whether they were called iconoclasts or whether, as in the 9th century, they rejected iconoclasm, advocated a religious purpose *in* the society; the monastics rejected this possibility.[124] It was the opinion of the monastic zealots that serious doubt had to be cast on the *societal* ritual, on even the priesthood (including the priestly simulacrum of kingship), who was to them a false interpreter of the divine substances.[125] Opponents of the societal ritual could be as crude as the ordinary habit-fettered, complacent but intolerant and unproductive monk, or as intellectually acute as the Studites—Theodore, or later Simeon the New Theologian. Against the *ecclesia* these monastic theoreticians put *ascesis*; more, they might speak of blocking every road to salvation but the mystic-contemplative. Theodore's defense of icons was partially anti-Imperial, never crudely iconodule, for to him and to the antinomian enthusiasts who came after him the physical relict had only the function of a signal or code-key to the transcendent.[126] The common worshipper was not likely to understand this, and in any case was drawn into the antisocietal camp only under special strains and circumstances, but the tone and intent of that camp's muttered assault was always available.

(c) The Byzantine belief in and concern with the demonic is a side to their religious mentality that deserves close attention. The demon-figure itself has entwined and multiple roots. It serves as a means to objectify the nonhuman scale of powers, and to explain irrationality: as such it is an ancient device with a pedigree older than "classical" mythopoeia. Its forms are various: there is the ghost-demon or revenant, the spirit of the dead. There are the demons who appear with the great Hellenistic salvation-cults, combining all the forms that went before, and adding an element of organization, a demonology. To this was grafted a Judaeo-Christian idea of the demon as a focus for visible evil.[127]

Byzantine demonology provided a formula for dealing with a vast number of powerful psychological data. Within its compass

[124] See R. Jenkins, *Byzantium: The Imperial Centuries* (New York, 1966), 96–97, 100, on *economy* or dispensation versus the antisocietal monastic attitude.

[125] John of Damascus and Theodore of Studios, in Barker, *Social and Political Thought,* 86–88.

[126] On Simeon: B. Tatakis, *La Philosophie Byzantine* (2ième fasc. suppl. of E. Bréhier, ed. *Histoire de la Philosophie,* Paris, 1949), 140–151.

[127] See H. Webster, *Magic: A Sociological Study* (Stanford, 1948), esp. Ch. III, "Procedures and Techniques."

could be set the simplest problem of frustration, such as the familiar resistance or obstinacy of inanimate things (animated by being made demonic). Resistance to or confounding of the *human* will and all its purposes was easily laid to demonic beings, especially when the notion of the demon as carrier of sin—or as the sin itself—is superadded, for the demon as "devil" intrudes himself into the pathway to salvation in a number of interesting ways. Sickness, of course, both physical and mental, must be demon-carried (and again, the demon becomes the illness itself) since it involves a breakdown of the normal human condition or balance.[128]

The demonic is, however, a true, if crude, spiritual cement: a force with which the Byzantines were always involved. The very power of the demonic assault could be described so broadly and vividly because this assault was *controllable,* or at the least could be evaded or repelled. The modes of control or evasion are themselves extremely complex. On the most primitive level the lives of country saints are riddled with diabolic and demonic encounters of every sort, and in coming victorious out of these encounters the saint's sanctity is proven.[129] On another level the spells and books of exorcisms and incantations, which were used and circulated widely, involved the most elaborate use of demonic interventions: the controlled demon, who predicts and grants favors, mixed with signs and portents—in other words, a popular science of demonology—leads up to such constructions as Michael Psellos' *De operatione daemonum,* a recension of Neo-Platonist views on the subject.[130]The common element in all levels of theorizing about the demonic is the idea that no division can be created between human and inhuman or nonhuman, that all of creation is polyphonically related, so that will and act, rational intent and irrational impulse, dream and reality, are interwoven. Man is continually picked up in a flux that has its origin outside him but

[128] A. Delatte et Ch. Jusserand, "Contribution a l'étude de la démonologie byzantine," *Mélanges Bidez* (*Annuaire de l'Institut de Philologie et d'Histoire orientales et slaves,* **II**.1, 1933–34), 230.

[129] See, e.g., Theodore of Sicyon, in N. Baynes and E. Dawes, *Three Byzantine Saints* (Oxford, 1948), 147–148, 153, 158, 175.

[130] Delatte et Jusserand "Contribution," 207–208; Michael Psellos, *De operatione demonorum, Patrilogia Graeca,* **122**.

impinges on him in innumerable ways; in turn, he can affect this power—must affect it, if he is to keep his mental balance.

Any saintly individual would intersect and agitate the demonic hierarchy frequently, and the *Life* of almost any saint must have its encounters, in each of which a demonic agency stands in or behind a variety of phenomena, usually unpleasant. In the *Life* of Simeon the New Theologian, a Studite saint and a mystic of note, demons bring (or appear in, as perceptible apparitions) night-visions to try the saint; they also inspire the jealousy of colleagues and the malignancy of neighbors. The chief demon ("the" demon, the Evil One—*o poneros*) caused, the *Life* says, the "accident" by which a certain Frankish bishop, who was at the monastery doing penance, killed a child. The saint also, in performing the common task of curing a possessed child, had to expel the demon possessor.[131]

Simeon is a "city" saint, and his matches with the demonic are comparatively rare, though absolutely typical of the genre. Theodore of Sicyon on the other hand was undoubtedly a country saint, whose *Life* is a series of drastic challenges by a host of demonic adversaries. They are stirred from the ground or from graves (more precisely, gravestones—pagan sarcophagae) and have to be laid again; they possess both people and oxen; they attack the saint and are repulsed with a blast of holy fire; they manifest themselves by knocking or rock-throwing, as garden-variety poltergeists. They are extraordinarily active, in their proper (or improper) persons as well as through their instruments.[132] In other *Lives,* such as those of the "establishment" saints Terasius and Nicephoras, both ex-bureaucrats and patriarchs of Constantinople, little contact with the world of demons is shown: this doesn't mean that they were free of them. As educated men they accepted the existence and the power of demons as literally as did the commonest parish priest.[133]

131 I. Hausherr et G. Horn, eds., "Un grand mystique byzantin: Vie de Symeon le Nouveau Théologien, par Nicetas Stéthatos," *Orientalia et Christiana* **45** (July-Sept. 1928), 23–25, 70 ff, 153, 169.

132 Baynes and Dawes, *Three Byzantine Saints,* 147, 158, 175; for other poltergeists see the Life of Daniel the Stylite in the same work: p. 15.

133 Da Costa-Louillet, "Saintes de Constantinople," *Byzantion* **24** (1954), 217–229 for Tarasius; 246–255 for Nicephoras.

One of the vivid indicators of the persistence and deep impress of demon-belief in Byzantine life is the variety of paraphernalia that was called upon to control them. The exorcisms (collected into books for handy reference), proverbs, folk-sayings and spoken charms show one type of command or prophylactic defense; there are also protective objects—amulets, phylacteries, and magical relics. These survive from every period and every level of Byzantine life, and they reveal the dark richness of this side of the Byzantine psyche.[134]

Three important factors gave knowledge and possibly the ability to restrict or even direct: name, embodiment, and powers. The three interlocked, but *naming* was most meaningful, because recognition had to come before any action could be taken. The name was absolutely necessary in incantory magic, where the demon was called upon to perform a task or give a sign—a most dangerous and illegal procedure. The names show the deep antiquity and wide provenance of these powerful beings: some were directly identified as pagan deities, especially the old earth-gods—Artemis, Rhea, Cybele, Dionysos; some came from the Judaeo-Christian tradition—Ashtaroth, Lucifer, and Pontius Pilate. The names of the greater number of individually identified demons were non-Greek.[135]

The demonic form was various and much debated. The appearance might be only that (*phantasma*) or might be a shadow; most demons were incorporeal or if corporeal, "subtle," and many changed forms freely. To gain power over them they had to be first identified, then revealed or given form; this might be done by proper feeding (smoke and blood were effective, though some demons wanted milk and honey).[136]

Their powers were the heart of the matter. They ruled over the inhuman and the unearthly, the places of taboo and fear—mountains, woods, cemeteries, doorways and crossroads, swamps, the subterranean. They were potent at night and at high noon. In

134 Delatte et Jusserand, "Contribution," *loc. cit.;* M. A. Andreeva, "Politicheskii i obshchestvennii element Vizantiisko-slavyanskikh gadatel'nikh knig," *Byzantinoslavica* V (1933), 122 ff.

135 Leo VI, *Novel* 65 (Noialles et Dain, *Les Novelles,* 236–239); Delatte et Jusserand, "Contribution," 213–214.

136 Delatte et Jusserand, "Contribution," 211–212, 217, 219.

the hierarchy devised by the Neo-Platonists they ascended to the planets, the stars, and the spheres, and had power over the seasons as well; this had some interest for the ordinary Byzantine, but of more poignant concern to him was the multitude of perceptible evils that were laid to their cause.[137] All maladies were demonic, all pests, all faults of wind and weather, insanity and irrationality, crop failure and epizoötics, moral laxity *and* the temptations that fed moral laxity.[138] Demons became, in other words, an objectification of the entire range of that which bore down on man, of all the traumata of life. They had to a degree the power of chastising the soul, within the Christian tradition; they also embodied the equalizing, Fatal power that fell on Classical man. But more than all this, they proved a most comforting invention: an intermediary force that was understandable and cognizable. Pure evil is a theological construct without meaning to the masses; an absolutely indifferent nature is almost as unbelievable. The demon, or the whole range of demons, makes evil both understandable and supportable. There is a sort of comfort in the confusion and mixture of recognizable opponents that every man can expect to encounter, standing behind all ills from mischief to disaster.

A Note: The Statue-Demons of the city. Constantinople imported every sort of demon-belief from the countryside, and had in addition a special focus for this superstition in the statue. Constantine the Great had decorated his city with statuary to reinforce its troubled image as New Rome; more was added by the Theodosians and the emperors of the 5th century: these were mainly Imperial icons—personal memorials in the older Roman sense; solid reminders of a Life and a Reign. The last statue in the "Roman" vein was the great equestrian piece erected by the Emperor Justinian in the Augusteon, between the Sacred Palace and the Great Church.[139]

Besides the imperial statues and those transferred to the city as a cosmetic measure—to create an idea of a civic art, and simply to beautify—there were a number of carved or cast-metal images

[137] *Ibid.,* 222–224.
[138] *Ibid.,* 230 ff.
[139] Janin, *Constantinople,* 73.

that originally served other purposes—a form of advertising in some cases. There were several Modii in the fora: a grain-measure cast in bronze, held by two hands, an encrypt for Imperial provision and prosperity or *plenitudo*.[140] There were others that were more frankly symbolic-magical, or at least this is how the population read them. For a number we have no explanation of their original uses or meanings. *All* these forms in the round, however, became objects of special attention. All of them were conceived as possessing powers, and in many these powers were projections of the demonic.

The *eidola* or images were endowed with a variety of attributes and potencies. Some were regarded as merely eerie, rather unnatural, since the craft of sculpture itself had died out, and the relics of another time remained without the ordinary familiarizing knowledge of techniques and the dusty, dreary labor of the workshops and foundries. The three-dimensional image itself had fallen out of the civilization. The natural inclination of the Byzantines was to transfer their suspicions of the insubstantial world of the demonic to the frozen substance of the statues, which became either the shell within which the spirit lurked, or the demon him- or herself. When pagan gods or goddesses were figured the identification was all too simple. *Eidolon* as a description carries a strong supernatural coloration, and a piece of statuary that had been an *objet d'art* and not a cult image was returned, in the popular imagination, to its beginnings: as the *eidolon* "which the pagans worshipped."[141]

A curious and valuable little document, the so-called *Patria* of Constantinople, which dates from the end of the 10th century, is much concerned with the powers of demon-ridden or purely magical statues, which it describes in terms the commons of the city undoubtedly used.[142] These were images in the Hippodrome, according to the *Patria*, monstrous themselves, which "give birth to monsters and devour men."[143] Another group of images near

[140] *Ibid.*, 66, 104.
[141] The *Patria: Pseudo-Codinus origines continuens; adiecta est forma urbis Constantinopolis,* in Th. Praeger, ed., *Scriptores originiens Constantinopolitanarum.* **II.** Fasc. Alter (Lipsiae, 1907), 258.
[142] *Patria,* passim.
[143] *Ibid.*, 190.

the Strategion were ordered thrown down by the Caesar Bardas, thus cleansing the site, "for it was a place of magic."[144] For good measure a Tyche of the City was knocked down as well; there were evidently several Tyches, and they suffered a great deal of abuse.[145]

The great Imperial images could hold no specifically demonic powers, since their significance fell strongly into other categories, but as symbols of the Type of the Ruler they were particularly vulnerable to popular superstitions. When a particularly selective earth tremor toppled one of them the city could be put into a terrific fright, for no other interpretation was for it but that the reign and perhaps the Empire was close to its end. More far-fetched readings (almost certainly after the event) were made of such incidents as the falling of a statue in the quarter called Deuteron in 865 A.D., which had to mean the approaching fall of the "second" man (*deuteron*) in the Empire—that is, the Caesar Bardas.[146] Such associations move sympathetic magic one step toward abstraction, since the particular statue in this case was not important, merely a potent indicator. Ordinarily the statue is more closely connected to the man. It was said (and so reported by the Continuator of Theophanes) that the arch-enemy Symeon of Bulgaria was represented by a statue standing in Constantinople, and that the Emperor (Romanus Lecapenus), following the advice of certain intimates had the image beheaded. "In that hour" Symeon, of course, died.[147] If the statue existed, whether or not it was ceremoniously decapitated, is not the point: the people *thought* that this sort of action was effective. In much the same vein it is reported of the Emperor Michael I Rhangabe that when faced with popular revolt he had the hands of the (or a) Tyche of the City cut off.[148] The people, who were the "hands" of the city, subsided, their power of action amputated with the image's hands. The citizenry also were firmly convinced (the *Patria* attests) that certain pests and vermin—invariably impelled by demonic appetites or personifying the demon himself—were con-

[144] *Ibid.,* 189.
[145] Janin, *Constantinople,* 63, 117; *Patria,* 160, 257.
[146] Theophanes Continuatus, 197.
[147] Theophanes Continuatus, 411.
[148] *Patria,* 160.

trolled in the city because bronze images of them "fixed" them: prevented their proliferation. Images of a Snake and a Fly are mentioned.[149]

The oddest and one of the most important popular beliefs was again connected with the statuary of the city, especially the Imperial images. The beginnings of the city were not mythic—that is, not beyond the reach of history—but had been mythized—transmogrified, rearranged to suit the mythopoetic faculty of successive generations of citizens. The foundation ceremonies of Constantine the Great, who became the Great Magician, passed from the category of state ritual to that of magical exercise. To secure the *terminus* of the city according to the people, the founder had brought the Palladium from Rome to his own Forum; more, he placed near the Milion a chain, securely locked with its key buried in the base of the monument. So long as the chain's circuit was complete, the city would endure.[150] But other monuments, scattered about the capital, contained encrypted messages that the initiated could read, telling always of the End: *ta eschata tes poleos, ton eschaton hemeron tas historias*—"the end of the City, of the last days of history."[151]

To find in this *Patria* of the 10th century a popular apocalypticism contrasting with the normal or official Byzantine view of the city's fate is extremely significant. The normative official view sidestepped the Christian or Christian-patristic view of temporality, the linear movement that had to point to the end of days, and built in the city a theory of sempiternality, of time dissolved in eternalized, ritual forms. The serial time of the ordinary Christian schema was itself a replacement of the earlier short-time or revelatory-prophetic view, which held to a belief in the immanence of the Last Days, and this reading of the uses of time sprang both from a sensation of exalted, neurotic superiority—a spiritual élitism—and a reaction away from the most severe secular pressures. Throughout the history of Christianity (and especially throughout the history of Christian heresy) millenarism was seen

[149] *Patria,* 250.
[150] *Patria,* 166, 174.
[151] Ch. Diehl, "De quelques croyances byzantines sur la fin de Constantinople," *Byzantinische Zeitschrift* **XXX** (1929–30), 196; *Patria,* 176.

when a given society felt enough pressure to release millenarian reactions. Ordinarily Byzantium was not prone to millenarian theories or the excitations they produced, and to find the population of the chief center of the Empire obsessed by prophecies of collapse and the end of history—the history of the saeculum—at a time when presumably the secular power of the city was at its height, is foreboding.

The *Patria* is explicit in at least one case: the equestrian statue in the Forum Taurus bore an inscription which when properly deciphered predicted the fall of Constantinople to the Russians. It is true that the Russians struck into the popular imagination; the city's first knowledge of them was catastrophic (their attack from the sea in 860 A.D. was a complete surprise), and by the time the *Patria* was compiled the unknown writer or writers may have been responding to the campaigns of Svyatoslav against the city—or even to the presence of the Varangian Guard in the city.[152]

152 Diehl, "De quelques croyances," 195.

Execution of a rebel (one of Bardas Phocas's co-conspirators) by wild animals. (Courtesy of Dr. S. Cirac Estopanan.)

FIVE

The Aristocracy

When the day dawned, he said his prayers, took his weapons, mounted his horse and rode out against the warrior. The warrior too had risen. He mounted and, turning toward Melik, charged at him. Why prolong the tale? They fought with every weapon, but neither could win. At the end, the warrior grabbed Melik Danismend by the belt and tried to throw him from his horse, but could not. He tried three times in vain. It was the turn of Melik Danismend: he set his feet in the stirrups, grabbed the warrior by the belt and pulled, saying "In the name of God and by the pure light of Muhammed-Mustafa!" He threw the man from his horse and, dismounting at the same time, placed his foot on his chest. He took his dagger for the *coup-de-grâce*. The warrior had fainted; Melik Danismend saw that he was a young man with a face fair as the moon and was seized by pity. The young man came to himself, opened his eyes and heaved a sigh.

"Become a Moslem," Melik Danismend said to him, "and I will set you free!"

Kiṣṣā-i Melik Dāniṣmend

OUTSIDE THE CHARMED CIRCLE, THE ARISTOCRACY

Definitions. According to the dominant theory of the Imperial polity, there could be no aristocracy in Byzantium outside the Center, or outside the definition that the Center made of "best" or "highest." Honor and rank were allocated through membership in the Sacred Hierarchy by the Emperor, and no *aristoi* but the members of that Sacred Hierarchy could be possible. These were the "best" and "highest," as the Emperor might choose.[1]

[1] R. Guilland, "Études sur l'histoire administrative de Byzance," *Byzantina-Metabyzantina* I(1), (1946): 170–171.

Constitutionally they were the Senatorial Order, but this term is subject to the usual Byzantine multiple readings and the superposition of several historical levels over one another. The *ceremonial* Senate was at all times more significant than the constitutional Senate.[2]

There are several working definitions of "aristocracy." One says that an aristocracy is a socio-political phenemenon that works toward apoliticality, basing itself on and drawing sustenance from the countryside as a favorable environment. There its élite status depends on a generational, blood-carried, agraphic, and antigraphic "history" of dominance.[3] If this dominance has a material base—which according to the self-generated definitions of the aristocrat it need not have—this base is land. The traditions of aristocratic stocks, however, usually have as their authenticating foundation the epical rather than the mythical seizure of the land as a battleprize; the beginning of a land-based economic domination by the "best" is the respectable, noneconomic act of war. The aristocratic founding myth, then, depends on an intrusion, whether historical or not; a triumph of victor over vanquished, of effective over ineffective warrior. The line between inner (winner) and outer (loser) is then maintained as a constant, always exposed to pressure.[4] This aristocracy either conceives of itself as a warrior class, or conceives of its domination and consequent economic or noneconomic rewards as verifications of a military past. Its service to the State, if it is drawn into service (and often it fails to recognize a higher, politicized sovereignty beyond itself) is limited to a military service or to "arms," vaguely defined.[5]

The accidents of Byzantine history seem first to have destroyed the remnants of one aristocracy and then to have created another. The existence of a landed aristocracy is postulated for the late 6th and early 7th century on the basis of the presence of estate-type or latifundial land tenure. If this nonbureaucratic, landed élite existed in the shifting scene of the Empire of that period, its

[2] Leo VI, *Novel* 97 (Dain et Noailles, *Les Novelles,* 185–187); for the senate in general, L. Bréhier, *Les institutions,* 181–184.
[3] Eisenstadt, *Political Systems of Empires,* 177–180, 182.
[4] As e.g. in the case of Sparta.
[5] Most visible in the "feudal" systems; I am specifically excepting here the so-called "bureaucratic aristocracy," with its origins in civil service.

habits of service were extremely circumscribed; the Byzantine army in the late 6th century was still heavily mercenary, and its military command tended to be mercenary as well.[6] The shattering blows of the early 7th century, which lopped off provinces (like Egypt, which had been heavily latifundial in its system of land use) and emptied others, disrupted all property rights and arrangements and, so far as we can tell, effectively destroyed what was left of estate-type agriculture.[7] In the repairs that the soldier-emperors of the 7th and 8th centuries made in the Empire *all* strata were shaken and mixed, and the structure that was erected eliminated all élites but service élites, and furthermore was predicated on an atomization of landholding, with both the taxload and essential military service tied to small or small-to-medium landholdings. In almost every territory or province remaining to the Empire economic modes, micro-political activities, and hierarchies of loyalty were replaced or readjusted. Leadership within the reformed system was shifted to the Center, and from the Center came the viceregal generals who held delegated power in the provincial subgovernments.[8]

Whatever tradition or actuality of "aristocracy" had been visible in the early 7th century Empire was totally disrupted, and yet an aristocracy is newly visible in the late 8th and early 9th century. It seems to have sprung from two conflicting but mutually reinforcing Imperial policies.

The Empire, first, searched for and found allies and recruits in several of the isolated, still tribalized or politically primitive cultures that lay near it. The most significant of these was Armenia, though Khazaria has perhaps been underestimated as a recruiting ground. From these small societies whole classes of élites were borrowed or transferred wholesale, and these élites brought an arsenal of aristocratic patterns with them: the *nakharars* of Armenia are a case in point.[9] Habits and traditions of dominance according to unwritten rules sought outlet in Byzantium, and in

[6] E. Stein, *Studien zur Geschichte des byzantinisches Reiches, vornehmlich unter den Kaisern Justinus II und Tiberius Constantinus* (Stuttgart, 1919), 140 ff.

[7] Rouillard, *La vie rurale,* 90 ff.

[8] Zakythinos, "Étatisme byzantin," 678.

[9] P. Charanis, *Armenians,* 13 ff; S. der Nersessian, *Armenia and the Byzantine Empire* (Cambridge, Mass., 1945), 15.

Byzantium's frequent wars and other crises. The Empire needed military leadership at all costs, especially in the middle ranges of command, and a borrowed sword-aristocracy exactly filled the bill.

At the same time, the dangers of a completely heterogeneous, unstabilized, or unordered polity were clear. The social fluxes within the Empire, the massive injections of new immigrants, some under control and many not, the tremendous pressures of war and economic stringency, could have broken the Empire at every seam and pulled it apart into fragments for the Arabs or the Slavs and Turkic tribes to quarrel over. The Imperial cement was strong enough to forestall this, and it was immeasurably aided by the cultural prestige and normalizing radiation of the capital. Adherence to a cultural norm was rewarded by trust and power, and the imported aristocracy was able, if it wished, to dig itself deeper into the Imperial society by adopting a language-carried cultural pattern. There was strong pressure in this direction. Also, the very multiplicity of the groups drawn into service helped the Empire control them. One major migration of a military or tribal-military people might have swamped the control points—the city and central administration—but a series of additions and migrations could be and were directed and counterbalanced.

A third point involves the relationship of a reconstructed bureaucracy to ambitious exogenous elements. It became clear to the immigrants that ambitious men could find advancement in this service area, as well as in the military. To a degree, then, the élites who had known only the traditional, ascriptive support of land and family were recruited into a different élite with a different system of support: a structure or *regulum* of service and reward. Thus it is possible to bureaucratize, to attract and hold men who came out of an aristocratic background, but the converse works as well. In Byzantium's predecessor (if not progenitor), the older Roman Empire, the Senatorial order, with its vague ambiance of genuine aristocracy, was long the reward of distinguished civil servants. The "native" Roman aristocracy, in fact, was strongly connected to State service—civil service—from the 1st century A.D. In time the temporary and provisional ennobling of superannuated bureaucrats grew into something solider and more separate from the apparatus of State. The Roman civilian-senator had a later parallel in the Byzantine civil servant who tried to convert his service nobility to one carried by hereditary right and somehow freed of the Emperor's choice and supervision. Ordinarily he could not do this in the city, but when he struck his roots into the countryside his élite status could be stabilized and with luck even made permanent. As foreign elements were engrafted onto the bureaucracy and passed out of the feudalized modes they had brought with them, the upper ranks of the bureaucracy often attempted to move in reverse, to hypostasize their positions and at the same time make them concrete and, most important, hereditary.[10]

Origins. The growth of an aristocratic élite within a social mix (as compared with a catastrophic intrusion) is extremely difficult to objectify and analyze. The nature of the aristocratic mythology blocks off self-analysis, since in this mythology "history" is extraneous or even dangerous if it involves the test of rationality (the appeal to written geneology is a proof of the extreme and decrepit old age of any aristocracy). An aristocracy should be secure in an inner knowledge that it is coterminous with the land it holds or, more properly, leads; it requires this fiction more deeply than any other.

In Byzantium the advent of a nonbureaucratic, landholding aristocracy is indicated (not proved) in the appearance of true family names in the documents and sources, names that are identifiable because of later distinction and continuation, although the important aspect of their appearance is simply that they are there. The earliest and the most numerous citations are in the Anatolian themes, for good reason: in the eastern provinces were settled most of the imported élites or foreigners with strong feudal inclinations, and here a degree of decentralized power was developed at least a century before the same phenomenon appeared in "Europe"—the Balkan lands and their Greek extension —after that area was believed secure.[11]

Of the family names extracted from the whole range of sources —historical-chronographic, sigillographic, and documentary, even

[10] Eisenstadt, *Political Systems of Empires,* 176, 284.

[11] S. Vryonis, "Byzantium: The Social Basis of Decline in the Eleventh Century," *Greek, Roman, and Byzantine Studies* II.2 (1959), 161.

hagiographic—over half are in view by the 9th century: Phokas, Maleinos, Dukas, Argyrus, Scleros, Musele, Botaniates, Malissenus, Tzimiskes, Curcuas, Melias.[12] Of these all but Argyrus and Botaniates are identified either positively or with reasonable certainty as Armenian in origin, an identification made sometimes because they are tagged as such in the sources (either Greek or Armenian), sometimes because of the continued use in the family of Armenian given names, such as Bardas (Vrdat) or Simbatios (Smbat) or saints' names with Armenian connections (Gregory or David).[13] As Armenian by "nationality" the families were certainly descended from the Armenian feudal, petty nobility, the *nakharar* class and its supporters, which came into the Empire in strength from the 6th century on: the Emperor Maurice was reported as having recruited 30,000 Armenian cavalrymen.[14] In the 10th century new names were added to the list (Bourtzos, Comnenus, Diogenes, Dalassenus, Cecaumenos) and in the 11th others (Synadenos, Maniaces, Paleologos). The Armenian element in these later arrivals was less marked.[15] These were grandees, knightly families, whose military occupation had originally been provided them by the Emperor. By the time the first of these names appears it is certain that Imperial control in the Anatolian themes was even less complete than it had been when the purposive decentralization and concentration of viceregal power there was begun in the 7th century. The viceregal office itself—the position of *strategos*—was taken more and more firmly into the hands of these Anatolian magnates, who might be manipulated more than directly controlled from the Center.[16]

The aristocracy of the European themes was a later growth and a lesser one. Dynastic aristocratic families had appeared there by the 9th century: Vryonis identifies Rentacios, Tessaracontopechys, Bryennius, Choerosphactes, Monomachus.[17] Choerosphactes, we

[12] Vryonis, *ibid.*

[13] Charanis, *Armenians*, 22, 23, 26, 28 e.g.

[14] Dolger, *Regesten* I, 12/94.

[15] Vryonis, "Byzantium: The Social Basis of Decline," 160–161.

[16] H. Glykatzi-Ahrweiler, *Recherches sur l'administration de l'empire Byzantin aux IX–XI siècles* (Bulletin de Correspondance hellénique, LXXXIV) (Athens and Paris, 1960), 36–45.

[17] Vryonis, "Byzantium: The Social Basis of Decline," 161–162.

know, founded a dynasty on the basis of his prominence in the civil service, but his family had already been prominent in its own place.[18] The names and families that are seen from the 10th century are also few (recalling that this was not a populous or especially prosperous part of the Empire) and three of them—Tornikios, Taronites, Curticius—are definitely Armenian.[19] Why the Armenian nobility is prominent in the 10th century rather than earlier is uncertain; perhaps these were peregrines from Anatolia who looked for a little more room than their compatriots at home would give them. The European themes were poorer in most respects and some areas were still frontier or nonproductive; there was a real shortage of usable land, even though the population competing for it was smaller. The home grounds or domainal lands of the European magnates were likely to have been in Thrace or Thessaly or the Macedonian plain.

Sources of power. The aristocracy that grew out of the social flux of the early Byzantine period could show no historical continuity, no generation-fed stasis in the provinces where the individual families might have found themselves. The origins of their strength have to be assigned to Imperial policies of the period of the Empire's most massive crisis. The Emperor at this instant needed effective, reasonably loyal and committed military lieutenants: men to command in the emergency districts—the new themes—where in the face of looming peril all authority, civil and military, had to devolve on one representative of the Center.[20] The genesis of aristocratic power, then, was an accidental part of an Imperial act, though obviously the new class filled a vital need in the new provincial structure. In any case the developing aristocracy will not make a point of emphasizing its service origins, or, indeed, any artificial origin at all. It conceives of itself in terms of its own timelessness and its own ritual.

The inception of what had to be before the aristocracy could

[18] Kolias, *Léon Choerosphactès,* 16.

[19] For Corticius, see Charanis, *Armenians,* 29, 44–45; for Taronites, N. Adontz, "Les Taronites," passim; for Tornikios, Charanis, *Armenians,* 46.

[20] J. Karyannopoulos, *Die Enstehung der byzantinischen Themenordnung* (Munich, 1959).

define itself as such—the modes of control and a base of operations—is difficult to reconstruct. The first Imperial act (one spread in time over a century or more) gave immense but devolved or representative power to certain men. The natural logic of the theme system—the system that was the result of that act—worked toward a stabilization of command as a corollary to the stabilization of recruitment and deployment; that is, the troops of the line, settled on the land granted them, could not be officered by total strangers sent from the Center—or not for long. The subformations into which the thematic corps were divided—*taxeis, phylla, banda* or whatever the terminology was as time went on—must soon have been led by men settled in the territories which, under ordinary circumstances, they administered as well. Military formations and territorial divisions were inextricably confused, in fact, and this very confusion seems to show the uses to which the subordinate officers were put.[21]

These underofficers would have been rewarded proportionately to their services. While the ranks of the *strategoi* were filled from the top, by fiat of the directing Throne, subordinate commands were taken over by "native" officers, and it is just here that we can look for an aristocracy in the process of being secured in both its resources—land—and its position of military and consequently of political leadership.[22] This process must have been perceptibly more rapid in areas, such as Anatolia, where the weight of migration from already feudalized or traditional-hierarchic satellites was felt, and a ready-made chain of command was already in existence.

The first move being taken, the proto-aristocratic families were in a position to try to build their second stage or support. This stage has a dimension in space, related to the extent of the land-resource that the proto-aristocracy could control and convert to its own uses. Military service continued to be the indispensible justification, insofar as the Emperor's objectives were concerned, for allowing sizable rewards in land to go to this group. In turn the group had no interest at this point in attempting to convert

21 Bury, *Imperial Administrative System*, 42; Glykatzi-Ahrweiler, *Recherches*.
22 Dendias, "études" 134–136.

its public service, which supported the survival of the State, to any private military objectives. Its own existence continued to be threatened along with that of the State, and the troops it led were bound to their officers only by the established necessities of military discipline, though possibly more private loyalties could be seen in the germ.

The dimension of control in *time* with which the proto-aristocracy was concerned was partly pragmatic, partly mythic. Their irrepressible aim was to insure the continuation within the family of the rank, prestige, and actuality of leadership, to establish authority as a habit within the family, and to safeguard this habit from intrusion by outside agencies of any sort. The safeguards were principally marriage and personal-familial ties (including adoption, godfather-godchild relationships, and sworn friendships) between themselves and the rest of the group.[23] The group was defined as those who governed and held land, at base, yet a more significant judgment probably aimed at a unanimity of thought and attitude: the group was made up of those who looked at the world in the same fashion. All aristocracies must finally evolve this fiction of blood-thought, which only becomes ludicrous when the aristocratic élite is senile or superfluous.

Every marriage, with its rituals of exchange and familial (not, of course, personal) juncture and consequent fruitfulness, and its all-important dowry and bride-price arrangements, cemented social and economic ties more firmly in and among the group, and separated it as a distinct social entity from the nonaristocratic person of *any* level, whether peasant or bureaucrat in the city. The sons of aristocratic families had to expect that their fathers' positions, or a very near approximation, would come to them as a matter of course, and with the position status, power, and a continuation of the resonance of the family name.[24] All this was a very practical concern, but the burgeoning landholding aristocracy also had to deal with its own beginnings—with time in the historical sense. By inference, substitution, and an exercise in nonhistory, the group obscured the awkward fact that at a point in time (some time in the 7th century, we suppose) the family

[23] Eisenstadt, *Political Systems of Empires,* 177, 181–182.
[24] *Ibid.,* 178.

or an ancestor occupied an Imperial grant or, in some cases, was elevated from more obscure origins to take a particular command and the estates that accompanied it. The mythicizing of this punctual event erased fact and punctual time by, first, defining use of the land as a literal constant: as the land had existed forever so the family must have always occupied it, and "time out of mind" —out of history—the two were joined.

The genesis of the dynasty was taken back into myth-time, to founding fathers or figures who filled out the same part as the god or hero ancestors of the Greek aristocracy of the Archaic period.[25] The great Armenian houses of the 9th century, to whom many Byzantine dynasts had direct affinities, claimed to trace their origins to Joshua, David the King, Assyrian monarchs and, of course, the Armenian Arsacid line.[26] These royal progenitors are considered by the aristocrat as exactly that, however: founders not of an idea of kingship but of a line, a sacred series of generations; their royalty is measured by their potency in the most direct possible fashion. And, the propaganda of aristocracy claimed not only that blood-time eliminated data-time or history, but also that power—pure or *mana*-authority—inhered not in mere property or economic base, but in the abstracted Name of the family, expressing a sovereignty, a ruling force, over the abstracted Land —the area within which this power was eternally effective.

The result of these processes was the creation of a countermyth to that of the city, a countermyth that opposed its own nonhistoric reading of the significances of time and space. In place of the city's ritual existence in durative time, measured by eternally reënergized cycles and directed by the always renewed type of the King-Emperor, the aristocratic time-myth substitutes the renewal cycle of the generations, of time measured by blood and semen. In place of the city's hyperstasizing of its material shell, its evolution of the iconic formula that allows to every significant mass or matter the means to escape itself, the aristocrat etherealizes his own base, theorizes himself free of the solidity of the land

[25] G. Glotz, *The Greek City and Its Institutions* (New York, 1929), 39 ff, 46 ff.

[26] L. Laurent, *L'Arménie entre Byzance et l'Islam depuis la conquète Arabe jusqu'en 886* (Paris, 1919), 69 ff.

into a dream of naked *mana*, filled with the reverberations of his Name.

The Byzantine landed aristocracy was never allowed to take a completely feudal stance, and this was true partly because other alternatives were kept open to them—for example, entrance into and service in the civil bureaucracy.[27] Still, the "Imperial centuries," when the dominance of the city and the Emperor in the city were most complexly and completely worked out, showed evidence of other possibilities and the tentative growth of powers other than the Imperial.

(a) The very existence of an identifiable landed aristocracy, the fact that it flourished and could not be uprooted, was significant enough.

(b) The growing antagonism of this nobility to the dominant Center, or more especially to the hierarchy of bureaucrats that operated from there, was visible already in the 10th century.[28] It was explicit in the acts of the military emperors, of Nicephoras Phokas and John Tzimiskes—both Armeno-Greeks and aristocrats—and implicit in the attitude of some of the historian-chronographers. Even Basil II, the last effective ruler of the Macedonian house, was enough influenced by the exigencies and mental sets of war and the soldier to be indifferent, if not hostile, to his bureaucracy.

(c) The military posture of the State, at the moment of its greatest successes, was slowly moving off the bases set up in earlier centuries, and was being strongly affected by certain centrifugal social currents.

Any movement toward a feudal decentralization, or a major breakup or fracture of State powers is liable to be seen first in the area where the State mobilizes its armed strength, and both points (b) and (c) bear on this possibility in Byzantium. In the 10th century, after long years in which both the tradition and theory of Imperial warmaking was defensive, the Byzantines went over to an offensive posture and moved in strength beyond the

[27] E. Kantorowicz, "Byzantine Feudalism," in R. Coulborn, ed., *Feudalism in History* (Princeton, 1956), 151–152.
[28] Dendias, "Études," 137.

Taurus and into northern Syria and Mesopotamia. By the end of the century they were campaigning in the north as well, and the Bulgarian kingdom would be nearly erased before they were done. Byzantine high strategy, in other words, turned 180°, and though the Empire did not seek expansion as an end in itself, it showed marked tendencies in this direction.[29] Why was this so?

One reason was the tempting fragmentation of the Caliphate, the Old Enemy, whose northern exposure was less and less well protected by secessionist emirates—and yet Byzantium did not launch a crusade, much less a Holy War, unless the campaigns of the fanatic Nicephoras Phokas fall under this heading.[30] The Bulgars to the north were also alternately weak and truculent, and an Emperor-general like Basil II might have been moved by either reaction to rationalize the threatened frontier by giving up an elaborate defensive diplomacy and moving his borders smartly up to the line of the Danube again. But more than strategic considerations were involved. In the case of the Byzantine move southward it is suggested that the military élite of the State, the great families of the border who had guarded the frontier for so long, made their move to increase the land available to them for exploitation.[31] The land, in this view, was an area of investment, the only one open in a society where commerce was severely restricted, and so Byzantine expansionism sprang from the land hunger of cramped nobles who also happened to lead the thematic corps—the old militia army.

That army itself was changed in composition, in effectiveness, and in its loyalties to the State. By the end of the 10th century, even by the middle of that century, it is clear that the thematic troops of the great Anatolian themes were loyal first to their commanders, the representatives of the magnate families of the theme, and then to the Throne. The Macedonian dynasty lost the battle for the loyaly of its smallholder peasant soldiers; these could not be protected from the land appetite of the nobility by

[29] We note that while Antioch was taken, no serious attempt was made on Jerusalem, which had no strategic value in Syria-Palestine.

[30] For Nicephoros as "crusader" see CMH **IV**, 1, 149–150; also G. Schlumberger, *Un empereur byzantin au dixième siècle, Nicéphore Phocas* (Paris, 1890).

[31] C. Neumann, *Die Weltstellung des byzantinischen Reiches vor den Kreuzzugen* (Leipzig, 1894), 24.

any functional Imperial legislation, no matter how often the edicts went out against encroachment.[32] More, the Imperial house had lost another battle, for the *dynatoi* had made their appeal to the imagination of the countryside and won.

The famous edict of Nicephoras Phokas, which established the value of a military estate (*stratiotika ktema*) at twelve gold pounds rather than four as earlier, shows that the composition of the thematic armies had changed—certainly their armament was increased, and with it their tactics, and their numbers were fewer.[33] In any case their dubious loyalty was decisive in convincing the Imperial house that it must rely on other troops, recruited in other ways. The *tagmata* or Guards regiments based in Constantinople had always included foreigners, but not in tactically significant numbers. Basil II, however, resorted to the hiring of foreign mercenaries *en masse*—the 6000 Slavo-Norse "Varangians" lent by Vladimir of Kiev—to put down the aristocratic rebel Bardas Phocas, and thereafter professional mercenaries formed the nucleus of the Byzantine army in its declining years.[34] With the adoption of a mercenary army for the first time in four centuries, the cost of waging war naturally increased, and with it the strain on the treasury. The inefficiency of the new system, especially when combined with the sad and disaffected remains of the old theme system, was seen on the disastrous field of Manzikert in 1071. The collapse of the military effectiveness of the themes, which began with the alienation from the Center of the smallholder militia, was naturally followed by a collapse of administrative responsibilities in the provinces, and eventually by the appearance of the semifeudal *pronoia* system of the late 11th century and after, which handed over military responsibilities and administrative action on the estate-sized *pronoia* to some "knight."[35]

"Byzantine feudalism" will develop as a forced alternative to re-

[32] See especially Romanus I Lecapenus' novels of 922 and 934 (Dolger, *Regesten* I, 72, 77); Constantine VII's edict of 947 (Dolger, *Regesten* I, 656).

[33] Neumann, *Weltstellung*, 56.

[34] Vasilievskii, "Druzhina," passim; Ostrogorsky, *History of the Byzantine State*, 293.

[35] G. Ostrogorskij, *Pour l'histoire de la féodalité byzantine* (*Corpus Bruxellense Historiae Byzantinae*, subs. I, Brussels, 1954), 9 ff.

sponsible central authority, a makeshift device to shore up the defenses of the State and to provide administrative services—services no longer extended from the Center—in return for freedom from taxation. In the 10th century, the great century of the city, the way was being prepared for this fatal diminution of responsibility. The city was separating itself from its hinterland, leaving that hinterland in the control of a greedy and ambitious landed nobility. The social and political conditions necessary to produce a true "feudal" hierarchy were not present, but the prejudices and fixed views that would fatally sever country from city were there on the land.[36]

Decentralization and rebellion. A centrifugal tendency in a landbased and military aristocracy, its movement away from the core of monarchic power, is most dramatically represented by rebellion and other sure proofs of disaffection. A rebellion, however, is a complex reaction involving a series of motives and accidents; it may be the culmination of an urge to pull away, to escape the gravitational force of the Center; it may also be an attempt to seize that Center in order to control it. Insofar as the developing aristocracy expressed itself in rebellion, we can see a pendular movement from one motive to the other, a hesitation, but the important fact is the aristocracy's willingness to undertake *apostasia*—the "standing away."

This thrust of the aristocracy toward the perverse release of rebellion is clear enough in the 9th and 10th century sources. In the century between the accession of the Macedonian house and the accession of the aristocrat Nicephoras Phokas, the Imperial domestic peace was shattered, generation after generation, by the gentry. The patrician Romanus Curcuas, of the Armenian warrior family, rebelled, failed, and was blinded in 877;[37] Nicephoras Phokas (ancestor of the Emperor) in 897;[38] Andronicos and Constantine Dukas and Eustathios Argyros;[39] Leo Phokas,[40] Bardas Boelas (*Strategos* of Chaldia),[41] Basil Pateinos and his fellow

[36] *Ibid.*, 14.
[37] Cedrenus **II**, 213.
[38] *Ibid.*, 256–257.
[39] *Ibid.*, 263–264, 267–269, 278.
[40] *Ibid.*, 288–295.
[41] *Ibid.*, 302.

conspirators—ranked as patricians, one of the family of Lips.[42] This list does not count the successful coups, as when Marianos Argyros, Nicephoras and Leo Phokas, and two of the Tornikios family overthrew the sons of Romanus I Lecapenus and replaced Constantine VII, of the legitimate Macedonian line, on the throne[43]—or pseudo-aristocratic uprisings, such as that led by Basil "called the Macedonian" who pretended to be the lost but risen Constantine Dukas and gathered support on these grounds alone.[44] Nor does the list include the reign of Basil II, when the great rebellions of Bardas Skleros and Bardas Phokas wrecked the theme system forever.

Admittedly the *centrifugal* tendency of the aristocratic defection remains to be proved. Other attempted coups aimed directly at the Center and were staged by disgruntled or ill-rewarded bureaucrats such as Anastasius the Sacellarius in 920,[45] or John Mystikos and Cosmas the Logothete in 925.[46] The Dukades struck directly at Constantinople, and we can take it that in no case did a rebel plan *de jure* secession from the Empire: there was no vocabulary to describe secession or the territorial dissolution of the body politic. In most cases, also, our information is extremely scanty; we have merely the names of ringleaders, their rank, and the disposition of their cases when they failed—mutilation, exile, forced entry into a monastery, sometimes death—but we do not have the slogans they used or what, if anything, they intended to reform.

It must be true that rebels who were identifiably connected with the administration of the themes used the thematic troops to back their rebellion, and when this occurred (as in the case of Bardas Boelas, and later Bardas Skleros and Bardas Phokas) a rupture of any effective political linkage between city and theme was clear. The thematic troops may have marched to readjust what their leaders saw as deficiencies in the Imperial headquarters, or to enforce a different reading of the will of God, in

[42] *Ibid.*, 327.
[43] *Ibid.*, 324; see S. Runciman, *The Emperor Romanus Lecapenus and His Reign* (Cambridge, 1963), 232–237.
[44] Cedrenus **II**, 315.
[45] *Ibid.*, 298.
[46] *Ibid.*, 307.

the time-honored Byzantine fashion, by changing Emperors. This was "constitutional," in the Byzantine sense. But the act of rebellion must also be a celebration of a separate mode of power, and every aristocratic rebel-general pulled his men farther from the Imperial idea of a unitary state. The great double rebellion of Phokas and Skleros was the most dramatic representation of aristocratic centrifugism, for the houses of the *dynatoi*, their appetites whetted by their compeers, the Emperors Nicephoras Phokas and John Tzimiskes, had no intention of being excluded from the exercise of power: when Basil II obstructed them and, later, the civil service occupied and monopolized the places of power, the magnates strengthened their position on the land and dismantled the last remnants of the old loyalty of the theme to the provident city. When the magnates moved back into the city and into power again after Manzikert—a disaster they helped to prepare—the defensive and administrative network in the Anatolian provinces was moribund; the ganglial network of government no longer operated, because a great part of the society no longer responded to impulses from the Center.[47]

The decentralizing movement of the landed nobility went forward on a number of levels: one was more purely economic, involving the agglomeration of smaller holdings into larger estates by whatever means, and the accompanying reduction of the smallholders (whether peasant militiamen or members of the communes) to a sort of dependence, in the face of Imperial legislation and the Imperial plan and will.[48] Land, in this fashion, was converted to power, power separated from its theoretical source in the Throne. Another level was administrative, as the *strategoi* of the themes readapted their offices to their own private or socially separate purposes, using their delegated power as absolute power within their jurisdiction.[49] A third level was emotional: the myth of the city was opposed by other myths, the propaganda of Imperial solidarity and unity was opposed by appeals to family and name, a warrior ethic, a noncity or anticity

[47] R. Jenkins, *The Byzantine Empire on the Eve of the Crusades* (London, 1953), 17.

[48] Ostrogorskij, *Pour l'histoire*, 12 ff.

[49] Eisenstadt, *Political Systems of Empires*, 177, 180, 183.

behavioral pattern and way of life and thought. This is an important separate problem in itself.

The allies of the aristocracy. The separatism of the aristocracy, as it acted against the concentrative and unitary instincts and actions of the Imperial office, was dangerously reinforced when joined with other dissident elements. The problem here does not center so much on those groups within the Byzantine structure that were attracted by the aristocracy and, because of this, moved "outward"—to the periphery of the society, as it were—into temporary or permanent alliance. The fact that the landed aristocracy did at last absorb the loyalties of the smallholder is important, and also that the bureaucracy, or segments of it, would occasionally be tempted by the *panache* and visible power of the nobility. These groups provided mass support, or valuable skills, but they did not themselves pull the aristocracy away from the core of the society. Other groups might do this, especially "national" minorities—groups partially defined by their own, consciously received cultural heritage, and partially defined by labels attached to them by the Center, of which the most inclusive was *exotikoi*—strangers. The unrealistic arrogance of such a label was particularly threatening to the health of the Empire when the "strange" people were as closely interwoven into the fabric of Empire as were the Armenians.

The flow of Armenians into Byzantium from the 6th century onward, and their energetic intervention in the history of the Byzantine state has been often underscored: the Empire of the 9th and 10th centuries has even been labeled "Graeco-Armenian," because of the numbers and the prominence of Armenian personalities, or, more precisely, of identifiable Armenian names and families.[50] Researches aimed at outlining or filling out an Armenian prosopography in Byzantium, however, merely touch the surface of a problem at once social and "national." The degree of acceptance or assimilation of a strong Armenian minority depended on a number of conditions, one of the most consequential being the social level of the migrant—if it can be determined. An Armenian of a lower social stratum, once he had broken his traditional familial ties, would accept a culture that promised him

50 Charanis, *Armenians,* 57.

upward mobility—would Hellenize—more rapidly and completely than an Armenian of, for example, the *nakharar* class, whose status was already set by his adherence to the forms and attitudes of Armenian feudalism. No social formula can be cut and dried when our data are as illusive and fragmentary as they are, but it is probable that Armenians—especially the *nakharar* cavalry—who passed over into the Empire and were settled in the hinterland, in the embattled themes, could and would maintain their national-cultural identity and with it their imported social hierarchy more easily than other groups. In *this* group germinated the great Armenian families who began to dominate the Anatolian, and later the European, theme governments: the Phokades, Dukades, Skleroi, Tornikioi. Armenians of lower status were more likely to be attracted to the Imperial capital, where they had nothing to lose and much to gain by entering the city-centered bureaucracy, or otherwise adapting themselves to the cultural and political schema of the Empire. Most prominent among these were, of course, the two adventurers Basil, founder of the Macedonian line, and Romanus Lecapenus, both of whom rose from obscure (but definitely Armenian) origins to the Imperial office, and stood for the most comprehensive Byzantine autocracy and statism.[51]

If there was, as is likely, a social or socio-economic determinant in the separation of Armenian immigrants into more or less assimilable types, this determinant was not absolute. The Macedonian house did not abjure its Armenian connections; on the contrary, Armenians found good positions under Basil—who had himself been befriended by an official of Armenian extraction—and the rest of his house.[52] Armenians in the central bureaucracy, as we know in at least one instance, kept up their own language.[53] Armenians of the military aristocracy also were found in the city, and took up positions there. The point is that Armenian connections, when combined with aristocratic birth and the likelihood of high provincial office that was increasingly associated with

[51] Der Nersessian, *Armenia and the Byzantine Empire*, 21.
[52] Charanis, *Armenians,* 25 n. 70.
[53] The case of Krikorikios: Charanis, *Armenians,* 41; Adontz, "Les Taronites," 535–540.

aristocratic birth, added another divisive element to those already deforming the relationship between countryside and city. Romanus Lecapenus, who had outmaneuvered one Armeno-Greek aristocrat, Leo Phokas, to gain the throne, soon faced a serious rising under the *strategos* of the Chaldian theme, Bardas Boelas, an Armenian in a heavily Armenized territory, whose revolt was assisted by Adrianos the "Chaldian" and Tatzates the Armenian.[54] The revolts of Bardas Skleros and Bardas Phokas were heavily dependent on Armenian troops, especially that of Skleros.[55] Some years before the Byzantine elimination of the independent Armenian principalities and the transfer of masses of Armenians to Cappadocia and Cilicia—an event often blamed for the enmity that burst out between the two cultures—the Armenian minority was expressing its hostility to the State, especially in border areas where the degree of assimilation into the Imperial society of that minority was slight, and Armenian nationality most resistant. This mutual hostility reinforced, if it did not cause, the separatist gestures of a landed military aristocracy that was largely Armenian. The response of the government to this dangerous inclination was, in part, to assure a system of rewards to those who *did* show loyalty to the Throne, but also, it seems, to recruit more widely among other minorities, especially Syrian Arabs and Turks. We have the examples in the 10th century of Samonas, the Byzantine Fouché; also the admiral Nasar,[56] the patrician Abessalom, son of Arotras,[57] the Hetairarch Theodore Zuphinezer,[58] while Turkic names become more common in the lower bureaucratic ranks, and at least one Governor-General was known to have been of Turkish origin (John Bogas, *strategos* of Cherson).[59]

The exclusive but expansive nature of Byzantine civilization, its arrogant political egocentrism, guaranteed that the more culturally complex or resistant minorities would rebel from time to time if leadership were generated or made available. At the

[54] Cedrenus **II**, 302.
[55] Charanis, *Armenians,* 34.
[56] Theophanes Cont., 298 ff.
[57] Cedrenus **II**, 281.
[58] *Ibid.,* 291.
[59] See G. Moravcsik, *Byzantinoturcica* **II**, 92, s.v.

beginning of the 9th century the great rebellion of Thomas the Sclavonian drew on every minority in Anatolia—Saracens, "Indians," "Medes," Assyrians, "Egyptians," Abasgians, Zichs, Chaldoi, "Vandals," "Getae," Alans, Armenians, and heretical minorities such as Paulicians and Athinganoi.[60] Thomas was no dissident magnate and his rebellion was more in the nature of a class war, a *jacquerie*, which is said to have traumatized and dispossessed the lower classes so severely that the spread of aristocratic domainal holdings in Anatolia was sharply accelerated. Following on Thomas' rising the separatistic feelings of minorities—especially the Armenians—shifted and recoalesced around the rising military aristocracy. The Macedonian dynasty fought for the loyalty of these minority groups—again, especially the Armenians—as it fought for the smallholders and the peasant militia, offering the protection of the Imperial system against the landlust of the Powerful, offering the opportunities and upward mobility within the city, and opposing a counterpropaganda to the attractions of the aristocratic ideal. Their offers were eventually rejected—not by a "nation" of Armenians, but by individuals who felt that the Greek Empire, and the great capital of that Empire, did not welcome them, or exacted too high a price for its welcome.

Another minority that stood outside the city and in its own way recruited adherents for the cause of the military aristocracy, was the mixture of heretical sects whose base was in Anatolia. Armenians who kept allegiance to their own faith do not fall into this category, though the non-Chalcedonian Armenian church was regarded by the Greeks as nonorthodox and nonorthodox Armenians were segregated within the city like the other nonorthodox sects.[61] The most dramatic opponents to oecumenical—Orthodox—Christianity in the eastern themes were dualistic Paulicians, mentioned with the smaller group of the Athinganoi in the roster of Thomas the Sclavonian's rebels. The Paulicians were recognized as an enemy of the Empire in the early 8th century, and in their main breeding ground on the upper Euphrates were accused of "poisoning the Armenians"; and they were anathematized by

[60] Theophanes Continuatus 55.
[61] See Chapt. 1, footnote 37.

each successive Armenian *catholikos* as well as by the Orthodox hierarchy. As in the case of most heresies, their doctrines are difficult to reconstruct out of the welter of orthodox polemic that was directed against them; they were certainly dualist, anti-sacramentarian, iconoclastic, and puritanical.[62] Unlike most dualistic or Manichaean sects they appealed to the sword, and with resounding success. They created a flourishing network of fortress-towns in the *Zwischenland* between the territories of the Empire and those of the Caliphate, and when the Empire, in the 9th century, attempted to reduce them they fought back with ferocity and considerable success. The Paulicians allied themselves with the Arabs, and only a series of major campaigns (and the death of their most brilliant general) broke their resistance. Remnants of their sect lingered along the border for a century, until John Tzimiskes transferred them to Thrace.[63]

There is no direct and provable tie between the Paulician heresy and the rise of the feudalizing military aristocracy in Anatolia. The Paulicians fell in with the classes that supported Thomas the Sclavonian in the early 9th century, and presumably the terrible persecution that pursued them had the same effect as the social war waged against Thomas: that of emptying the countryside, impoverishing the smallholders, and aiding the spread of large-estate holdings. Many of the Paulicians were certainly Armenian, but their appeal reached the Greeks as well: both Carbeas and Chrysocheir, the great warchiefs of the sect, were of Greek ancestry.[64] Nor is there any way to determine whether or not the dualistic puritanism of the Paulicians appealed to the military aristocracy. *If* we can assume that the military classes of Anatolia were infected through and through with iconoclastic poisons, which is not at all certain, then some sympathy for the iconoclastic Paulicians may have lingered along the border and among the bordering nobles.

The parallels between the Anatolian military aristocracy and the militant sect are found in ideas and attitudes. Both removed

[62] S. Runciman, *The Medieval Manichee: A Study of the Christian Dualist Heresy* (Cambridge, 1955), 49–51.
[63] *Ibid.*, 44.
[64] *Ibid.*, 41.

themselves far from the Center dominated by the Emperor and his bureaucracy; both found the borders, the inaccessible frontier zones, congenial; both found relations with their fellow frontiersmen on the Arab side of the border easy and attractive. Some sort of fellow-feeling is certain, for in the epic-balladic celebration of aristocratic mores and virtues in, especially, the cycle called Akritic, involving the archetypal border noble, Digenes Akritas, the Paulicians appear, and their resistance to Imperial power, if not their doctrines, is indirectly praised.

Aristocratic Culture

City myth and country epic. The secession of the military aristocracy from the city, their creation of a detached, decentralized political mode and a separate societal view, was not possible without widespread support. To gain this support the landed Powerful had to build and maintain their own *topos* and mode of life; they then had to create a myth as well, one of their own devising celebrating their values and accomplishments. This myth moved to counter the myth of the Center: the myth of Imperial unity, supreme and unquestioned power in the oecumene, sacred and secular excellence.

The literature that powerfully prepared the way for the popular acceptance of aristocratic mores was not disseminated as propaganda, however well it succeeded as propaganda. Its origins are obscure, springing from the country courts held by provincial magnates and, more important, from the land itself, from the peasant communes and frontier villages. Eventually balladic and epic fragments might be combined to make a whole, by unknown "authors." The source of this literature is not as important to this study, at least, as what it says and when it appears, and the effect it obviously had on the popular consciousness of Byzantium.[65]

The chronology of the so-called "heroic age" of Byzantium can be deduced from the epic songs; identifiable events and identifiable figures place the first of them in the early 9th century, when great blows were being struck at one another by both Islam and the Empire across the Anatolian massif. The dramatic and trau-

[65] See J. Mavrogordato's introduction to *Digenis Akritas* (Oxford, 1956), xv, xxvi, lxxix ff.

matic siege of Amorium is one epic incident, and later the expedition of Michael III across the Euphrates.[66] Michael III, assiduously slandered and his memory damned by the Macedonian house-historians, had his revenge in the developing epic, for after him the Emperor-hero retreats to a subsidiary rôle, replaced by a protagonist who is of noble family and who upholds a knightly ideal. The family of the Argyri is already seen in one of the early ballads, but the aristocrats most beloved of the epic poet-bards were the Dukades. The adventurous lives and tragic fates of Andronikos and Constantine Dukas, who rebelled against Leo VI, formed the core of several ballads: Constantine was transmogrified into the "foe of the tyrant," who fought and lost and became the Prisoner.[67] Constantine's fate was obviously the stuff of legend, so that another rebel (Basil, a "Macedonian") could rally popular support by claiming to be Constantine returned from death.

The arch-noble family of Dukas also has a leading rôle in the great Akritic cycle: the epic of Digenes the Borderer. Digenes himself is a Dukas (or a Kinnamos, another aristocratic family name) on his mother's side: her father is Andronikos, her brother, Constantine. Digenes' wife too is a Dukas, daughter of "Dukas the General." On his father's side the "Twy-Born" Digenes is Arab, though two of his uncles have been tentatively identified not as Arabs but as Paulician generals (Chrysoberges or Chrysoherpes=Chrysocheir; Karoes=Carbeas).[68] Another historical figure who resurfaces in a strange guise in the Akritic ballads is the great Armenian general Melias (Mleh), here called Melimitzes.[69] There is also an Emperor (Basil or Romanos) in a very subsidiary rôle.

The importance of the Digenid cycle does not lie in names and identifications; these are deceptively readable points in the palimpsest. The cycle describes attitudes and, if not a way of life, a knightly dream of a way of life, which deserts the city and its materialized rituals for a separated state, one ruled by other im-

[66] H. Gregoire, "L'Âge héroique de Byzance," *Mélanges offerts à M. Nicolas Iorga* (Paris, 1933), 388.
[67] *Ibid.*, 390–395.
[68] See the geneology of Digenes; Mavrogordato, *Digenes Akrites* 254–255.
[69] *Digenes Akrites,* 189, line 2888; see Intro., liii.

peratives. Digenes is a noble (*ex eugenōn Romaiōn*) and his epic existence is a reprise of aristocratic dream-images.[70] Even his Christianity sits lightly on him, for spiritually as well as physically he crosses the border between Orthodoxy and Islam; he is certainly no crusader. His life is spent hobnobbing with Saracen and Christian alike, and his funeral draws mourners from both sides of the frontier: "Charzanians, Kappadokians . . . Tarsites, Marounites . . . Elect Bagdadis . . . Nobles from Babylon, many from Amida . . . ."[71] More Moslem than Christian placenames are mentioned in this list, and one observer has said that most of Digenes' named opponents are "nominally" Christian.[72] The Paulician influence detected in the poem is certainly not doctrinal, and there is no dualistic influence at all.[73]

Digenes' life is, in fact, Arabized without being Islamized; his attitude toward religion is that of the Anatolian frontier nobleman who fled to the Caliphate at need and had been known to apostasize. Conversion in the epic is casual. Digenes defends his own territory against all comers, and the combats take place between warrior-knights, not ideologues. Though the Type of the "borderer," Digenes is barely effective as such; he is assigned a territory but nowhere in the epic does he actually protect the frontier against the raging hordes of Islam. Digenes is first an aristocrat, then a knightly warrior. As an aristocrat, he is defined by his bloodline—placed in a generational context, according to kinship ties—then provided with a task: a working out of the individualized *areté* of the noble.

The Borderer chooses a life far from any city; for most of his brief life he lives in a tent, in the middle of a vaguely paradisical wilderness. He challenges and is challenged to knightly combat. He carries off and marries a noble Girl, who provides little more than a slight erotic edge to the tale. He is given two opportunities to stray sexually and takes reasonably prompt advantage of both, but in neither is any emotional complexity visible (whatever the psychic roots of the Amazon who appears in the tale), and abso-

70 The phrase "well-born" is repeated some fifty times in Mavrogordato's edition.

71 *Digenes Akrites*, 245, lines 3741–3746.

72 *Digenes Akrites*, Intro., xvi.

73 *Digenes Akrites*, Intro., lxiv.

lutely nothing of the love-death neuroses of the chivalric literature of the medieval West—quite the contrary.[74] His adventures are carried out with superhuman *brio* but he has only one supernatural foe, and there are no allegorical convolutions. In the text that survives to us he eventually builds a noble mansion, loses both parents, then his wife, and dies.

The aristocratic dream existence described in the Digenid sounds trifling when briefly outlined; it seems to be condensation of uncomplex, dramatically naïve fantastications. So it undoubtedly is. The epic quality, however, is there: a virility and cheerful bloodlust, a warrior ethos and a moral simplicity. And, as a fantasy of the military nobility of the frontier the Digenid and its fellows had an impact that both reflected and reinforced the centrifugal currents of the 9th and 10th centuries. In the Digenid the young hero-aristocrat, whose fame has spread everywhere, is visited by the Emperor—Digenes himself does not go to the city. He lectures the monarch on the responsibilities of kingship, performs a feat or two, and leaves the storybook king marveling. He receives the wardenship of the marches as his reward.[75] Other than this Digenes has no contact with the abstractions of power; his aristocracy is implicit and confident, without any hint of tragic confrontations or alternative possibilities.

The Digenid epic obviously shows a nobility firmly entrenched in its own self-defined cosmos. Authority in this cosmos comes with birth and blood and is recognized, not generated or authenticated, by a monarchy that is distant and exotic. Place and status are ascriptive and implicit, and are reinforced by personal excellence—there is a fine epic recollection of the old Greek confusion of physical and moral beauty. The aristocratic definition replaces any idea of citizenship or nationality as membership in a state. There is no opposition between *Romaios* and *Sarakenos*; the epic itself is known to borrow from Arab types, especially the *Gesta* of the frontier hero Sidi Baṭṭal, but in the Digenid a true amalgam is reached between a tone of relaxed sensuality and the

[74] D. de Rougemont, *Love in the Western World* (New York, 1956), 32–35, 42 ff.
[75] *Digenes Akrites,* 133–141, lines 2050–2168.

muscular and athletic obsessions that are more typically Greek.[76] The aristocratic definition also eliminates the confrontation between Christian and Moslem. The culture of nobility is tolerant, sensual, athletic—often bilingual (both Digenes and his father use both Greek and Arabic, and no one has much difficulty communicating with the opposition).[77] The relaxation shown in the Digenid was not to continue forever, of course, and could be called a victim of the passing of power from Arabic to Turkic Islam in the 11th century.

The point to be remembered about the Digenes poems and the rest of the literature connected to an aristocratic culture is this: the poetry was popular, and the images it drew were impressed on the imagination of the mass of Byzantines, rivaling, overshadowing, and even replacing the myths that emanated from the Center. The decline of the city's attractive myths had to weaken the city itself, and the attraction of a noncity ethos for the country population had to push city and village even farther apart. This process could go on only so far before the rupture of vital lines of reinforcement and efficient power doomed both city and village and the unity of Empire they constituted.

[76] *Digenes Akrites,* Intro., lxii ff.
[77] *Ibid.,* lxxix.

Epilog: The Failure of the City

A difficulty—perhaps *the* difficulty—in recreating the modular structure that approximately represents the forces and objects, the ideas and institutions of some state-in-history, is that once recreated this modular structure claims a place of its own, a real existence we as its contrivers are reluctant to deny. Students of Byzantine history and civilization are pressed or impressed even more strongly by their recreations, because the state and society they examine was declared invalid and immaterial by modern Western historiography as that historiography made its first assumptions. Byzantium was debunked before it began; its growth was attached in advance to the decline, the long regretted degenerescence, of the Antique World. By the time the fate of the "Later Roman Empire" or "Bas-empire" was reexamined and began to claim its own specialists, the damage was nearly done. Byzantium received only a little more justice from the liberal historiographical schools of the 19th century than it had from Gibbon, and by the mid-20th century, despite the accumulation of a respectably vast number of data and analyses of data, historians concerned with the Empire still have to push aside or patiently explain away dense masses of pseudo-metaphors and plain misconceptions about their subject: the noncreativity and cultural nullity of the Empire, its theological rigidity and absurdism, its unmanly diplomacy, its sly and subtle—un-Western—social and cultural tone, and so on and so on. Defending themselves from these prejudices against the Realm of Blood, Byzantinists can easily become petulant and intellectually resistant and crossgrained. Their recreations or models become more fragile and more precious than all others, and are defended with more scholastic—or Byzantine—ferocity. I hope I have avoided this.

This study has tried to describe the organism of a great city, the capital of a great Empire, at the top of its historical parabola, at a time when its shapes and powers were clearest. Implicit in the description of this organism is its fallibility or failure, its failure to endure in time, for Constantinople—and Byzantium—declined from the preëminence it held in the oecumene of what I have vaguely called the 10th century, and it declined catastrophically. As an historical datum, composed of perceivable and evidential fact, the catastrophic decline is deceptively easy to describe, and has been frequently described.[1] It is also easy to produce, by simple description, a rich dramatic coda: the majesty and preëminent power of the Empire at the death of Basil II, in 1025, can be put over against the equally manifest inability of the same Empire to recover from the pressures exerted on it as the century wore on. "Suddenly" all the vital juices are gone. The Empire slips from its prime to senility without any intervening stages. If this cannot be accepted, then the "prime" of the Empire becomes suspect. Was Byzantium under Basil really as strong as it appeared to be? Obviously not, and we have to ask why not.

If the parabolic pattern of Byzantine historical development is somewhat flattened a fair amount of drama escapes. Certainly the tenacity of the truncated and mutilated Empire after 1071, and again after the Latin occupation of 1204–1269, has to be admitted, together with the cultural vitality that always seems to have returned, to produce rich things in a small space. Nor was this tenacity simply the stubborn inertia of senile dissolution. Byzantium made its way between the neurotic strength of the Medieval West and the new powers of Asia by showing more flexibility and inventiveness than a senile society should or could have shown. But as this is recognized, the accomplishments of the

[1] C. Neumann, *Die Weltstellung des byzantinisches Reiches vor den Kreuzzugen* (Leipzig, 1894); J. Hussey, "The Byzantine Empire in the Eleventh Century: Some Different Interpretations," *Transactions of the Royal Historical Society,* Fourth Series (XXXII, 1950), 71–85; P. Charanis, "The Byzantine Empire in the Eleventh Century," *A History of the Crusades,* ed. Setton and Baldwin, I (Philadelphia, 1958), 177–219; Sp. Vryonis, "Byzantium: The Social Basis of Decline in the Eleventh Century," *Greek, Roman and Byzantine Studies* 2 (1959), 159–175; R. Jenkins, *The Byzantine Empire on the Eve of the Crusades* (London, 1953).

10th century too must be reevaluated and diluted, and it is especially necessary to see the unfortunate long-range results of the aggressive expansionism of the soldier-emperors, and the reality of the insufficient base of resources that was supposed to support this expansionism and could not. This fault lies on the level of policy of state, and there are others.

To return to the subject of this study: it might be profitable to examine the hypothesis that the failure of the Empire depended strongly on the failure of the city. The most singular construction of Byzantine civilization was its city, a point that metaphorically compressed and included all, and recapitulated the Empire. As both a synchronic and diachronic historical phenomenon the city drew into itself so much of the life of the Empire that it must not have been merely a capital, an administrative and cultural center, but a synecdoche—or at least this is what it aimed to be in a healthy state. When the state was *not* healthy, the city must bear responsibility to some degree. How true is this in Constantinople's case? How did the Myth of the City fail?

Constantinople was conceived as a city-icon, where mass and spirit reinforced one another. Its material power and its spiritual force were regarded both from within the city and from the Empire at large, as perfected and central. But the centrality of the city gradually hardened and became sclerotic; the icon began to be worshipped in its own right by those who lived in it; even more, by those—specifically the bureaucracy—who felt that the city was not so much an icon, vibratory and luminescent, but a mechanism, a machine that they operated, a series of techniques that they commanded. These city dwellers gladly acted to separate the city from what they regarded as the inert matter outside it. The attitudes of Michael Psellos are typical enough of bureaucratic group feeling and snobbery, though Psellos added a hyperintellectualism and egoism all his own.

The bureaucrat could ignore the nonurban population, but he could not ignore another power group, the military aristocracy. These he resented, schemed against, hoped to drive from the seat of power. The bureaucracy of the 10th century had been forced to the side while the soldiers marched and the boundaries of the Empire moved outward. Then, at Basil II's death, the bureaucrats did their best to dismantle the military machine that had gained the victories. The fact that the frontiers were not secure, that there were as always new enemies, was kept from them by their isolation in the impregnable city. The lines of communication to the hinterland had atrophied, the living pulse that had tied province and capital together was weak and thready.

The very culture of the city, nurtured by the bureaucratic obsession with graphic patterns, received traditions, more or less subtle rhetorical statement, proved too precious, in the wrong sense, to keep a broad attractive value. Byzantine high culture was never, of course, widely disseminated, any more than any high culture is, but the mandarinesque rigidifying of cultural attitudes visible in men like Psellos marked a new level of inwardness and resistance to change or influence. The *Greek* emphasis of this culture was probably no more notable than in other periods in the Empire's cultural life, but it was less tolerant, less accessible, more organized. Hellenisticism—"scholastic" Hellenism—stood more and more as a barrier, rather than acting as a lure, to peoples who at other times had found more welcome in Byzantium.

The most important exogenous element in the Empire, the Armenians, encountered such antagonism in the half-century between Basil's death and the battle of Manzikert that "race war" between Armenian and Greek has been seen.[2] Undoubtedly much of the abrasion between the two groups came from massive Armenian migration—many times forced—into rural areas where they soon came to dominate, but there was also rioting in Constantinople, and the antimilitary reaction of the bureaucratic clique that took power after 1025 was certainly tainted by anti-Armenian feeling. This feeling was based on more than cultural exclusivism; it stemmed from resentment and fear of the Armenian military dynasts who had won almost undisputed control of the great Anatolian themes and were potent in Europe as well. Thus the absorptive, transmuting power of the Imperial City was decreased, and the unitary civilization that had added the Christian definition of citizenship to older Imperial patterns, stiffened its back against new recruits and retreated deeper into the citadel.

[2] Jenkins, *The Byzantine Empire,* 11–12; Vryonis, "Byzantium, The Social Basis of Decline," 167–173.

Michael Psellos opposed *to politikon*—the civic, bureaucratic élite—to *to stratiotikon*—the military arm—and in this opposition there is more than a hint of a primitive racism.[3] The "city" Greek felt that he could afford to despise the "county" Armenian.

The economic policies that commanded in the Imperial City led to isolation by another way: by cutting or helping to cut the strands of economic interrelationship that gave the capital its resources. Put very simply, when the loyalty of the theme governments failed, or when for whatever reason administration in the provinces passed beyond the purview of Imperial authority, the smallholders and *stratiotai* threw in their lot with the landed gentry, and the Imperial tax-base failed as well. More, the old antagonism of the Center to native commerce brought in more and more merchant-adventurers, mostly Italians, who from their privileged position reduced this area of economic vitality to an enclave controlled by them. The decline in the native mercantile class cut back the tax-base even further; it naturally reduced economic opportunity, and eventually made the city almost a colonial dependency of foreign commercial interests. Economic dependence bred more antagonism against the exploiting outsider, and Byzantium could not make up the absolute economic loss involved, even from its fabulous storehouse of treasure. The noneconomic imperatives that directed Imperial policy—the actualization of the desire to harmonize and ritualize the human cosmos—were too successfully carried out, for after a certain crucial point the drained and insufficiently replenished Sacred Treasury was not able to sustain the necessary, real expenses of Empire. The city as Eden had a number of snakes, but a particularly venomous one was economic stringency—and eventually Eden went broke.

The sudden debilitation of the city's responses has been explained, pleonastically, as a result of the "onset of exhaustion."[4] This explanation might be better supported by referring directly to the anticausal Spenglerian schema of human-organic (or botanic) growth: civilizations are born, grow, metastasize, and die: in the midst of life we are in death. But in Byzantium's case

[3] Psellos, *Chronographia,* VII.1.
[4] Jenkins, *The Byzantine Empire,* 7.

there is insufficient evidence for exhaustion, or at least for exhaustion visible throughout the entire Imperial structure. Energy seems to be plentifully available, but it is more and more either uncontrolled or overcontrolled, and if this is true the city, which sets itself up as the point of spatial and temporal control, has failed. If the vast vitality that had fueled the Empire during darker days than would follow the disaster at Manzikert was no longer effective, it was because this vitality was either drained off into self-contained, provincial channels, modes, objectives—or was isolated and overrarified in the city, whose myth had finally collapsed in on itself.

The collapse of the city's myth must be closely involved with some fatal weakness in the Imperial figure himself, who was so closely bound up with the crystallized power of the city. Yet the fault that appeared in the Imperial control of all aspects of Empire does not seem to come from the Byzantine tradition of omnipotent, autocratic responsibility, but from a digression from this tradition. We might say that the very success of the Macedonian dynasty proved to be the undoing—however temporarily—of the Imperial office at a crucial point in time. The very establishment of a true dynasty, of an acceptance of the descent of authority in one family, interrupted the normal process of selection and testing. The Byzantine autocratic office that was in God's gift—a prize luring every sort of adventurer seeking to prove himself the new instrumentality of God—still had given space to astonishing talents, especially when the supporting élites of the State, civil and military, remained responsive and to some degree dependent. The isolation and futile gestures of the last remnants of the Macedonian house and their associates, then, stemmed partly from Byzantine overconfidence in a "lucky" house, partly from the self-separation of the bureaucratic élite from its essential loyalty and from its service roles—all added to the disaffection of the native military aristocracy. Perhaps the burden of total responsibility, total control of all modes of creativity, was too much to ask of any one man, and yet this responsibility was accepted with singular results throughout the life of the Empire, and when the responsibility was diluted the fabric of the Empire could not be kept intact.

The universalism of the Byzantine theory of state was not itself incapable of competing with and withstanding "the plurality of the middle ages."[5] Universalism was not peculiar to the Empire; the medieval West had its own universal dreams. The cultural exclusivism of the Byzantines undoubtedly rasped foreign nerves, but it was also immensely attractive. The weakness at the heart of the Byzantine system was in a hardening—whether avoidable or not we cannot say—of the iconic image, a stopping down of the systolic and diastolic flow of vitality between Center and periphery. The walls of the city had grown too high, too impermeable, and the city itself became merely a miser's horde, a store of treasure that could not move or create, waiting for the more active power that would come and seize it.

[5] *Ibid.,* 8–9.

Bibliography

PRIMARY SOURCES

Greek

Constantine Porphyrogenitus. *De administrando imperio,* ed. Moravcsik. Translated by Jenkins. Budapest, 1949.
———. *De ceremoniis aulae byzantinae,* ed. Reisk. Bonn, CSHB, 1829.
———. *Le livre des cérémonies,* ed. and transl. A. Vogt. 2 vols. and *Commentaire.* Paris, 1935.
τὸ επαρχικὸν βιβλίον. "The Book of the Prefect." Translated by A. E. R. Boak. *Journal of Economic and Business History* I (1929), 547–619.
———. Ed. Nicole. Geneva, 1893.
Eusebius of Caesarea. *Triakontaeterikos,* ed. Haekel. Leipzig, 1902.
Eustathius of Thessalonike. *Oratio ad manuelem imperator,* ed. Regel. *Fontes rerum byzantinarum* I.1, Petropoli, 1892.
Fourny, M.-H. and M. Leroy (transl.). "La Vie de S. Philarète." *Byzantion* 9 (1934), 85–170.
Geoponica sive Cassieni Bassi Scholastici de re rustica eclogae, ed. Beckh. Teubner, Lipsiae, 1895.
George Cedrenus. *Historiarum compendium,* ed. Bekker. 2 vols. Bonn, CSHB, 1838–1839.
John Cinnamus. *Historia,* ed. Meineke. Bonn, CSHB, 1836.
John Malalas. *Chronographia,* ed. Dindorf. Bonn, CSHB, 1831.
Karlin-Hayter, R. (transl.). "Vita S. Euthemii." *Byzantion* **25–27** (1955–57), 1–172, 747–778.
Leo Diaconus. *Historiae libri decem,* ed. Hase. Bonn, CSHB, 1828.
Mavrogordato, J. (ed. and transl.). *Digenes Akritas.* Oxford, 1956.
Michael Psellos, *Chronographia,* ed. Sathas. London, 1899.
———. *Chronography.* Translated by Sewter. London, 1953.
———. *De omnifaria doctrina,* ed. Westerink. Utrecht, 1948.
———. *De operatione demonorum.* Migne, PG 122.
———. *Michael Psellos Chronographie, ou Histoire d'un siècle de Byzance* (977–1077), ed. Renauld. 2 vols. Paris, 1926.
Noailles, P. and A. Dain (transl.). *Les Novelles de Leon VI le Sage. Texte et traduction publiés.* Paris, 1944.
Photius. *The Homilies of Photius Patriarch of Constantinople.* Translated by C. Mango. Cambridge, Mass., 1958.

Procopius of Caesarea. *Buildings,* ed. Haury. Translated by Dewling. (Loeb Classical Library, 1954).

Scriptores originum Constantinopolitanarum: Pseudo-Codinus origines continuens; adiecta est forma urbis Constantinopolis. II fasc. Alter. Teubner, Lipsiae, 1907.

Stethatos, Niketas. "Un grand mystique byzantin: Vie de Simeon le Nouveau Theologien, par Nicetas Stethatos." *Orientalia Christiana* **45** (July–September, 1928).

Suidas. *Suidae Lexikon,* ed. Adler. 5 vols. Leipzig, 1928–1938.

Theophanes. *Chronographia,* ed. de Boor. 2 vols. Leipzig, 1883.

Theophanes Continuatus. *Chronographia,* ed. Niebuhr. Bonn, CSHB, 1838.

Zepos, J. and P. (eds.). *Jus graecoromanum.* 8 vols. Athens, 1931.

Other Sources

Al-Husain, in Vasiliev, *Byzance et les Arabes* **II**, 425–426.

Amalarius of Metz. *Versus marini. Monumenta Germaniae Historica.* PLAC **I**, 427, 1. 38–40.

Arculfus. *The Pilgrimage of Arculfus.* (Palestine Pilgrim Text Society, **3**). London, 1897.

Harun Ibn-Yahya, in A. A. Vasiliev, "Harun Ibn-Yahya and his Description of Constantinople," *Seminarium Kondakovianum* **5** (1932), 149–163.

Liutprand of Cremona. *Legatio* and *Antapodosis,* in *The Works of Liutprand of Cremona.* Translated by Wright. London, 1930.

Marvazi, in V. Minorsky, "Marvazi on the Byzantines." *Mélanges Grégoire* II. 445–469.

Melikoff, I. (transl.). *Kissā-i Melik Dānişmend. La Geste de Melik Dānişmend.* (Bibliothèque Archéologique et Historique de l'Institut Français d'Archéologie d'Istanbul, **X**). Paris, 1960.

Michael the Syrian. *Chronique de Michel le Syrien, patriarche jacobite de Antioche: 1166–1199.* Translated by Chabot. 6 vols. Paris, 1899–1910.

Sebeos. *Histoire universelle.* Translated by Macler. Paris, 1904.

Sherbowitz-Wetzor, O. P. and S. H. Cross (eds. and transl.). *The Russian Primary Chronicle: Laurentian Text.* Cambridge, Mass., 1953.

SECONDARY SOURCES

Abel, A. "L'Apocalypse de Baḥira," *Annales de l'Institut de Philologie et d'Histoire Orientales et Slaves de l'Université de Bruxelles* **III** (1935), 1–12.

Adams, R. W. *The Evolution of Urban Society.* Chicago, 1966.

Adontz, N. "Les Taronites en Arménie et à Byzance." *Byzantion* **X** (1935), 531–551.

Andreadès, A. "Byzance, paradis du monopole et du privilège." *Byzantion* **IX** (1934), 171–181.

———. "The Jews in the Byzantine Empire." *Economic History* **III**, No. 9 (January 1934), 1–23.

———. "De la population de Constantinople sous les empereurs byzantines." *Metron* I, 2 (1920), 1–56.

Andreava, M. A. "Politicheskii i obshchestvennii element Vizantiisko-slavyanskikh gadatel'nikh knig." *Byzantinoslavica* II (1930), 47–73.

Antoniades-Bibicou, H. *Recherches sur les Douanes à Byzance.* Paris, 1963.

Bach, E. "Les lois agraires byzantines du Xiéme siècle," *Classica et Medievalia* V (1942), 70–91.

Barker, E. *Social and Political Thought in Byzantium.* Oxford, 1957.

Baynes, N. *Byzantine Studies and Other Essays.* London, 1960.

———. *The Hellenistic Civilization and East Rome.* Oxford, 1946.

——— and E. Dawes. *Three Byzantine Saints.* Oxford, 1948.

——— and H. S. B. Moss. *Byzantium.* Oxford, 1948.

Beck, H.-G. "Der byzantinische 'Ministerprasident'." *Byzantinische Zeitschrift* **48** (1955), 309–338.

Bellinger, A. R. "Coins and Byzantine Imperial Policy." *Speculum* **XXXI** (1956), 70–81.

Bloch, M. *Le roi thaumaturge: étude sur le caractère surnaturel attribué à la pussance royale particulièrement en France et an Angleterre.* Paris, 1961.

Bratianu, L. "Empire et 'démocratie' à Byzance." *Études byzantines d'histoire économique et sociale.* (Universitea mihăileană din Iaşi, IV. Paris, 1938), 93–128.

———. "Études sur l'approvisionnement de Constantinople et le monopole du blé à l'époque byzantine et ottomane." *Études byzantines,* 129–154.

———."La politique fiscale de Nicéphore Ier ou Ubu Roi à Byzance." *Études byzantines,* 183–216.

Bréhier, L. "La femme dans la famille à Byzance." *Mélanges Grégoire* **I** (Annuaire de l'Institut de Philologie et d'Histoire orientale de l'Université de Bruxelles IX, 1949), 105–108.

———. "La marine de Byzance de VIIIe au XIe siecle." *Byzantion* **19** (1949), 1–16.

———. *Le monde byzantin. La civilisation byzantine.* Paris, 1950.

———. *Le monde byzantin. Les institutions de l'Empire byzantin.* Paris, 1949.

———. "Notes sur l'histoire de l'enseignement supérieur à Constantinople." *Byzantion* **III** (1926), 73–94.

Boak, A. E. R. *The Master of Offices in the Later Roman and Byzantine Empires.* New York, 1919.

Bury, J. B. *The Constitution of the Later Roman Empire.* Cambridge, 1910.

———. *The Imperial Administrative System in the Ninth Century.* New York, 1959.

———. *Romances of Chivalry on Greek Soil.* (Romanes Lectures for 1911). Oxford, 1911.

Charanis, P. *The Armenians in the Byzantine Empire.* (Calouste Gulbenkian Foundation Armenian Library.) Lisboa, 1963.

———. "The Byzantine Empire in the Eleventh Century." Setton and Baldwin, eds., *A History of the Crusades.* Philadelphia, 1958.

———. "Some Aspects of Daily Life in Byzantium." *Greek Orthodox Theological Review* **VIII**/1, 2 (Summer 1962—Winter 1962–63): 53–70.

———. "Some Remarks on the Changes in Byzantium in the Seventh Century." *Zbornik Radova* 8, 1 (1963).

———. "The Transfer of Populations as a Policy in the Byzantine Empire." *Comparative Studies in Society and History* **III** (2) January, 1961, 140–154.

Child, V. Gordon. "The Urban Revolution." *Town Planning Review* **21** (1950), 3–17.

Choisy, A. *L'Art de batir chez les Byzantins.* Paris, 1883.

Cohen, G. "Épopée byzantine et épopée française." *Mélanges Grégoire* **II** (Annuaire de l'Institut de Philologie et d'Histoire orientale de l'Université de Bruxelles X), Brussels, 1950, 143–160.

Cousin, M. *Histoire de Constantinople jusqu'à la fin de l'Empire. Translaté sur les Originals grecs de M. Cousin.* 4 vols. Paris, 1672–1674.

Da Costa-Louillet, G. "Saints de Constantinople aux VIIIe, IXe et Xe siècles." *Byzantion* **25–27** (1955–57), fasc. 2, 783–852; *Byzantion* **24** (1954), 179–264.

De Beylie, L. *L'Habitation byzantine: Recherches sur l'architecture civile des Byzantins et son influence en Europe.* Grenoble-Paris, 1902.

Delahaye, H. "Byzantine Monasticism." In Baynes and Moss, *Byzantium.*

Delatte, A. and Ch. Josserand. "Contribution a l'étude de la démonologie byzantine." *Mélanges Bidez* (Annuaire de l'Institut de Philologie et d'Histoire orientales et slave) 1933/34.

Demus, O. *Byzantine Mosaic Decoration.* London, 1948.

Dendias, M. "Études sur le gouvernement et l'administration à Byzance." *Atti del V Congresso Internazionale di Studi Bizantini* (Studi Bizantini e Neoellenici V), Roma, 1939, 122–140.

Der Nersessian, S. *Armenia and the Byzantine Empire: A Brief Study of Armenian Art and Civilization.* Cambridge, Mass., 1945.

De Rougemont, D. *Love in the Western World.* New York, 1956.

Diehl, Ch. "De quelques croyances byzantines sur la fin de Constantinople." *Byzantinische Zeitschrift* **30** (1929–1930), 192–196.

Dölger, F. *Beitrage zur Geschichte der byzantinischen Finanzverwaltung, besonders des 10. und 11. Jahrhundert.* (Byzantinisches Arkhiv, Heft 9) Leipzig-Berlin, 1927.

———. *Corpus der griechischen Urkunden des Mittelalters und des Neuern Zeit. Reihe A: Regesten. Abt I: Regesten der Kaiserurkunden des oströmischen Reiches.* 1 *teil: Regesten von 565–1025.* Munchen-Berlin, 1924.

Dumezil, G. *Mitra-Varuna: essai sur deux représentations indo-européennes de la souveraineté.* Paris, 1948.

Dvornik, F. "The Circus Parties in Byzantium." *Byzantina-Metabyzantina* **I** (1946/1), 119–133.

———. *Les Légendes de Constantin et de Méthode: vues de Byzance.* (*Byzantinoslavica* Suppl. I). Prague, 1933.

Ebersolt, J. *Les arts somptuaires de Byzance*. Paris, 1923.
Eisenstadt, S. N. *The Political Systems of Empires*. Glencoe, Ill., 1963.
Eisler, R. *Orphisch-Dionysisch Mysterein-Gedanken in der christlichen Antike*. Hildesheim, 1966.
Eliade, M. "Centre du monde, Temple, Maison." *Le Symbolisme cosmique des monuments religieux*. (Serie Orientale Roma XIV), Roma, 1957.
———. *Cosmos and History: The Myth of the Eternal Return*. New York, 1959.
———. *Images and Symbols*. London, 1961.
———. *Patterns in Comparative Religion*. New York, 1958.
Engnell, I. *Studies in Divine Kingship in the Ancient Near East*. Uppsala, 1943.
Frances, E. "L'Empereur Nicéphore Ier et le commerce maritime byzantin." *Byzantinoslavica* **XXVII** (1/1966), 41–47.
Frankfort, H. *Kingship and the Gods*. Chicago, 1962.
Freud, S. *Civilization and Its Discontents*. New York, 1962.
Gadd, C. J. *Ideas of Divine Rule in the Ancient East*. (Schweik Lectures in Biblical Archaeology, 1945), London, 1948.
Gaster, T. *Thespis: Ritual, Myth, and Drama in the Ancient Near East*. 2nd ed. New York, 1961.
Gerland, E. "Das Wohnhaus der Byzantiner." *Burgwart* **16** (1915), 10–19.
Ghirshman, R. *Iran* (Penguin) Baltimore, 1961.
Glotz, G. *The Greek City and Its Institutions*. New York, 1929.
Glykatzi-Ahrweller, H. *Recherches sur l'administration de l'empire byzantin aux IX–XIe* siècles (Bulletin de correspondance hellénique, LXXXIV), Athens-Paris, 1960.
Gorianov, L. *Sbornik dokumentov po sotsial'no-ekonomicheskoi istorii Vizantii*. Moskva, 1951.
Grabar, A. *Byzantine Painting*. (Skira) New York, 1953.
———. *L'Empereur dans l'art byzantine. Recherches sur l'art officiel de l'empire d'Orient*. Paris, 1936.
———. *L'Iconoclasme byzantine: dossier archéologique*. Paris, 1957.
Granet, M. *Chinese Civilization*. New York, 1930.
Grégoire, H. "L'âge héroique de Byzance." *Mélanges offert à M. Nicolas Iorga*. Paris, 1933, 383–397.
———. "Nouvelles chansons épiques des IXe et Xe siècles." *Byzantion* **XIV** (1939), 235–263.
———. "Notes on the Byzantine Epic." *Byzantion* **XV**.
Grierson, P. "Coinage and Money in the Byzantine Empire." *Moneta e Scambi nell'alto Medievo* (Centro Italiano di Studi sull'alto Medievo; Settimani di Studio VIII), Spoleto, 1961, 411–453.
Guilland, E. "La collation et la perte ou la déchéance des titres nobiliaires à Byzance." *Revue des Études Byzantines* **IV** (1946), 24–69.
———. "Études sur l'Hippodrome de Byzance." *Byzantinoslavica* **XXVII** (1/1966), 289–307; *Byzantinoslavica* **XXVII** (2/1966), 26–40.
———. "Études sur l'histoire administrative de Byzance." *Byzantina-Metabyzantina* **I** (1) (1946), 165–179.

———. "Les eunuques dans l'Empire byzantin." *Revue des Études Byzantines* **I** (1943), 197–238.
———. "Fonctions et dignités des eunuques." *Revue des Études Byzantines* **II** (1944), 185–225.
———. "Vénalité et favoritisme à Byzance." *Revue des Études Byzantines* **X** (1952), 35–46.
Gylii, Petri. *De topographia Constantinoplis,* liber **III**, in Banduri, *Imperium Orientale, sive Antiquitates Constantinopolitanae,* t. 1. Venice, 1720.
Handlin, O. and C. Burchard (eds.). *The Historian and the City.* Cambridge, Mass., 1963.
Hauteceour, L. *Mystique et architecture: symbolisme du cercle et de la coupole.* Paris, 1954.
Hobsbawm, E. L. *Primitive Rebels.* Manchester, 1959.
Hocart, A. M. *Kingship.* Oxford, 1927.
Hussey, J. "The Byzantine Empire in the Eleventh Century: Some Different Interpretations." *Transactions of the Royal Historical Society,* Fourth Series, **XXXII** (1950), 71–85.
———. *Church and Learning in the Byzantine Empire: 867–1185.* Oxford, 1937.
Iorga, N. "Constantinople et la thalassocratie byzantine." *Études byzantines* **I** (Bucharest, 1939), 51–65.
———. "L'Homme byzantin." *Études byzantines* **I**, 313–325.
———. "La vie de province dans l'empire byzantin." *Études byzantines* **II** (Bucharest, 1940), 147–171.
———. *Histoire de la vie byzantine. Empire et Civilisation; d'après les sources, illustrée par les monnaies.* **II**. Bucharest, 1934.
Janin, R. *Constantinople byzantine: Développement urbaine et répertoire topographique.* 2ième ed. (Institut Francais d'Études Byzantines). Paris, 1964.
Jenkins, R. J. H. *Byzantium: The Imperial Centuries: 610–1701.* New York, 1966.
———. *The Byzantine Empire on the Eve of the Crusades.* London, 1953.
———. "The Flight of Samonas." *Speculum* **23** (1948), 217–235.
Joannou, P. "Psellos et le monastère τὰ Ναρτοῦ." *Byzantinische Zeitschrift* **44** (1951), 283–290.
Kaegi, W. "The Byzantine Army and Iconoclasm." *Byzantinoslavica* **XXVII** (1/1966), 48–70.
Kantorowicz, E. "Byzantine Feudalism." In Coulborn (ed.), *Feudalism in History.* Princeton, 1956.
———. *Selected Studies.* Locust Valley, New York, 1965.
Kazhdan, A. P. "Sotsial'nii sostav naseleniya vizantiiskikh gorodov v IX–X vv." *Vizantiiskii Vremennik* **VIII** (1950).
———. "Vizantiiskie goroda v VII–XI vekach." *Sovietskaya Arkheologiya* **21** (1954), 164–183.
Kirsten, E. "Die byzantinische Stadt." *Berichte zum XI Internationalen Byzantinischen-Kongres.* Munich, 1958.

Kolias, G. *Léon Choerosphactès, Magistre, Proconsul et Patrice.* (Texte und Forschungen zur Byzantinisch-neugriechischen Philologie, no. 31). Athens, 1939.

Koukoules, Ph. βυζαντινῶν βίος καὶ Πολιτισμός. 5 vols. Athens, 1948–55.

———. "τά λουτρά τῶν βυζαντινῶν." *Epiteiris Eteiris Byzantinōn Spoudon.* **XI** (1935), 192–238.

Laurent, L. *L'Arménie entre Byzance et l'Islam depuis la conquète Arabe jusqu'en 886.* Paris, 1919.

Lechner, K. "Hellenen und Barbaren im Weltbild der Byzantiner. Die alten Bezeichnungen als Ausdruck einer neuen Kulterbewutzseins." Dissert. Munchen, 1954.

Lipshits, E. Ya. "K izucheniyu ekonomiki prigorodov Konstantinopolya v X v." *Vizantiiskii Vremennik* **XIV** (1958), 81–85.

———. "K voprosu o gorode v Vizantii VIII–IX vv." *Vizantiiskii Vremennik* **VI** (1953).

———. *Ocherki istorii vizantiiskogo obschestva i kultury VIII pervaya polovina IX v.*" Moskva-Leningrad, 1961.

Lopez, R. S. "The Crossroads Within the Walls." In Handlin and Burchard, *The Historian and the City.*

———. "Silk Industry in the Byzantine Empire." *Speculum* **XX**, 1 (January, 1945), 1–42.

Luckenbill, D. D. *Ancient Records of Assyria.* 2 vols. Chicago, 1927.

Lynch, K. "The Form of Cities." *Scientific American* **190–191** (1954), 55–63.

———. *The Image of the City.* Cambridge, Mass., 1960.

Macri, C. M. *L'Organization de l'économie urbaine dans Byzance.* Paris, 1929.

Malafosse, J. de. *Les lois agraires a l'èpoque byzantine. Traduction et exégèse.* Toulouse, 1949.

Malinin, V. *Starets Eleazarova Monastyrya Filofei i ego poslaniya.* Kiev, 1901.

Manojlović, M. "Le peuple de Constantinople de 400 à 800 après J.C. Étude spèciale de ses forces armées, des élements qui le composaient et son rôle constitutionnel pendent cette période." *Byzantion* **11** (1936), 617–716.

Mathew, D. *Byzantine Aesthetics.* London, 1963.

Melaart, J. *Earliest Civilizations of the Near East.* London, 1965.

Miller, D. A. "The Logothete of the Drome in the Middle Byzantine Period." *Byzantion* **36** (1966), fasc. 2, 438–470.

Monnier, H. *Les Novelles de Léon le Sage.* Bordeaux-Paris, 1923.

Moravcsik, Gy. *Byzantinoturcica.* 2 vols. Berlin, 1958.

Müller, W. *Die heilige Stadt: Roma quadrata, himmlischen Jerusalem und die Mythe vom Weltnabel.* Stuttgart, 1961.

Mumford, L. In *City Invincible: A Symposium on Urbanization and Cultural Development in the Ancient Near East.* Chicago, 1960, 224–246.

———. *The City in History.* New York, 1961.

Neumann, C. *Die Weltstellung des byzantinischen Reiches vor den Kreuzzugen*. Leipzig, 1894.

Onians, R. *Origins of European Thought*. Cambridge, 1951.

Ostrogorsky, G. "Agrarian Conditions in the Byzantine Empire in the Middle Ages." *Cambridge Economic History* **I** (Cambridge, 1966), 205–234.

———. "Byzantine Cities in the Early Middle Ages." *Dumbarton Oaks Papers* **13** (1959), 45–66.

———. *History of the Byzantine State*. New Brunswick, New Jersey, 1957.

———. *Mélanges G. Ostrogorskij* **I**. Paris, 1963.

———. *Pour l'histoire de la féodalité byzantine*. Translated by H. Grégoire. (Corpus Bruxellense Historiae Byzantinae. Subs. I). Bruxelles, 1954.

———. "Das Steursystem im byzantinischen Altertum und Mittelalter." *Byzantion* **XI** (1931), 229–240.

Pargoire, J. "St. Mamas: le quartier russe de Constantinople." *Echos d'Orient* **XI** (1908), 203–210.

Pasini, A. *Il tesoro di San Marco*. Venice, 1889.

Pedersen, J. *Israel, Its Life and Culture*. 2 vols. Oxford, 1926.

Poëte, M. *Introduction à l'Urbanisme: L'Évolution des Villes: La Leçon de l'Antiquité*. Paris, 1929.

Redfield, R. *Peasant Society and Culture*. Chicago, 1956.

———. *The Primitive World and Its Transformations*. (Cornell) Ithaca, New York, 1957.

Reik, T. *Ritual: Psycho-analytic Studies*. New York, 1958.

Rice, D. T. *The Art of Byzantium*. London, 1959.

Robinson, H. S. and Weinberg, S. "Excavations at Corinth: 1959." Hesperia **XXIX**/3 (July–September 1960), 225–253.

———. "Excavations at Corinth: 1960." *Hesperia* **XXXI**/2 (April–June 1962), 95–133.

Roheim, G. "Die Wilde Jagd." *Imago* **XII** (1926), 401–450.

———. *Gates of the Dream*. New York, 1952.

Rouillard, G. *La vie rurale dans l'empire Byzantin*. Paris, 1953.

Runciman, S. *The Medieval Manichee: A Study of the Christian Dualist Heresy*. Cambridge, 1955.

———. *The Emperor Romanus Lecapenus and His Reign*. Cambridge, 1963.

Schlumberger, G. *Un empereur byzantin au dixième siècle, Nicéphore Phocas*. Paris, 1890.

Sebillot, R. *Le Folklore de France*. 4 vols. Paris, 1900–1907.

Segré, A. "Essays on Byzantine Economic History." *Byzantion* **XVI** (1942–43), 393–444.

Seidler, G. L. *Soziale Ideen in Byzance*. (Berliner Byzantinische Arbeiten, bild 24). Berlin, 1960.

Setton, K. M. "On the Importance of Land Tenure and Agrarian Taxation in the Byzantine Empire, From the Fourth Century to the Fourth Crusade." *American Journal of Philology* **LXXIV** (1953), 225–259.

Skyllitzes Matritensis, t. 1: *Reproducciones y miniaturas*. Comm. S. C. Estopanan, Barcelona-Madrid, 1965.

Sorlin, I. "Les traités de Byzance avec la Russie au Xe siècle." *Cahiers du Monde Russe et Soviétique* **II** (3) (1961), 313–360, (4), 447–475.

Starr, J. *The Jews in the Byzantine Empire: 641–1204*. (Texte und Forschungen zur byzantinisch-neugriechischen Philologie, XXX). Athens, 1939.

Stein, E. *Studien zur Geschichte des byzantinisches Reiches, vornehmlich unter den Kaisern Justinus II und Tiberius Constantinus*. Stuttgart, 1919.

———. *Untersuchungen zur spatbyzantinischen Verfassungs- und Wirtschaftsgeschichte*. Hanover, 1925.

Syuzyumov, M. Ya. "Ekonomika prigorodov vizantiiskikh krupnikh gorodov." *Vizantiiskii Vremennik* **XI** (1956), 55–81.

Tarn, W. W. *Hellenistic Civilization*. 3rd ed. London, 1952.

Tatakis, B. *La philosophie byzantine*. 2ième fascicule supplément de E. Bréhier, *Histoire de la Philosophie*. Paris, 1949.

Teall, J. L. "The Grain Supply of the Byzantine Empire: 330–1025." *Dumbarton Oaks Papers* **13** (1959), 87–139.

Texier, C. and Pullen, R. P. *Byzantine Architecture*. London, 1864.

Thompson, J. A. K. *Greeks and Barbarians*. New York, 1921.

Thrupp, S. "The City as the Idea of Social Order." In Handlin and Burchard, *The Historian and the City*.

Treitinger, O. *Die ostromische Kaiser- und Reichsidee nach ihrer Gestaltung im hofischen zeremoniell*. Jena, 1938.

Van Millingen, A. *Byzantine Constantinople. The Walls of the City and Adjoining Historical Sites*. London, 1910.

Vasiliev, A. A. *Byzance et les Arabes*. *II*ième partie: *Le dynastie macédonienne*. Brussels, 1936.

———. "Harun Ibn-Yahya and His Description of Constantinople." *Seminarium Kondakovianum* **V** (1932), 1, 149–163.

———. "Medieval Ideas of the End of the World East and West." *Byzantion* **XVI** (1942–43), 462–502.

Vasilievskii, V. G. "Varyago-russkaya i varyago-angliiskaya druzhina v Konstantinopolye XI i XII vv." In his *Trudy*, **I**, St. Petersburg, 1908.

Vogt, A. "Études sur le theátre byzantin." *Byzantion* **VI** (1931), 37–74, 623–640.

von Falke, O. *Decorative Silks*. New York, 1936.

Vryonis, Sp. "An Attic Hoard of Byzantine Gold Coins (668–741) from the Thomas Whittemore Collection and the Numismatic Evidence for the Urban History of Byzantium." *Mélanges G. Ostrogorskij* **I** (1963), 291–300.

———. "Byzantium: The Social Basis of Decline in the Eleventh Century." *Greek, Roman and Byzantine Studies* **II**, 2 (1959), 159–175.

Weber, M. *The City*. Glencoe, Ill., 1958.

Webster, H. *Magic: A Sociological Study*. Stanford, 1948.

Wittvogel, K. *Oriental Despotism.* New Haven, 1957.
Wolff, R. L. "The Three Romes: The Migration of an Ideology and the Making of an Autocrat." *Daedalus* 88 (1959), 291–311.
Yakobson, A. L. "O chislennosti naseleniya srednovekogo Chersonesa." *Vizantiiskii Vremennik* 19 (1961), 154–165.
Zakythinos, D. "Étatisme byzantin et expérience hellénistique." *Annuaire de l'Institut de Philologie et d'Histoire orientales et slaves* X (1950), 667–680.

INDEX